The Future of Adam and Eve

Finding the Lost Gift

The Future of Adam and Eve

Finding the Lost Gift

Mary Rosera Joyce

LifeCom

Published by

LifeCom

St. Cloud, Minnesota, USA

© 2009   Mary Rosera Joyce

All rights reserved

ISBN 978-0-578-03415-7

No part of this book may be used or reproduced in any manner whatsoever without written permission. No part of this book may be stored in a retrieval system or transmitted in any form or by any means including electronic, electrostatic, magnetic tape, mechanical, photocopying, recording or otherwise without the prior permission of the publisher.

For information, address *LifeCom*, Box 1832, St. Cloud, MN 56302

Contents

Preface		vii
Introduction		ix
Reading Guide and List of Conversations		xi
Note		xii
Chapter 1	The Storyline	1
Chapter 2	Adam's Puritan-Playboy America	5
Chapter 3	The Missing Person	13
Chapter 4	Searching for Our Missing Personhood	25
Chapter 5	Finding Our Missing Personhood	37
Chapter 6	The Human Person in a New Light	45
Chapter 7	Finding our Power for Wisdom	55
Chapter 8	Turning Up the Light	65
Chapter 9	Finding our Power for Love	75
Chapter 10	Emotional Health and the Puritan	87
Chapter 11	Good Character and the Playboy	95
Chapter 12	The Healing of Human Sexuality	103
Chapter 13	In the Likeness of God	119
Chapter 14	True Sexual Freedom	135

Chapter 15	The Friendship of Man and Woman	149
Chapter 16	The Spousal-Parental Heart of Society	157
Chapter 17	No Family is an Island	171
Chapter 18	When the Wandering Cultures Meet	179
Chapter 19	Adam's America and the Lost Gift	187
Chapter 20	The Future of Adam and Eve	195

Developmental Reflections

A. The Meaning of Personhood in Trinitarian Theology	205
B. The Paradoxical Logic of Wisdom	223
C. A Little Less than the Angels	229
D. The Background Storyline	241

Words and Meanings
249

References
257

Endnotes
263

Preface

"I wish my husband would just hold me sometimes. He can't do so without wanting sex." This is what a woman said to me after a talk I had given on the friendship of man and woman. Quite obviously, her husband was impulse-driven. Without a reflective growth in wisdom about love, this couple's relationship would remain at a standstill.

Their story would be similar to the one that has been told about a stray baby eagle that fell among prairie chickens and learned how to be just like them. One day this supposedly new prairie chicken saw an eagle soaring majestically high in the sky. "What is that?" he inquired of an elder. "That's a different kind of bird than we are," was the reply. Thus persuaded by his surrounding culture, the little eagle continued to think he was a prairie chicken. Never did he discover the true power of his wings.

We, too, live in a culture that will not let us know who we really are. The world around us has little to say about living with our impulses other than "buy now," "call today," or "do it immediately before you forget." In other words, don't go below the surface of things. And whatever you do, don't raise your wings by stopping to think."

In the meantime, most of our brain-power is dying, while our low-brain impulses are firing themselves away. But this is not how we really want to live when we consult with ourselves in our better moments of awareness.

We have within us a miraculous power to know things we do not know we know until we realize it. This is our power to know that something *is* and that we *are*. As much as animals sense more than we do, such as a bird sensing a worm thriving below the surface of the ground, no animal can know the *is* of what it senses.

No bird or beast knows that it, itself, exists. If one of them could know the *is* of anything—or of its own self—that creature would not be an animal; it would be a person. By knowing *is,* persons, even if they do not realize they know it, can wonder *what* a thing is, *where* it came from, *how* and *when* it got there, and, most importantly, *why* it exists at all.

In order to develop our potential for "raising our wings and soaring in this way," we need to act by common sense and wisdom more than by impulses. Common sense is wisdom in its ordinary, everyday light. It is the eagle in the nest before it learns how to fly. High-brain power for wisdom about love is the "eagle" within us finally becoming capable of the fullness of its powers.

Chapters 7 and 8 of this book show how we know the *being* of the things we know. Other chapters focus on the culture in which we live and how it both resists and supports our journey into the future.

This book is a search more than research. Its happiest reader will be one who cherishes common sense, wisdom, and insight beyond eyesight.

* * * * * *

I am grateful for the encouraging words of Pope John Paul II in *Fides et Ratio*, his encyclical on faith and reason, where he asks philosophers "to explore more comprehensively the dimensions of the true, the good, and the beautiful to which the word of God gives access." He says that this attention to philosophy should be an "original contribution in service of the new evangelization." I interpret these statements as a call for deeper and original searching into reality.

Also, I want to thank my best friend and husband, Robert, for the influence of his original philosophy of creation in Chapter 20 and in Reflection C at the end of the book, as well as for his careful editing of the entire manuscript.

I am grateful to readers of the manuscript who offered their helpful comments and to my other supportive friends. All have been witnesses to the importance of friendship as affirmed by this book's venture into the meaning of love.

Introduction

The story of Adam and Eve tells us we are all in one family. In some important way, our parents and their parents back to the original are still within us. All are longing for the happiness and wholeness our first parents were given as they came into being by the power of God. Their story tells us they failed to *receive fully* the gift. Since their beginning, and through their ongoing family, they have been trying to recover what they lost. We, too, even if unconsciously, want to join in the search.

The gift is both simpler than simple and richer than rich. It is a paradox: an integration of opposites. As paradoxical, the lost gift is an exciting challenge to our usual way of thinking.

Ordinarily, we prefer to file different things into separate boxes or categories of the mind. That manner of sorting produces practical knowledge and an ever-expanding multitude of technologies, but not the warming light that comes from the heart within the mind and the mind within the heart.

Adam within us is less inclined than Eve to think with the heart. He wants to know things in order to name them. He asks what, how, when, why, and where more readily than Eve. He tends to search and research outward; she tends inward. He excels in exploration, explanation, and invention. He is the one who said "Sail on, sail on." Far away amidst the dangers of the ocean, the Eve within us might be more inclined to say, "Let's go home."

While Adam loves to analyze things by breaking them down into their parts, Eve relates more spontaneously to their wholeness. She wants to synthesize what he analyzes. When he differentiates, she tends to integrate. Whether a man or a woman, each one of us has within us these Adam-Eve aptitudes. A man, of course, is more like the Adam within him, and a woman is more like the Eve within her. Each, with an emphasis opposite from the other, shares in the other's predominant attributes.

Unfortunately, by being unaware, we strongly tend to oversimplify what we know. For example, we either separate men and women into different categories or roles in life, or we see them as basically the same. Historically, we have tried both views only to suffer deeply the consequences of our shortsights. Adam and Eve within each one of us are neither separate nor identical. They are integrally paradoxical.

Within all women and men, Eve is especially sensitive to the deep emptiness between herself and Adam. In the beginning, she was first to lose the gift and first to suffer its loss. Awakening in the darkness, she is first to realize that something is missing. She, especially, wants to find it.

As Eve opens her eyes in the area of her being where she is sensitive to the wholeness of things, she feels the loss of the gift. She knows that if she ever found it, she could not welcome it alone. So, Eve invites Adam to join her in their quest. She wants him to find and receive the gift together with her *in us*—their sons and daughters. But how?

Reading Guide

This book proceeds on two levels. The first level moves along the storyline. The second goes deeper into the meaning of the story.

The reader might prefer to follow the storyline chapters first, then follow up with those that are more concerned with the meaning of the story.

The chapters closest to the storyline are:

    Chapters 1 through 4

    9 through 12

    14 through 20

Those that are more philosophical and theological are:

    5 through 8, and 13

    Developmental Reflections A through D

Conversations

Eve and the Puritan	Chapter 10	88-91
Adam and the Playboy	Chapter 11	95-97
Adam and Eve	Chapter 13	120-133
Adam and the Playboy	Chapter 14	135-137
Adam and the Playboy	Chapter 14	139-140
Adam, Eve, and the Playboy	Chapter 14	144-147
Adam, Eve, Puritan and Playboy	Chapter 16	159-161
Adam, Eve, and the Reader	Chapter 20	195-204

Note

Until the Middle Ages, reason was the humble servant of the Christian faith. Metaphysical philosophy provided a foundation for defending divine revelation against numerous heresies. Not long after St. Bonaventure and St. Thomas Aquinas, metaphysics began to lose its life. Since then, the West has been alternately weakening and strengthening in the faith. In the overall trend, however, the faith has been steadily losing ground. Western culture no longer takes seriously divine revelation. Although religious fervor is increasing in the rest of the world today, it needs deeper roots in reason, as well as in faith.

Metaphysical philosophy has been the highest accomplishment of the *rational animal*. But, because of this biology-based concept of human nature and intelligence, metaphysics gradually lost its cultural influence. Man, because of the male organization of his brain, feels satisfied with a "rational animal" concept of himself. But man, together with woman, realizes his way of thinking is not complete.

Another step in philosophy is required. Called a new ontology, this way of searching for truth begins in the spontaneously intuitive judgments of the mind ordinarily recognized as common sense. Then it searches for the inner source of these intuitions and finds it at one level deeper than the starting point of metaphysics. The result is a turnaround in the way we see everything. This new ontology sees the whole of being, including the cosmic universe, as person-based.

Man and woman must find a way through hardened masculine walls. Together we can do it. Within the subsequent "sunburst," everything shifts in meaning for the better. We have only to set out on the journey with readiness to receive the gift.

Chapter 1

The Storyline

In the beginning, the man of *Genesis* was alone with the animals. These were his only companions in the universe. After creating all of them, God warmly affirmed their goodness, but had reservations about the aloneness of Adam. So God created Eve, the woman of *Genesis*, from a bone close to Adam's heart.

Then Eve began to hear a strange voice that sounded intrigued about her obvious likeness to God. Someone was trying to sink his serpentine teeth into her special gift. Active receptivity. He wanted her receptivity to collapse into passivity so that she no longer could receive divine grace.

If Satan could get at her receptivity, the dominant power in Eve's feminine nature, he would have access to Adam's less dominant gift of receptivity. The brilliant dissembler knew exactly where to strike.

He convinced the woman that, by being more assertive, she would become like God. Eve swallowed the deception. Then she persuaded her soulmate to do the same. When he did so, his aloneness became far worse than it was at first.

Expelled from Eden, the two began to search for what they had lost: their original personhood in friendship with God and with each other. But their cultural influence continued to reveal profound alienation between them. Their estranged feminine and masculine mentalities developed in opposite directions.

The feminine spirit of Eve went East into the Orient. In India, she sought her lost self in God, only to lose herself in the passivity of pantheism. In China, she tried to find herself in the natural world and abandoned herself to the impersonal Tao (Way) of Taoism.

Wandering through the Middle East, Adam moved away from the immanent God of Eastern pantheism toward the transcendent God of

2   The Future of Adam and Eve

Abraham and Moses. He discovered himself to be an image and likeness of the Divine. Eventually, his transcendent God became incarnately immanent within human nature, while remaining also transcendent.

Proceeding west into Europe, Adam *still* tried to find himself among the animals—his former companions. He began to think of himself as being an animal having a rational difference. He was profoundly ambivalent about who he really was.

In that condition, he eventually became an individualist who finally lost himself in the extreme individualism of the Puritan character. He became so self-assertive that he wanted no cultural surrounding but his own. So he, in his progeny, sailed to America.

There he began to dream of "a shining city on a hill." He yearned so ardently to make his dream come true that he became a model of ingenuity and inventiveness. He even rocketed to the moon and walked on its surface. After that he sent technological explorers to Mars, and beyond, everywhere searching for the bountiful goodness he had lost in the beginning.

No matter what we think and do as Americans, we are sons and daughters of the Puritan Adam, the rebellious spiritual adolescent who left his home in Europe and sailed across an ocean to settle in the wilderness of another continent. In America, the too-masculine mentality of the Puritan soon became reactive and revolutionary. His revolt against European monarchy caused him to start the American Revolution. Eventually, he *invented* a new form of government—a democratic republic based on constitutional law.

The Constitution, by emphasizing rights, depended on the culture for the responsibilities that would balance these rights. The culture, however, was not as stable as the Constitution. It moved from the Puritan Adam to his playboy son who rebelled against the principles and willpower of his parent. The compulsive parent begot the impulsive child who became willful, instead, about his own self-centered preferences.

Compulsive willpower, as demonstrated by the Puritan, ignores feelings for the sake of acting correctly. The compulsive person is a perfectionist who says "Feelings don't count." Oppositely, the playboy's impulsive willfulness ignores feelings by acting from them without adequate evaluation. The impulsive person says "If it feels good do it."

Because Puritan individualism is excessively masculine, it causes the culture to try to find balance by swinging between extremes. Neither the Puritan's principles nor the playboy's preferences can integrate with its opposite and heal Adam's inner ambivalence.

The integrating power is feminine: *active receptivity*. This serpent-targeted source within human personhood has long been lost, and is still missing in the cultures of East and West.

Active receptivity makes possible the kind of love that affirms the very *being* of persons. Receptive affirmation is the missing core of love that can integrate, and thus begin to heal, Adam and Eve within us.

Once regained, this receptivity enables them to face three barriers, or walls, that resulted from their estrangement in the beginning. Passing through these walls, finally, their gift of active receptivity can be intensified toward its original glory.

Facing Three Walls

At the present point in their story, Adam and Eve are facing three ancient walls through which they need to pass on their way toward the fullness of the lost gift. They, however, will not be able to do so by climbing over, by tunneling under, or by breaking through them in any way. The only way to move into their future is first to find the doors in these walls and carefully open them by exercising their *active receptivity*.

The first of these interior blockages is their self-constricting view of themselves as either part of God (Eve's pantheism) or as part of the animal kingdom (Adam's biologism). The door in this wall is the human intellect's power to know what *is* as *being*. Opening this door is an actively receptive access to their sorely missing personhood and its feminine-masculine integration.

The next wall is God as seeming to be all-masculine: Father, Son, and Holy Spirit. This foreground face of God is a special problem for Eve in understanding her likeness to God. Consequently, the likeness to God of the Adam-Eve relationship has been virtually invisible. The door in this second wall is the authentic meaning of personhood. Opening this door is an actively receptive access to the spousal model (beyond the traditional parental model) of the divine interior life.

The final barrier is the wall between the two creations: the one featured in *Genesis*, and the one obviously missing. The missing creation includes the beginning of the angels. The door in this wall is the difference between the *being* of created persons and their *existence*. Eve and Adam opening this door is their actively receptive access to a liberating awareness of their origin in *being*.

The missing person, the missing depth in their likeness to God, and the missing creation are three major forms of darkness that resulted from the original loss of active receptivity. Eve, the first to lose the gift and its splendors, is the first to want to find the doors in these walls. But she cannot pass through them without Adam going with her. This is how their storyline leads to their future.

We, the people, now face a decision. Will we continue to pursue our preferences without an awareness of our true personhood? Or will we react against the culture of the self-centered playboy and swing back again toward the culture of the self-righteous Puritan?

Or will we turn up the light and see a way through ancient and traditional walls blocking our recovery from what we lost? In the land where their wandering cultures meet, will the lonely Adam and desperate Eve within us seek for and discover together something similar to the bountiful goodness they shared before their separate cultural journeys began?

Chapter 2

Adam's Puritan-Playboy America

America is the only nation on earth that has been conceived, born, and developed within Puritan individualism. Our roots are Biblical, revolutionary, idealistic, resourceful, self-conscious, and extremely masculine. If the American character is anything, it is an expression of the alienated Adam at his best.

The character of a culture is formed most deeply by its view of the ultimate reality. Consequently, the Puritan interpretation of God is the most significant of our cultural roots. For the original American Puritan, God was a hyper-transcendent, inscrutable, masculine, and stern lawgiver for a *depraved* humanity. God's will was so arbitrary as to *choose* who will, and who will not, be saved. Anxiety resulted. The Puritan asked, "Am I one of the chosen? How can I know?"

The tortured soul found an answer in thinking, "If I can actually *experience* grace, become righteous and industrious, and especially if I am prosperous, I must be one of the divinely chosen." So, work, achievement, and thrift became the answer to the Puritan dilemma. The result became the self-proving, driven, American individualist.

How could the cold, hard God of Puritanism spontaneously and warmly affirm the goodness of anyone? How could any Puritan individual spontaneously affirm the goodness of others who were viewed as depraved and arbitrarily chosen by a voluntaristic God? And how could an individual with that kind of self-concept feel affirmed by either God or anyone else?

Merely choosing by the will is not spontaneous affirmation from the heart.

Nevertheless, the Puritans believed they were predestined and thus numbered among the chosen people of God. As such, they were heroic, passionate, and determined to be superb achievers. Their self-proving drive became the *hyperactive* (passive-reactive) source of their energy.[1] Their drive was inspired by a vision of creating on earth an image and likeness of the Bible's luminous "city on a hill," a kind of heaven on earth—America, the beautiful.

Also significant was the rebellious quality of the Puritan character that originated in Europe with a religious reaction against Rome. Luther's individualistic "Here I stand" reverberated through Calvin and other protestors. They would not allow what they viewed as Papal interference in their personal interpretation of the Bible. Divine revelation became viewed as exclusively Biblical, and its interpretation became the role of the individual. Their situation became reminiscent of Adam's aloneness in Eden and his loneliness thereafter.

Then, some of the Calvinist Puritans became so adamant in their beliefs that they decided to get away from what they viewed as a corrupt European culture. Boarding the Mayflower, they sailed to a new world.

At first, they were European colonists. Even as they had declared, while in Europe, their religious independence from Rome, they now demanded, in America, their governmental independence from England's throne, and fought a revolutionary war to secure it.

Soon after, they established a union of states under a Constitution that became a sacred ideal of individual liberty confirmed in law.

Puritan Distress

Unlike the Latin cultures of southern Europe, the Puritans were emotionally reserved and cool. They were more inclined to regard their emotional life as part of human depravity than to express their emotions freely as part of their humanity.

Profoundly influenced by that kind of mentality, we are a people uncomfortable with our feelings. We do not know how to live well with them. Often we ignore them, hoping they will just go away.

And so, we have special problems in our relationships. No other nation on earth has so many psychiatrists and counselors. Even with massive attention to psychological disturbances, there is an ever growing need for those who truly understand the emotional life.

Qualities like self-control and self-reliance, when not balanced sufficiently by other good qualities, can become deadening. In the Puritan character, these virtues produced the raw individualism of "the self-made man." "I am the master of my fate, the captain of my soul," said William Ernest Henley, a British poet (*Invictus*, 1875), driving Luther's individualistic implication to its final expression.

When John Calvin became Luther's theologian, the Puritan era of the lonely crowd began. With this era—continuing yet—the natural feeling of connection between persons suffered a heavy blow.

Because they saw us as depraved and perverse, the Puritans, and especially the Victorians, thought human nature and feelings had to be rigidly controlled. People were not supposed to touch each other any more than they had to, and certainly not in public. "Hands off" meant keep your distance. Discipline and work were supremely important. Enjoyment and play were suspect.

The idea that feelings and emotions are unimportant creates a special kind of distress. The violence, crime, alcoholism, and drug abuse in our society are, to some extent, traceable to our historically predominant Puritan attitude toward life.

When Puritanism became Victorian, an extreme kind of feminine influence increased the lace in clothing and the curves in furniture. But women remained emotionally reserved, prudish, and frigid. Emotional problems increased to such an extent that medical doctors wondered what was causing so much insanity.

From Puritan to Playboy

At the beginning of the 20th century, Sigmund Freud (1856-1939) noticed the disturbed psychological condition of the people around him. Under the influence of Newtonian mechanics, he tried to explain the human psyche in a scientific—viewed as mechanistic—manner. His resultant theory reduced everything human to the level of a sexually driven tissue energy that develops psycho-dynamics and defense mechanisms. He identified one of these "mechanisms," which he called repression, as being the main cause of mental and emotional illness.

An extreme *fear* of sexual repression became the result. But fear of repression became itself repressive. Thus, the reaction against repression became an impulsive expression. The resolution of the dilemma, a healthy restraint of impulses, got lost in the cultural oscillation from one extreme to the other.

The opposite extreme from too much control of anything is not enough control. During and since the 1960s, in reacting against Victorian Puritanism, many people went wild. "Do as you please and have fun doing it," became their cry of liberation.

After that, nothing could stop the playboy revolution. Cool above and hot below, this "son" of the Puritan inherited his father's performance anxiety. The importance of performance shifted from work into play. Short-term fun without long-term happiness seemed like the "happy" way to go.

The playboy offspring of the original Puritan was, and still is, as excessively masculine as his forebear. And so, today, the creeping cultural chill is getting progressively colder. Most people adapt to the "temperature" and do not realize that both a cultural "ice age" and "dark age" are upon us and within us.

Lacking inner receptivity (the authentic and emphatic power of Eve), the lonely Adam in both the Puritan and playboy does not know how to relate with feelings and impulses. As the Puritan became compulsive about achievement in work, the playboy became impulsive about fun in play. As the one became a master of self-proving performance in highly inventive industrial and technological accomplishments, the other became a master of sexual maneuvers and self-gratifying entertainment.[2]

And we wonder why there is so much emotional and character disturbance in America, and why we need so many psychologists, counselors, and therapists who, themselves, are conditioned by the same culture. In a situation such as this, how could there be anything but a profound emptiness that people hopelessly try to fill? Outward performance without a deep inner receptivity for transcendental realities is characteristic of Adam without Eve, no matter how many women live in that kind of culture.

From Freud to Friedan

Thoroughly masculine in his mechanistic psychology, Freud was mystified by women. "What does a woman want?" he wondered. In the context of his theory of depraved, irrational, and rationalizing human nature, he thought that women really want to be men. In *The Feminine Mystique*, Betty Friedan denied that women want to be men, and asserted that women only want to be human. She said that women suffer from "a problem that has no name," because they are confined to "the comfortable concentration camp" of domestic chores. In the Puritan-playboy culture of Friedan's time, leaving the "camp" and finally becoming human meant becoming *more like men*. Ironically, the masculinization of women was inevitable.

Authentically sensing a deep emptiness in Victorian women that neither Freud nor the playboy could fill, Friedan launched the women's liberation movement of the '60s. But her shortsighted view of liberation only sent women straight into the work ethic of the Puritan and the sex ideology of the playboy.

More than ever, women became almost hopelessly enslaved by the masculine mentality. Trying to control their own bodies, they lost to the dissolute playboy the control of their own minds.

From Individualist to Selfist

From Freudian and other sources in Europe, the sexual revolution crossed the Atlantic to America. Carried along by its subversive current, the American playboy revolted against the Puritan.

Tough individualism based on *principle* melted down into a suave, sophisticated, selfist version of individualism based on *preference*.[3] Adam's loneliness shifted into another way of attempting to fill a vacuum: an emptiness between God and his own soul, and between himself and everyone else.

The emptiness in the Puritan Adam drove him to prove to himself that he was one of the elect. When he became a playboy, he retained this self-validating characteristic, but in a more juvenile manner.

As a result, he transformed the female from the passive *property* of the male to his passive *plaything*. But what he conceives in her body would have to be *her* property alone. She would have to be free to treat the result of sex as nothing more than a malignant tumor unfortunately induced by him.

So, by moving through the courts, the playboy began to assert his irresponsible privacy "rights," in *her* name, against the Puritan-inspired Constitution. By using the language of women's liberation, he began his legal move against the Puritan in 1965 when the High Court, in the *Griswold v. Connecticut* decision, nullified that state's law prohibiting the sale and distribution of contraceptives. Only seven years later, in 1972, the same Court's *Eisenstadt v. Baird* supported contraceptive use by the unmarried. At the beginning of the very next year, January 22, 1973, *Roe v. Wade* coupled with *Doe v. Bolton* legalized abortion until birth.

Other abortion-related decisions followed until the year 2000, when the *Stenberg v. Carhart* decision protected the grisly atrocity euphemistically called partial birth abortion. This "procedure," more accurately called brain-suction infanticide, is an attack on a child rivaled only by a terrorist beheading. Seven years later, *Carhart* was finally reversed by a 5 to 4 Supreme Court decision. But the full force of *Roe* remained untouched.

In this relentless trip down the shining city's hill, the arbitrary willfulness of the Puritan God descended into the willpower of the Puritan. Then, the Puritan's voluntarism continued down the slope into the willfulness of the playboy and his glorification of his playmate's "choice." Her "reproductive choices" of who should *live* and who should *die* is a culturally consequential image and likeness of the Puritan God's choice of who should enter eternal *life* and who should be condemned to eternal *death*.

While playmate-feminists fancy they are finally free, Eve is still submerged in the playboy culture. If the female does not submit to the male's erotic imagination, he facilely labels her a frigid vestige of Victorian Puritanism. When she naively describes the abortive removal of his sex-induced "growths" from her body as her final liberation from his control, her childish words are "paradisal" music to his selfist ears.

So, in order to secure the sound of this music in the nation's supreme covenant, the impulsive playboy (seven of nine Supreme Court males) gave to his playmate the "privacy rights" that he suddenly imagined to exist in the darkest and remotest implications of the Constitution. With all of this masculine control of the playmate's mind, Eve could not be more captive to the original serpentine voice that deceived her.

Power in the Roots

Adam, Eve, Puritan, and playboy, though real people, are also cultural symbols of a supreme and overarching (archetypal) nature. They tend to live a life of their own apart from the original Adam, Eve, Puritan, and playboy. These super-symbols, like underground roots, become power sources in the subconscious mind. They serve as culture-generating images within the vital connection between intuitive intellection and the imagination. They represent some of the deepest aspects of our relational being, and from their depth, express themselves in the culture, a society's way of thinking and living.

A culture is not only a society's character and "personality," but its lived interpretation of reality. Its root images are formed in the depth of our nature where we try to *concretize* our intuitions in our imagination before we express them in concepts and words. These deep-set archetypal images *influence* our primal judgments and values—powerfully.

One of the deepest intuitions of the human mind is that *something is the ultimate source of everything else*. Wanting to know what that something is, *not abstractly, but really*, the intuitive mind initially concretizes its intuition in the imagination, and only subsequently works out its intuition in reasons.

Consequently, some ancient cultures thought the sun is the source of everything else. The Greeks imagined all kinds of gods on Mount Olympus. On their way to the Promised Land, the ancient Hebrews even worshipped a calf they made out of gold. Something they probably assimilated unconsciously in Egypt worked its way to the surface out there in the stressful desert.

Nothing forms a culture like a people's shared image of the ultimate reality they believe to be causing everything else. If the ultimate reality of a culture is impersonal, that culture will be impersonal. If the ultimate is either feminine or masculine in its characteristics, the "personality" of the people develops accordingly.

From their primal roots, even if not consciously recognized, all the cultures of history took form in their own time and place. Each tended, in its own unique way, toward regaining what was originally lost when the man and woman of *Genesis* abandoned their active receptivity. Without this tendency toward recovery, history has no ultimate meaning. It is a story that is going nowhere.

Thus far, whether predominantly feminine or masculine, cultures have been unintegrated and largely impersonal. Eve and Adam, though longing to discover each other, have not yet regained the intimate friendship they seek. Clearly, not in America.

Whether they are compulsive or impulsive or both at once, self-conscious, self-proving people are trying to fill an emptiness with something that cannot fill it. Work cannot fill it. Sex cannot. No performance on earth can fill the emptiness in human personhood.

People are unconsciously yearning for a special kind of love. They want to discover the root-cause of the emptiness. They need, finally, not just to fill it, but to receive and heal it.

Chapter 3

The Missing Person

Our fathers brought forth upon this continent a nation conceived in, and dedicated to, Western individualism. Their bold assertion of independence from popes and kings, and their hallowed ideals of life, liberty, and pursuit of happiness released tremendous energy and optimism in the people.

Individualism had, and continues to have, its practical advantages. But America has been paying the resultant price. The cost to our vulnerable national character is the profoundly missing personhood of the human individual.[4]

Essentially relational, personhood is *within*, *with*, and *for*. A person is a being who, knowing *is,* is aware that "I am, you are, we are." Knowing *being* in this way, persons exist for the sake of loving communion with all that is. Loving communion is a mutuality of giving and receiving.

Individualism, however, is I-centered. Though the Puritan-deist character that begot the American Constitution had a unitive impulse evident in the union of families, colonies, and states, it was based on the triumph of individual rights. The difference between personhood and individualism is immensely significant for understanding not only America's cultural crisis, but also its possibility for healing.

The Paradox of Personhood

A paradox is a union of opposites. Mutual giving and receiving is an example. The absence of personhood in our national character results in a division between opposites, not their union.

Our culture is divided between two kinds of individualists: the original individualist and the subsequent selfist. The original (the Puritan) is dedicated to do-good principles, and the selfist (the playboy) is dedicated to feel-good preferences. Both are extremely masculine reactions against passivity. Thus, both are driven.

Neither individualists nor selfists have the feminine receptivity that integrates opposites. Individualists do not care much about feelings. And selfists do not care much about principles. Both lack the basis of personhood: receptivity for feelings and principles together.

So, receptivity is really what is lacking. Eve and her healing relationship with Adam await our awareness. Until she awakens in America, Adam's culture will remain divided between its masculine extremes.

Eve's original relationship with Adam *signifies* the essence of personhood. This essence is the paradoxical relationship between the receiving and giving that makes love possible.

Receiving, signified by Eve, is inner-directed and emphatically feminine. Giving, correlatively signified by Adam, is other-directed and emphatically masculine. So, withinness and otherness mutually interpermeate and are inseparable.

The withinness-otherness of receiving and giving is the feminine-masculine paradox of personhood. In the integrative heart of this paradox we receive in a giving way, and we give in a receiving way. Active receiving means receiving in a giving way, not in a passive way.

An example is listening as different from hearing. Hearing can be passive. We can hear without listening. We do not necessarily attend to what we hear. But listening is attentive and active. It is a giving way of receiving.

Manhood and womanhood originate in the paradox of personhood, that is, in its essence of receiving (as receptive withinness) and in its essence of giving (as expressive otherness). The being of a man in soul and soul-deep body emphasizes the other-directed or expressive pole of personhood while including its inner-directed or receptive opposite. And a woman's being emphasizes the receptive pole while including its expressive opposite.

In the feminine-masculine relationship *within* a person, one of these opposites makes their union possible. *The feminine withinness of active receptivity is the integrating source.* By actively receiving both feelings and principles we are able to bring them together harmoniously.

When individual*ism* sets in, the feminine-masculine paradox collapses. Withinness becomes insideness, and otherness becomes outsideness. Things become objects *over there*, no longer present within. The inside and outside separate from each other and tend to become extremes that generate more extremes. Thus the historical separation between the cultures of Eve and Adam resulted in Adam's Puritan (individualist) and playboy (selfist) extremes in America.

But when receptivity becomes active and integrates withinness and otherness, these extremes recede. Then the paradoxical wholeness of personhood can be regained.

All finite persons are basically receptive in relation to the gift of being, and in relation to the Giver. That is the way they were created to be. Each male and female person needs to *respond* receptively (feminine) and become *responsible* for the gift (masculine).

A male person's *receptivity*, however, is a masculine kind of receptivity; itself paradoxical. And a female person's *responsibility* is feminine; also paradoxical.

Eve's initial failure to respond receptively to the gift of being, and Adam's irresponsible confirmation of that failure resulted in a fall of their active receptivity into passivity. This sadly passive condition remained predominant throughout the history of Eve.

In Adam's history passivity continued, but subdominantly. And he reacted against it. His reaction made him hyperactive in trying to prove himself to himself. This made him acutely self-aware. As a result, he eventually became an individualist, and finally a selfist, especially in America.

How Adam Tried to Find Himself

Wherever the spirit of Eve wandered, passivity was dominant. Especially in the Eastern world, humans experienced themselves either as parts of an impersonal ultimate reality, or as destined for the impersonal emptiness of *nirvana* where nothing is differentiated. In the emptiness of Nirvana, no individual being—as *individual*—is *ultimately* significant.

Adam suffered from a similar kind of passivity. But he was too miserable to bear it. His masculine emphasis could not remain so undifferentiated. Moving into the Middle East, he abandoned Eastern pantheism (the idea that we are part of God) and polytheism (that there are many gods). Instead, he became a theist, believing in one God as *other* than the world, and therefore as masculine and transcendent. And he saw himself as an image and likeness of this masculine God.

When the God of theism began talking intimately with Abraham as a friend (*James* 2:23), something interpersonal began to happen in Adam's history. And when Moses heard a voice in a burning bush that said "I am Who am," the nature of Abraham's God came into the clearing. Finally, when a virgin daughter of Abraham gave birth to a son who said, "Before Abraham came to be, I am," Adam's theism became, in Jesus, transcendent-immanent. The Incarnation of the transcendent God became the triumph of *being* in a paradoxical integration of all that *is*.

In the Son of God, Jesus of Nazareth, transcendent otherness and immanent withinness became, and remain, the supreme paradox. Thanks to his mother's active receptivity, and to his redemptive death on a cross, Adam, Eve, and their progeny were restored to God. That was a truly new beginning in the journey toward the recovery of their personhood.

Farther north and westward, in Greece, sons of Adam had been on a different course. About 600 B.C., some of them began to notice the world around them as an object of inquiry. They tried to explain everything in the material world as expressions of a single basic source.

One of these philosophers thought everything came from water. Another thought the source of everything is earth. Yet another, fire. Even air. Still others thought all things were reducible to atoms. This subject-object relationship involved a differentiation between the world "out there" and the observer trying to understand it.

By the time of Socrates (469-399 B.C.) and Plato (429-348) the relationship between the subject and object—the observer and the world—shifted into reverse. The subject became the object of inquiry. This new object, the human being, became viewed as a soul in a body.

Finally, in the philosophy of Aristotle, the human object became clearly defined as an individual among other individuals in the material world.

From Aristotle to Jefferson

Aristotle (384-322 B.C.) was the first to understand the individual as a substantial being that is really distinct, even separate, from other substantial beings. He understood this individual substance as a being composed of passive matter and an actuating form. He called the form of a living substance its soul. And he saw *passive matter* as the principle by which there are many individuals in one common nature.

Because of this passive and material base of individual beings, Aristotle defined the human object as a rational *animal*. He regarded human biology, not the human soul, as basic.

But the difference between an animal-base and a soul-base in the definition of our nature is absolutely momentous.

In the animal-based definition, it is as though Adam in the midst of the animals of Eden collapsed into Adam becoming one of them. Even to this day, Aristotle's biology-based concept of humanity remains both the philosophical and the scientific source of Western individualism.

When the eminent Catholic theologian, Thomas Aquinas (1225-1274), took Aristotle as his main philosophical mentor, his Christian intuition of personhood assimilated the pagan concept of the human individual. But the Thomistic union of the Judeo-Christian sense of personhood with Aristotelian individualism was not integrative enough. It could not prevent Adam's subsequent history from breaking down into biology-based empiricism on one side, and logic-based rationalism on the other. In this way, the senses and reason separated from each other. So, also, did faith and reason.

Why did these separations happen? Something integrative was missing. Aristotle had identified and named it the agent intellect (*De Anima* iii 5). He described this power metaphorically as a light that causes abstract knowledge of the natures of things without, itself, knowing anything. His major followers agreed, including Thomas Aquinas in the 13th century and a prominent Thomist philosopher in the 20th century, Jacques Maritain (1882-1973).

According to the metaphor, light does not see anything; it only makes seeing possible. This is true for the senses, but not for the intellect. Intellectually, the light would have to be a pre-conceptual act of knowing, not an unknowing *cause* of conceptual knowledge. In other words, the pre-conceptual act of knowing the *is* of an object, and that this object *has* a nature, *causes* the abstractive concept of *what* that nature is. If we did not intuitively know, *before* abstraction takes place, that a being *has* a nature, we could not even begin the abstractive process of forming a concept of that nature.

Instead of trying to understand that which the metaphor of light signified, the three philosophers mentioned above seemed satisfied to posit the agent intellect as the cause needed to explain the transition between the senses and the formation of abstract concepts, and leave it at that. What they left, however, was a serious gap between the senses and reason, a problem never solved, not even to this day. Because the light remained a handy metaphor, Western philosophy has endured a breakdown instead of a breakthrough.

Soon after Thomas Aquinas, John Duns Scotus (1266-1308) noticed that the abstracting agent intellect did not know individual beings as such; these were known supposedly only by the senses. Scotus rightly knew that something important was missing: our intellectual, not just our sensate, connection with individual beings. Instead of solving the problem of the gap at this crucial point of recognition, Scotus made it much worse. He logicalized the mind's understanding of *being* by changing it into a univocal concept. This hyper-masculinizing change was an intellectual disaster from which the philosophers never recovered.

As an unfortunate result, Scotus reduced to a virtual category the *thisness* of the individual being. By emphasizing the importance of the individual in this incomplete way, he initiated a definite surge in

Western individualism. The case of the missing person increased in urgency.

William of Occam (1290-1349) emphasized the importance of the individual so strongly that he reduced universal natures to mere names. His resultant nominalism (overemphasis on names) signaled the virtual demise of philosophical wisdom at that time.

Then Martin Luther (1483-1546) saw no basis for a union between faith and reason. The mind seemed too darkened, and the heart too depraved by sin to do other than believe without reasons. A Bible-based faith alone, and the individual's interpretation of its meaning, was all that mattered. Luther's forceful self-assertion in this way gave a powerful religious boost to Western individualism.

For Descartes (1596-1650), the senses and reason seemed to be worlds apart. Neither could be trusted. Only mathematics seemed beyond doubt. Driven by a desire for clear and distinct certitude in philosophy, he arrived at a starting judgment, "I think, therefore I am." From this subjectivist beginning, he *deduced,* among other things, the existence of his body as extending from himself like a mechanism. With this painfully impersonal and divided sense of self, he became the precursor of the Enlightenment's rationalistic and impersonal individualism. Ironically, Cartesian subjectivism only increased the problem of the missing person.

By championing the independence of science from religion, philosophers of the Enlightenment glorified the scientific method of observation and experimentation. They glorified, also, the one who did the observing and the experimenting. This one became, for the newly "enlightened," the experiential, self-conscious, impersonal, individualistic self.

Especially due to John Locke, with his Puritan heritage (1632-1704), and Thomas Jefferson, with his deistic inclinations, (1743-1826), the individualist Enlightenment reached its zenith in the American institution of Constitutional government.

The American culture, however, was religious. It was Biblical to the core. A culture of responsibilities balanced a Constitution of rights. In this way, America became a "shining city on a hill" where the person, as a person, was, and still is, missing.

From Abraham to Jefferson

More than philosophy was involved in Adam's trip into America. His experience with Abraham, Moses, Jesus of Nazareth, Peter and Paul, Luther, Calvin, and the Bible-dedicated Puritans was also involved.

Abraham was a tribal man whose friendship with the transcendent God made him an interpersonalist, not an individualist. Moses, too, spoke with God as a friend (*Exodus* 33:11), and received from his divine friend ten commandments that the Puritan Adam took with him to America.

These commandments contained the natural law understood by Jefferson and his associates to be, together with Locke's empirical version, an essential part of the carrying context for the American Constitution. Jefferson's powerful assertion of inalienable rights to life, liberty, and the pursuit of happiness given to individuals by their Creator, presupposed responsibilities contained in the Bible's divinely announced natural law.

Jefferson's explicit assertion of rights with implicit responsibilities was highly individualistic. But the Bible itself is not individualistic in that sense. Responsibilities, such as the Ten Commandments, are Biblically more explicit than rights.

The Judeo-Christian Bible, however, is more person-based than Jefferson's Enlightenment philosophy of government. Nowhere in Sacred Scripture does it say, or even suggest, that humanity is animal-based. Instead, the opening pages of *Genesis* identify our nature as a likeness of the transcendent and somewhat intimate God.

The split condition in Western civilization between the Judeo-Christian prophets and the Greek philosophers, or between the Biblical intimations of human personhood on one side, and "rational animal" individualism on the other, has been, and is, a major source of the cultural conflicts in Western civilization. One of these oppositions is the way in which the Bible-based Puritan begot the Enlightenment-based playboy.

Though personhood is strongly implied in the Bible, a "rational animal" kind of individualist interpreting it is not likely to get the implication. This is why the Biblical sense of human personhood has been weak in America, and why it has been rapidly receding.

Two Views of Human Nature

The difference between a "rational animal" and an "image and likeness of God" is profoundly significant. This difference must be understood before cultural healing becomes possible. The main source of the culture's problem is the animal base in Aristotle's definition of human nature.

According to the Aristotelian cosmological, or bodily, frame of reference, we do exist together with animals in the genus of sensient organisms. But what is implied in Biblical revelation is that we exist in a community of persons including humans, angels, and three divine Persons. This means that we are basically in the "genus" of persons, not of sensient organisms. We are not biology-based persons, but beings that have a person-based biology.

Because our knowledge is mediated through bodily senses, we are not only intuitive like all other persons, but also rational. No persons other than humans are rational in the sense of being discursive. Angels and the divine Persons know with intuitive immediacy. God's immediate knowledge is infinite. The angel's immediate knowledge is finite. Though we know intuitively *like* them, we also know rationally, *as different from them*. Therefore, we are *rational persons*, *not* rational animals.

Faced with these two views of human nature—the rational animal, and the image and likeness of God—we need to realize that we are much more like God in our spirit-soul-body personhood than we are even physically like the animals. Furthermore, when we understand our bodies as *person*-based, our perception of our likeness to the animals is modified accordingly. Likeness is not identity.

In both cases, however, we *are not* what we are like. So we need to become more aware of what and who we are as human persons.

The animal-versus-God dualism in our interpretation of our nature militates against recovering our personhood. Still more basically, the predominance of the animal-side in this duality *accentuates* the absence of our primary likeness to God. In thinking about ourselves as animal-based rather than person-based, our personhood could not be other than *missing*.

Logical Consequences

Once a culture becomes well-formed, its initiating judgments lead to cultural conclusions by the force of logic. Since the starting judgment of American individualism is an explicit assertion of rights without an equally explicit assertion of responsibilities, "me and my rights" selfism is the next logical step. Before a shift into a healthier culture becomes possible, a new starting point—a new first premise from which logical thinking proceeds—is required.

In the meantime, the American character continues to follow its original logic from an individualist premise to a selfist conclusion. This culture's emphasis on individual rights has been moving away from the Puritan's principled view of rights as reasonably balanced by responsibilities. The movement has been toward the playboy's irresponsible and preferential view of rights that are really wrongs. Logically, these so-called rights, especially the vastly over-extended claim to sexual privacy, have become supreme, and thus, extreme.

According to the selfist logic of sexual privacy, marriage is unnecessary for sexual fulfillment. Commitment is regarded as a matter of preference, not of principle. Pregnancy can be terminated legally. Women are "free" to choose abortion, but sex is impulsively compulsory. And marriage, if preferred, is definable as a *private* matter between consenting adults. Thus marriage becomes logically available to same-sex couples, even triples, and more.

The cultural-judicial situation is already disposed for this human disaster. Privacy rights have been used to legalize a whole train of aberrations: for example, contraception for the unmarried, abortion throughout pregnancy, and sodomy. Apparently, with no end in sight. Logically, privacy rights easily can be extended to any matter of preferential choice, including a gender-neutral and even a quantity-neutral, definition of marriage. Due to the rational animal's capacity for rationalization, almost any behavior can be rationalized as good and acceptable.

A sensibly limited right to privacy is present in the natural law of human persons as persons. This law is the basis of the Constitution.

Interpreted by individualists, however, it has not functioned as the natural law of relational personhood.

For example, John Locke did not see marriage as natural, but rather as a social convention imposed upon the natural (biology-based) relationship between a mother and her child. As Puritan-influenced, he still had the Bible to hold him to man-woman marriage. But his mainly empirical view of the natural law carried other implications, such as the woman *alone* (later in history) having a private "right to choose" to have an abortion.

Because our Constitution is not clearly and explicitly person-based, the value of life has been subjected to an extremely self-centered concept of liberty.

Human nature's conception-and-pregnancy relationship between father, mother, and child is violently reduced to the woman's selfist preference. This preference, gratuitously established in law, denies the inherent rights of the father and child. In this supposed Constitutional situation, the natural and cultural essence of the natural family is legally destroyed. Same-sex "marriage" and any other kind of "marriage," or living together without marriage, are logically implied.

Furthermore, extreme privacy rights that include abortion extend to so-called "scientific" embryonic harvesting, infanticide, assisted suicide, and euthanasia—all in the "wanted and unwanted" category of preferences.

Another way to expose the inexorable force of logic in American culture is to see how the selfist judgment that women are the same as men plays out. If that premise is true, women need to neutralize their most obvious difference from men: their pregnancy potential. Sameness with men has obvious same-sex implications that justify same-sex unions, and even marriage with an intrinsic dynamism for nuptials between three and more.

In the meantime, contraception, abortion, homoerotic expression, and other such contortions fly out of the closet. Morality is forced into it. Eventually, religion follows and the door is slammed shut. If we do not want this logical train of aberrant consequences, we need to return to the "starting gate": the hardwired folly that men and women are the same. At that point of recovery, we will need to establish a true first premise.

Considering the national emergency in our cultural pathology, a new American revolution is necessary. But where can we go for a philosophical, as well as Biblical, insight into the natural law of human personhood? Clearly, not to the animal-based sources of Western individualism.

A New American Revolution

When the fixation on the disabling concept of the "rational animal" is confronted, explicitly and emphatically once and for all, we will have taken a giant step toward being able to see and spread into the culture the true meaning of human personhood and the natural law.

A turnaround in our self-awareness from a biology-based person to a person-based biology would deeply increase our sense of bodily integrity. We would discover that the body of a person is soul-deep, and that heterosexuality is not just a biological appendage of the soul.

A person-based concept of our nature would be able to change everything human for the better. If we take seriously an explicit affirmation of our personhood, it could signal a new stage of maturation in the unique American character. Beyond adolescent individualism and childish selfism, the loneliness of Adam could yield to a better sense of who we are as man and woman in the image and likeness of God.

Chapter 4

Searching for Our Missing Personhood

In the search for America's missing person, Adam cannot go it alone. Once again, Eve needs to emerge from his bones and his soul, and become aware of who she really is. Together, if they choose, she and Adam might be able to restore in this land something like the life, liberty, and happiness for which God created them.

If the woman of *Genesis* were to open her eyes in America, she would be faced with Adam's Puritan-playboy culture. She would see how Adam, in his concept of himself, returned to his loneliness among the animals, and even identified with them in thinking that he is basically an animal. At the same time, he recognized himself as an image and likeness of God. "So much disintegration!" she would say to herself, feeling overwhelmed with repentance and compassion for her original part in his disintegrated condition.

Then she might say to Adam, "I see that you have made much progress on your journey from Eden. Your inventions are amazing and wonderful. Women have learned to use and enjoy them. But they have not been inventors like you.

"So, what is this strange notion about women being just like men? It's another case of alienation from the persons we really are. Adam, don't take seriously any idea of sameness between us.

"It is time that we become friends again, integral in our relational difference. Together, we can search for our long-lost personhood and, in so doing, find healing for our relationship and for America's Puritan-playboy culture."

Eve and the God of Abraham

Long before Adam's cultural emergence in the Middle East, Eve, through her Hindu pantheism, saw distortedly the immanence of God. She thought that everything actually *is* God in different forms.

This mistake encouraged the polytheism of Eastern and Middle Eastern cultures: a belief in god in many different forms. Eve's cultures also moved into the Nirvana of Buddhism: the peace of emptiness, indifferent about anything higher or lower than Self.

Without Adam, Eve's cultures could not detect the difference between the immanence and transcendence of God. By herself, Eve lacked a sense of the otherness of God. In her pantheistic cultures, Adam was submerged in Eve.

In relation to masculine transcendence or *otherness*, immanence is feminine. Immanence means the *withinness* of being.

When God began speaking to Abraham, there was a new kind of immanence in the intimacy between them. It was not the immanence of pantheism and polytheism. Nor was it the empty bliss of Nirvana. Between God and Abraham, something wonderfully interpersonal began to happen in human history. Friendship between persons, as persons, began like a sprouting seed.

Still, the God of Abraham was the Lord: the single, transcendent, One Alone. The Lord sent Abraham on a journey to another land, and promised him that his descendants would be far too numerous to count.

Through Abraham, Adam's cultural journey westward began and continued by leaving a trail of mighty masculine accomplishments. All along the way, Adam's Abrahamic cultures saw man as an image and likeness of the masculine face of God.

But Eve remained submerged in Adam. She needed to become her own person, recreated, as it were, by God from Adam. But she would still have to wonder how she, as a woman, is a direct image and likeness of God. Is there something in the Lord's intimacy with Abraham suggesting that God is in some way *feminine*?

Eve and the Mind of Aristotle

The first thing an awakened Eve would notice about the mind of Aristotle would be the importance of passivity in his way of thinking. She would recall how this condition began when she abandoned her own active receptivity, passed the defect to Adam, and suffered it herself in ages of pantheistic Hinduism, polytheism, and Buddhism. Seeing a different form of the same defect in Aristotle's view of the world, she could not avoid a sense of sorrow for her part in causing it to be. At the same time, she would greatly admire this accomplished philosopher's struggle to overcome the darkness of mind caused by her original failure in being.

According to Aristotle, dark passivity exists at the base of both the world and the mind. He saw matter as basically passive, which he called "prime matter." He also thought that the mind is basically passive, like a blank tablet, which he called the "passive intellect."

These two kinds of emptiness and darkness would constitute together Eve's primary concern. She would recognize in them her regrettable effect on Aristotle's philosophy. Noticing his profound influence on the mentality of Western civilization, her repentance would only deepen.

Though passivity in matter and passivity in the mind are both real, Aristotle's main problem was that he saw matter as the base of the mind. Unlike his forerunner, Plato, he took the matter of his body and the world around him as the primary object of his attention. Plato had been concerned, instead, about the objects of the mind, which he called forms. He thought he once knew these archetypal essences in another world before he was born in this world.

But Aristotle could not accept this other-world placement of the natures of things. Instead, he looked *outward* at the physical world in an objective (masculine) way. This is why Aristotle's philosophy became the source of the scientific inquiry so characteristic of the West.

The awakened Eve would notice how this outer-directed attention to the material universe placed the soul in the body and the mind behind the senses. If she were to reveal to Adam that the truth goes the other way around—the truth that they lost in the beginning—would he listen? Would he see that the body is more basically *within the soul* and the senses are more basically *within the mind*?

Adam might ask Eve how she knows this. "Through my gift of withinness," she would say. "You have this gift, too, Adam. But it is not as prominent in you. I am the keeper of withinness. You are the keeper of otherness. Our withinness is our initial access to our lost personhood. The rest of the way is in the interaction between us."

Adam would then know that he is called by his own withinness toward his better self. This inner call would not imply, however, that he, by way of Aristotle, should return to Plato's other-worldly frame of mind. Aristotle would need to turn around where he is in this world and notice what he is missing in his own objective frame of mind.

No, it is not subjectivity that is missing. It is receptivity: active, not passive.

Had he discovered the active receptivity of his own personhood, Aristotle would have been almost entirely different in his thinking. Such a different awareness would have been similar to Copernicus discovering that the earth travels around the sun instead of the sun going around the earth. What a shakeup in the senses that was! The opposite from what appeared to be true was actually the truth!

It surely looks and feels like the sun moves across the sky. Similarly, it looks and feels like the soul is in the body. Of course, this is true as far as it goes. But still truer is an awareness that the body is *within* the power of the soul, and that the body's senses are, therefore, *within* the power of the mind.

This inner turnaround frees us for seeing that the soul dynamically *receives* matter, instead of just forming matter, as Aristotle thought.

Eve and the God of Christians

Nothing could be more immanent-transcendent than God incarnate in human nature.

Born of a virgin in a stable, dying on a cross and rising from death, this incarnate God redeemed Adam and Eve in all of us. After two thousand years, however, the redeemed Eve in the Western world is still culturally embedded in Adam.

Why is it taking so long for her true self to emerge?

First of all, the world was barely ready to *receive* its redeemer. He came to earth as soon as he could after Abraham and Aristotle. A virgin descendant of Abraham said "Let it be done to me according

Searching for Our Missing Personhood

to your word" (*Luke* 1:38). But how could God-Incarnate tell the strictly monotheistic sons of Abraham that there is more than one Person in God, and that he, himself, is one of them? He could only imply it. But he did actually go so far as to say, "Before Abraham came to be, I am" (*John* 8:58).

This sounded too much like God saying to Moses "I am who am." And that was enough for rigid monotheists to condemn Jesus of Nazareth. When he was arrested, his followers fled and left him alone to be tortured, crucified, and drained of his blood.

Jesus is the new Adam; his mother, the new Eve. But most people on the planet do not know it yet.

With that kind of slowness and passivity, how could the Lord Jesus tell us any more than he did about the Person he is? Not until he was about to ascend into heaven did he finally name the three divine Persons: Father, Son, and Holy Spirit. No explanation was given. He simply left the Great Mystery to those who had previously abandoned him.

Soon they were challenged to defend their faith. They had to find some way to explain it to others. But how? Three Gods? "I and the Father are one" (*John* 10:30), he had said. Three-in-one must be the explanation: three Persons in one divine nature.

All three were revealed as masculine. Except for the uniqueness and profound influence of Mary, the new Eve, the original Eve was still culturally buried alive in Adam.

What Happened to Christianity?

Redeemed by God-Incarnate, the passivity of the human mind still needed to be healed. That was not to happen immediately, or even quickly. For the cultural Adam, healing would take many centuries of gradual awakening. He had to meet the challenge of trying to defend his Christian faith against all that tries to destroy it. He struggled his way through the blood of martyrs, then through Augustine's theology that used the philosophy of Plato to explain revealed truths of faith, then through Thomas Aquinas who used the philosophy of Aristotle in his consummate dialogue between faith and reason.

Adam's struggle to understand and defend his Christian faith—alone and without Eve: that is what happened to Christianity. The unfortunate result was that Christians viewed God overwhelmingly as masculine.

Adam's explanations, though a great blessing for his faith, carried within them the shortcoming of his going it alone. Faith, and his reasoning about it, lacked the *integrating receptivity* that would have successfully united thinking with believing.

For Adam's philosophers, receptivity meant passivity. And this passivity remained fundamental throughout their philosophies. Consequently, the acts of believing and reasoning—in spite of how closely these acts interrelated in the mind of Thomas Aquinas—were destined to part company. And that is what actually did happen. And quickly.

How Did It Happen?

Thomas Aquinas received wholeheartedly the Biblical revelations about creation and the triune nature of God. Faced with Aristotle's uncreated and eternal world, he nevertheless developed, in the light of faith, a concept of personhood and the immortality of the human soul.

But he also accepted Aristotle's view of both the world and the mind as basically passive. As a result, his view of the mind turned out to be an inadequate basis for faith in divine revelation. None of the philosophers who followed him overcame this inadequacy.

The kind of mind that is capable of both believing and explaining what is believed is not like the mind of Adam alone. Neither is it like the mind of Eve alone. Thomas brought together Abraham and Aristotle as close as Adam alone could bring them, but not close enough to prevent their subsequent straying from each other.

Adam in the philosophers wanted to know how the mind, through the senses, abstracts universal natures from individual things. His problem, from the outset, was that he was so much more interested in the abstract universals than in the concrete things.

This masculine preoccupation with universals blinded him to the *immediate* (actively receptive) way that the intellect knows the *being*, the *is*, of real individuals. Adam's philosophers did not even see or recognize any kind of *immediate intellectual* knowledge of individuals. According to the 20th century Thomists, Etienne Gilson and Jacques Maritain, material beings are known through the senses, and then through a post-conceptual "existential judgment." This judgment affirms the actual existence of the sensed object *out there*, but only after the initial concept of its nature is formed.

There can be no existential judgment, however, unless the *is* of the object is known *before* any concept of its nature is formed. The reason is that the immediate existential intuition *causes* the concept in the first place. This pre-conceptual act of agent intellection is more immediate and more active than any kind of sense knowledge; it contains and transforms our sense knowledge from an animal-based to an intensively intellectified person-based kind of sensing.

Unaware of this unique kind of sense knowledge, Adam's philosophers missed the starting point of wisdom. Duns Scotus tried to connect with this starting point by way of an intuitive knowledge of the singular. But he failed to do so by intuiting it *as* a singular (versus a universal), not as a unique being in itself, and by sending *being* into the passive realm of logic. As a result, universals became what William of Occam called them: mere names applied to singular entities.

Western philosophy suffered from these profound shortsights, eventually committed suicide, and was buried by mathematics and technology. Adam was at his wits end in the depths of loneliness.

The Great Turnaround that Intensified the Problem

At the end of the 15th century, an Italian named Christopher Columbus thought he could reach the East by sailing West. When his ships did not fall off the end of the earth, people started to realize that the earth is not as flat as it seems.

Several decades later, the sun "stopped moving across the sky" when a Polish astronomer, Nicolaus Copernicus, said that the earth revolves around the sun. That was a huge turnaround in the human consciousness that had been cast out of Eden. It changed the whole universe in the eyes of the people, and put them in a condition of uneasiness. No longer did they experience themselves living at the center of the world, nor did they trust their senses as much as before.

Some people, especially philosophers, became self-conscious and, at the same time, more aware of the physical world as a challenge to their understanding. A painfully split condition resulted. "Out there" and "in here" became two different worlds. Awareness of the human body-soul relationship plummeted into a new, more virulent, form of ancient dualism.

Aristotle's way of rescuing the human individual from Plato's body-soul dualism could not survive the Copernican crisis. His attempt to understand the unity of body and soul in terms of a matter-form (hylemorphic) relationship, though a giant step forward in philosophical insight, was basically incomplete. It was vulnerable, therefore, to cultural stresses that eventually would produce a disintegrated understanding of the relationship between the soul and body of the human person.

Shortly after Copernicus, Rene Descartes (1596-1650) wanted to find a starting point for philosophy that was more certain than sense knowledge. Due to the newly-apparent shortcomings of sensory evidence, objective *certainty* seemed to him to be out of the question. Pulling back from the senses, he discovered that he, himself, was doubting his senses. That is what he knew with certainty. At that illuminating point, he almost said, like God, "I am who am." Instead, "I think, therefore I am" became his radically *subjective* starting point. From there, he wanted ideas that were clearly and distinctly well formed. Clarity and separation of ideas (one from another) became his criterion for truth.

Previously, in classical thought, truth was based on the conviction that the mind, through the senses, conforms to things that exist independently of the mind. Descartes began, instead, with ideas in the mind itself. As a result, he thought that the human person is a self-conscious soul and that the human body, like a mechanistic appendage, is an attachment to the soul.

Ironically, this philosophical catastrophe was destined to happen. Aristotle's animal-based concept of human nature affected his view of the body-soul relationship in such a way as to imply something like the Cartesian predicament. The ancient philosopher who trusted

Searching for Our Missing Personhood

his senses too much would lead to the modern philosopher who could not trust his senses at all.

According to Aristotle's *soul-in-body view* of human nature, the soul seems enclosed in a biological closet. Consequently, according to his view, the mind is so sense-based and sense-bound that its connection with objects beyond the senses had to be assumed.

In spite of what he called the "light" of the agent intellect, Aristotle could not overcome his soul-in-body problem. He used this posited "light" to explain the abstraction of universals from sense knowledge *without also knowing intellectively*—immediately and directly—the particular realities from which the universals are supposedly abstracted. Consequently, his mind-reality connection amounted to Adam without Eve in his intellectual life. This means that Adam *produced* knowledge without Eve's initial and actively receptive knowing of the *real existence*—not just the sensible qualities—of that which is known.

In this traditional sense-bound setup, skepticism about the mind's connection with reality is implied. The Copernican challenge to the senses had forced this weakness in the mind-reality connection to rise to the surface and become explicit.

Therefore, in the history of Adam's philosophers, the "immediate predecessor" of the skeptical Descartes was really Aristotle. Almost two thousand years had passed between these two. But the earlier thinker's astute explanation of both body-soul unity and human knowledge was still so inadequate that it finally paid the price in Descartes' methodical doubt and body-soul disintegration.

In the only way that Adam could do it without Eve, Descartes retreated into his mind away from his senses. This retreat into consciousness made his body an object of his mind. The result became a separation between his soul and body so extreme that he allowed between them only a gland in his head. The pineal gland became his pathetically biological substitute for the mysterious "light" of the mind that Aristotle posited between the body and soul of the sense-bound rational animal.

After Descartes, the extremes of empiricism and rationalism were decisive in forming the modern era. An example of this divide between the senses and the mind is the modern interpretation of human consciousness. On the empirical side, Freud claimed that consciousness is so completely determined by unconscious forces that no real freedom is possible. On the other side, Jean Paul Sartre (1905-1980) insisted that we are "condemned to be free." The empiricist Freud reduced human nature to sexual energy. The existential rationalist Sartre reduced human nature to absolute choice. The cultural progeny of these far-out opposites has become the *Roe v. Wade* hijacking of the American Constitution.

The vivid contrast between the Freudian and Sartrean views of human nature clearly reveals the "split personality" of Western civilization. These are the opposites that came together culturally in what has been, and still is, called the sexual revolution.

The Crisis Today

The so-called "personalism" of contemporary philosophers and theologians is a direct descendant of Cartesian dualism. So, these "personalists" are really subjectivists who treat their own bodies like objects. This object is managed like an "instrument" of the subject rather than *received* within the person as an expression of the soul.

Treating the body as an object of the subject depersonalizes the body by biologizing it. Such mental treachery initiates a kind of logic that takes its own course—as logic always does—in spite of ardent denials along the way. The irrational "rational animal" rationalizes contraception, abortion, homoeroticism, assisted suicide, and euthanasia on the so-called basis of personalism. This basis—this starting point—is little more than selfist subjectivism.

Thus, the schizoid form of "personalism" that objectifies and biologizes the human body increasingly separates body and soul in a way that resembles their separation at death. This fraudulent sense of personhood—this ultimate condition of the missing person—is actually the source of the culture of death.

Western Civilization's cast-out-of-Eden search for our long-lost personhood has become, in our times, a crisis of psychotic-like proportions. Due to contemporary advancements in technology without a contextual understanding of human personhood, soul and body are more separated than ever. Our relationship with our biology, as a built in result, has become acutely paranoid. Without adequate discernment, huge quantities of drugs are being used by many to defend themselves against what they view as their alien, unruly, threatening bodies. In other ways, also, people are treating their bodies as objects, as things.

Where, then, can we find the integral human person *as a person*? Clearly not in the idea that we are rational animals. As history shows, that kind of "animal" is more likely to rationalize than to be truly rational.

A Clue in the Search

The missing person is one who is misunderstood as having a biology-based soul instead of having a soul-based biology. These are two different ways of seeing reality. One is like seeing the earth as flat; the other like seeing the earth as round.

From an eye-ball perspective, the earth looks flat and a human person looks body-based. From a fuller point of view, the earth *is* round and a human person *is* based on the soul. From their own perspectives, both views are true. Only one, however, is true to what actually *is*.

The real human person has a soul-based body. In other words, the body is an expression of the soul within the soul. This expression could not be such, however, unless the soul first *receives* the body, and does so actively, not passively. But a recognition of substantial receptivity in the soul is nowhere to be found in Adam's philosophy.

In our search for the missing person, we will have to pass through an ancient wall in our sense of ourselves. We will need to affirm our soul's active receptivity for our body. This affirming recognition requires the awakening of *Eve* in both woman and man together. Then, we will be able to find and receive the many-splendored gift of our God-like personhood.

Chapter 5

Finding Our Missing Personhood

After the light went out between Adam and Eve, she wanted it turned on again. But her quest was severely limited by her collapsed and passive way of thinking. Unable to see how she was a likeness of God, she began to think of herself as being a part of God. From her pantheistic point of view, enlightenment meant a *process* of leaving the darkness and returning to the light where she would lose her individuality in the impersonal Absolute.

For centuries in the Orient, Eve's philosophers thought the soul enters one body after another until it finally frees itself from matter, and becomes God—an actual fulfillment of the original deception. This cycling of the soul into and out of matter has been called "reincarnation." So, according to Eve's men of wisdom, there is no real unity of the human soul and body. Thus, there is no recovery of personhood.

In the West, Adam's philosophers discovered more soul-body unity than that. According to their objective way of thinking, the soul still *enters and leaves* the body. But it does so only once.

Both Eastern and Western ideas about the soul's relationship with the body are like thinking that the sun rises and sets because it looks and feels that way. The soul entering and leaving the body; the sun rising and setting. That is how the "rational animal" sees and thinks.

Therefore, Eve and Adam need something like a Copernican revolution. Their turnaround would have to occur in "inner space" and grace. Eve, the keeper of withinness, would need to connect with Mary of Nazareth who said "Let it be," meaning "I receive."

Twenty centuries ago, feminine receptivity was consummated in Mary's clear and glorious *fiat*. Eve in the world's philosophers has not heard it yet. Consequently, the cultures of the planet are in a desperate crisis, and masculinized feminism is one of the most troublesome results.

In the light of her redemption, Eve needs to turn around and actually see how she failed to *receive* God, not only in Eden, but also in the minds of her pantheistic philosophers. Because of their passivity, they think the soul disappears in God and becomes part of God. If Eve could see, instead, that the whole human person, soul and body, receives God while remaining *other* than God, she would be liberated from her oriental philosophers.

Then Eve would be free to relate with Adam in a way that would bring them together in a mutual adventure of discovery.

Eve and the Mind of Adam

The pantheistic Eve based the soul in God, not in matter. The individualistic Adam based the soul in matter, not in God. Neither one of the two, in their philosophers and theologians, sees the soul as receiving and immortalizing the body. Neither one of them—alone—can see the truth about their personhood.

Eve needs Adam to show how God is *other* than the soul. Without Adam, she falsely thinks that the soul is within God as a part of God.

And Adam needs Eve to show how the body is *within* the soul. Without Eve, he falsely thinks that the body is outside the soul as a part of the animal kingdom.

Eve's predominant interest in the soul is her way to the truth about the human person. If she would realize her emphasis in her relationship with Adam, she could relate with him, finally, on the level of their personhood. "Neither of us," she might say to Adam, "has recognized how our nature is based in our own kind of being. We are neither God nor an animal. So let us find out what we really are."

In spite of Adam helping Eve to realize the otherness of God, he would be likely to respond to her clarification by quoting Aristotle. Clinging, at first, to his identity with the animals, as secured by

Aristotle, Adam would wonder how his body could possibly be within his soul.

To clarify further, Eve could show that Aristotle's concept of the soul as the actuation of passive matter does not suggest survival after death. Plant and animal souls are also life principles that serve as forms of passive matter, and, for that reason alone, cannot survive death. Instead, their souls dissipate into the energies of nature when the passivity of their matter finally overcomes them.

From the surviving texts alone, we have little evidence that Aristotle supported the immortality of the individual human soul.

Thomas Aquinas, in spite of agreeing with Aristotle's matter-form view of the soul, and largely due to his own Christian faith, recognized the human soul as immortal. But, due to his acceptance of the body-based view of the soul (according to "the philosopher," as he called Aristotle), his interpretation of the relationship between soul and body was likewise inadequate.

In their "rational animal" (body-based) frame of reference, both Aristotle and Thomas accepted the archaic idea that the soul enters the body some weeks or months after conception. They did not have the scientific means for discovering the completeness of genetic structure at conception.

At their time in history, they also believed that the earth is flat and that, according to Ptolemy, the sun goes daily around it across the sky. Such ideas about both our inner and outer worlds are primitive and undeveloped. Yet some intellectuals who think of themselves as rational animals still accept delayed animation as true.

The cultural turnaround from the Ptolemaic to the Copernican view of outer space is only the beginning. Another revolution, still to come, must occur *within* us.

At this point in her journey, Eve can realize that her ancient idea about reincarnation is shortsighted. She can also see the grossness in Adam's body-based view of the human soul. With this kind of awareness, she can begin a turnaround from within.

Eve is able to see that the soul does not enter the body at all, because the body is not really outside the soul as something to be inhabited. Instead, the body is within the soul's *active receptivity* for matter.

This insight into the soul's *substantial* receptivity would be, however, startling news to Adam. He, in his philosophers, never thought of such a thing. For Adam, there could not possibly be substantial receptivity in an actuating form such as the human soul. He has no clue about receptivity as a kind of activity that is *not at all passive*.

Receptivity of the soul for matter would be Eve's primary insight into human personhood. So, realizing that she herself never thought differently before her awakening, she would have to ask Adam why he thinks that receiving is passive.

If Adam could see that his kind of outward action is not the only way of being active, he could open his mind to another way of being active. Eve might ask him, "Adam, are you aware that you can listen to what you are saying *while you are saying it*? When you are listening to yourself talk, and not just talking to an object, I become interested in listening to you. It's a subtle interaction, but it's real."

Listening is receptive in relation to speaking. But listening (giving one's attention) is just as active as speaking, though differently.

So, according to Eve—the keeper of withinness—receptivity, like listening, is not passive. There is no reason, then, why receptivity cannot be substantial in the soul.

Adam and the Mind of Eve

Finally, Adam needs to listen to the ontological (being-based) resonance of substantial receptivity in the human soul. If he were to do so, his masculine perspective would bring out something that Eve does not see clearly. He would notice how the soul is not only inner-directed, but also outer-directed. And he would point out to her how the soul *expresses* itself in the very structure of the body.

The soul not only receives the body according to the withinness noticed by Eve, but also ex-presses itself physically according to the otherness noticed by Adam. In the light of these two perspectives—both the withinness and otherness of the body in relation to the soul—Eve and Adam would be on the threshold of their personhood.

Finding Our Missing Personhood

As they would move toward their inmost core, Adam would have to face Eve with the weakness in her sense of individuality. Her previous identification of the soul with God would be intolerable for him. He would make clear to her that being a *likeness* of God in accord with theism is vastly different from being *part* of God according to pantheism. "Eve," he would say, "You are no more a part of God than you are a part of me. You are yourself, individually and uniquely."

Then Eve might respond, "Adam, do you still agree with Aristotle that matter is the principle of individuation? That is true only about plants and animals. If matter is the only principle of a person's individuation, no person could survive death. Therefore, the human soul, in its *substantial* receptivity—not the passivity of matter—is the principle of *human* individuation."

"Even if that is true, something is still missing," Adam would insist. "The soul would have to be as expressive as it is receptive. The individuation of the human person would have to be receptive-expressive."

He would continue, "I see my propensity toward individualism is incomplete because it fails to include the receptivity in the depths of my being. And your propensity toward anonymity is incomplete because it fails to include the expressivity in the depths of your being."

So, neither Eve nor Adam can become complete unless they do so together. And the *receptivity* they share is their mutually integrating power.

The Importance of Receptivity

Before Adam and Eve recognize the substantial receptivity of the soul for the body, Eve thinks she is a part of God, and Adam thinks he is basically an animal. Obviously, the two are far apart and have a major problem with their relationship. Physical intimacy attempts to bridge the chasm and temporarily seems to do so. Psychologically and spiritually, however, the distance remains. Ontologically, in their God-animal dichotomy their alienation is deepest.

By recognizing together the substantial receptivity of their soul for their body, Adam and Eve can become fully person-based in their sense of themselves as beings. The result in their lives can become a revolutionary ability to become friends between themselves, with God, with other persons, and with other creatures around them. Recognizing in this way the active receptivity of their being, they can find the lost gift of their personhood and its many splendors.

In our substantial depth of receptivity, we face both the infinite Giver and the finite gift of our being as persons. Paradoxically, we are called to receive together both the Giver and the gift. Both at once.

We can receive either gratefully, or indifferently, or not at all. Our daily way of living is the evidence of how we are exercising this receptive freedom of our personhood.

Active receptivity like this is our access to a rebirth in our way of living. It is also a rejuvenation of the metaphysical philosophy long thought to be dead. As indicated previously in this book, the philosophy of being—as being—died after the Middle Ages because the masculine mentality could not carry it alone.

An integration of the feminine with the masculine mentality about *being* would result in something more than metaphysics (beyond physics). This new way of thinking would include the *being* of the physical along with the *being* of everything else; it would become not metaphysics, but ontology.

Without a living ontological insight, through and beyond eyesight, Western civilization is destined to collapse into the darkness and emptiness of technology increasing and multiplying for its own sake. This is the inevitable destiny of Adam's individualism without the redeemed receptivity of Eve.

New light regarding the *radical difference between passivity and receptivity* is, therefore, a profound need in the philosophy that affects all areas of human existence. An interpersonal, feminine-masculine (no longer individualist), kind of philosophy is needed in theology, psychology, sociology, the arts, the church, the state, and family life. And this kind of wisdom is not possible without a clear understanding of the *integrative power of active receptivity*.

Receptivity is important everywhere. The actively receptive side of human personhood needs to be encouraged. Receiving in the

Finding Our Missing Personhood

heart is quite different from just taking and possessing with the hands.

The difference between a receptive and a possessive attitude seems highlighted in "Auguries of Innocence" by poet William Blake (1757-1827) when he refers to seeing a world in a grain of sand and heaven in a wild flower.

Something profound in us is awakened when we begin to *see* and to *hold* in this way. We can strengthen our ability to do so by giving it more attention. More awareness.

Then the feminine-masculine paradox of our personhood can come to life in our lives. The Eve and Adam within us can recover their active receptivity together. In the process of doing so, they will have an exciting and meaningful future.

Chapter 6

The Human Person in a New Light

In the super vastness of the universe, a human person seems like almost nothing. Quantitatively. But an individual person makes the whole cosmos seem like almost nothing. Qualitatively.

The universe has no idea why it exists, and is not even able to *wonder* why. But a one-celled human person has the natural, though not yet functional, ability to wonder why. Billions upon billions of stars in space, all different in glory and immensity, are far from the *quality* of one microscopic human life.

That personhood can be so important when appearing so small is a considerable challenge to our usual way of thinking. But this is only one of the mind-openers we face. In a person-based versus body-based frame of reference, everything about our personhood requires re-thinking. Especially the relationship between our soul and body.

How the Soul Receives the Body

The life principle or soul of simply organic beings is mortal and dissipates at death. But the soul of a *person* is spiritual, immortal, and personal forever.

This difference between mortal and immortal souls means that the human soul relates with matter in a profoundly different way than the soul of a plant or animal.

Mortal souls are individuations of organic energy. This energy materializes itself in many kinds of organisms, and in many organisms of each kind, then dematerializes each of them back again into organic energy. But immortal souls are not individuations of organic energy that disintegrate in this way.

Immortal souls are individually created by God to *receive* organic matter into their being, and to *express* their being as bodily persons. This deep receptivity—not present in mortal souls—*immortalizes* the essential *quality* of the body—not it's physical *quantity*. And this immortalized *quality* of the human body survives death. But the *quantitative expression* of the human soul—its physical matter—leaves the soul and disintegrates.

Though the *physical* expression of the person's body is mortal, that same body is *metaphysically* immortal. Only receptivity in the human soul for the body makes possible this qualitative immortality of the body.

Because of their masculine way of thinking about the human being, Adam's philosophers could not even suspect substantial receptivity in the human soul. Thomas Aquinas, Adam's stellar best, attributed immortality to the human soul, but saw it as able to subsist on its own after death. Logically, he was compelled to think that the soul leaves the body at death and becomes an incomplete substance, or incomplete person, until the resurrection of the body completes the person again.[5]

But the human person with a metaphysical body that becomes de-physicalized at death remains, in the most basic sense, a *complete* person. This person is incomplete only in a secondary sense.

Thomas needed more insight into receptivity as active rather than passive. He could have been more aware of the metaphysical inseparability of the human soul and body. Subsequently, the history of Adam's philosophers could have been a significantly different story.[6]

In writing about the human body, St. Paul had said, "If there is a physical body, there is also a spiritual body" (1 *Cor*. 15:44). The expression "spiritual body" can be another way of naming the metaphysical depths of the physical body. Without this spiritual (or ontologically metaphysical) body, the resurrection of the *same physical person* would not be possible.

Furthermore, the reality of the spiritual body makes impossible the reincarnation of the soul in one body after another. A soul entering a second body that has essential bodily qualities *different from* those

The Human Person in a New Light

already immortalized in that soul, and later entering sequentially still more bodies, is a multiple contradiction.

The human body, then, is soul-deep. It is not just an attachment that can be dispensed with like an object, and reattached in another "incarnation." One unique human body is subsistently constituted forever within the unique soul of each human person.

This soul-based perspective on the human body has tremendous implications for finding our missing personhood. For example, the body viewed as soul-deep undermines animal-based methods of bodily treatment as being radically inappropriate. Some of these high-class veterinarian procedures include sterilization, artificial insemination, *in vitro* fertilization, embryonic stem cell research, so-called "therapeutic cloning," and killing our prebirth little ones as if they were no more than biological tissue. All of these "procedures" are human perversions due largely to an ancient "Ptolemaic," long-outmoded, and dualistic, view of reality. Recovery will involve a discovery of the *true center of the solar system*, not far out in cosmic space, but right here on earth. The center is not the solar sun millions of miles away, but the "soular" sun of human personhood warm and luminous within us.

There is a place, however, where the light of our personhood is most hidden in darkness. If we could recognize and acknowledge personhood there, we would be facing the "soular" sun in its most challenging requirement for insight beyond eyesight. That place is where the human person begins to exist deep within the body of a woman.

What Happens at Conception?

Microscopic, totally vulnerable, and hidden in darkness, a new little person begins to exist. Even if conception occurs out of place under a microscope in a well-lit lab, most of this momentous event is invisible to the eye. Intense physical light makes little, if any, difference for the insight needed.

We can see what happens at the dawning of human personhood only by a different kind of light—an intuitive kind. Only intellectual intuition can reach the reality that exists deeper than what the eye can see.

On the surface of the one-celled conception event—biologically, not ontologically, called "fertilization"—Adam thinks that the sperm penetrates the ovum because it looks that way. Then he thinks the soul enters either the zygote that results, or the embryo that develops later, or the fetal organism still later, or even the organism at birth. With his eyeball fixation, he is not sure when humanization occurs.

If the soul *enters* the body at conception or sometime later, and *leaves* at death because it looks that way, the logic of eyesight prevails. But the opposite is truer. It is better to think that the body, not the soul, does the entering and leaving. Then we can see more clearly the soul-based body, and not remain prisoners of eyesight in what we construe as a body-based soul.

According to the soul-based turnaround, God creates the soul to express itself in a bodily manner. This does not mean that the soul is created first, then the body. God creates simultaneously the whole human person, not just the soul. The person is really and vitally one, not just a soul and body put together like parts of an artifact.

Therefore, the parents do not create the new person's body. God does. The parents present to God only a particular disposition of matter *through which* the soul causes its own body, as God creates that soul to express itself physically. Father and mother supply the naturally instrumental (gametic) causes. By the instrumental activity of these gametes, the soul is able to *receive* their causality and *express* itself as a bodily person.

At conception, then, something happens that is much more active and instantaneous than a sperm penetrating an ovum. Actually, there is no such thing as a "fertilized ovum." The sperm and ovum die together so that a new person might live. These generative cells, together with the human soul, become mutual *causes* of the new person's body. Cytoplasmic matter left over from the ovum remains to nourish the new human life.

We do not see, but can come to know, that the soul of the new person *receives and transforms* the material causes of its own body. These material causes include organic energy, the physical quantity of the sperm and ovum, and genetic information. The disintegration of the gametes releases into the power of the soul these material causes. Instantaneously, as the new bodily person begins to exist, the receptive-expressive soul receives and transforms these material causes. In the very same instant, the soul immortalizes all of these causes except the physical quantity of the body.

The almost invisible quantity (size) of the gametes and the unique individual quality of their information become, instantaneously, the new person's metaphysical and physical self-expression.

So, it is naive to think that the soul *enters* what appears to be a united ovum and sperm. Rather, the human soul receives the organic energy and matter of these co-active cells as they mutually lose their gametic individuality. The resultant genetic material is not that of the father and mother, but of the new person (or persons, in the case of twinning).[7] The new single-celled person *has*, not *is*, genes and chromosomes.

According to the ontological (being-based) perspective, then, there is no body for the soul to enter. Instead, there are at least nine interacting causes having one *simultaneous* effect. Nine causes; one effect. The instantaneous interaction of so many necessary causes is a consummation of being that is wondrous to contemplate.[8]

Since the body expresses the soul, the maleness or femaleness of the body is an expression of the sexual emphasis of the soul. As created by God, the spiritual soul is both feminine and masculine, but having either a feminine or masculine emphasis. This emphasis in the receptive-expressive power of the soul has a selective effect on the sperm cells that surround the surface of the ovum before conception takes place. Some of these sperm cells carry male, and others carry female, chromosomes. The soul's power means that, at the moment of conception, the feminine-emphatic soul actively receives an ovum and simultaneously causes it to selectively receive one of the XX (female) sperm cells that pre-conceptively surround the ovum. Similarly, the masculine-emphatic soul actively receives an ovum and simultaneously causes it to selectively receive one of the Xy (male) sperm cells. Thus, the soul, not the body, is the primary source of the sexuality of the human person. The gender of the body *expresses*, within the soul, the gender of the soul.

Amazingly, *the new person, who is only the size of a single cell, is almost totally pre-physical. As a bodily person, however, this little human being is complete*, not only metaphysically (causally), but also ontologically (personally). In one microscopically tiny cell, the *whole body* of the new person exists. Physically expressed as a zygote, the new person is not yet physically expressed in embryonic, fetal, infant, child, adolescent, and adult stages of development.

Clearly, then, the human person's body does not have to be physicalized, except for a single cell, in order to be the body of a complete human person. Seeing this truth is essential to finding our culturally missing personhood.

What Happens at Death?

The traditional animal-based concept of human nature demands an animal-based interpretation of death. According to that view, the soul completely separates from the body. But body-soul separation at death means that, even while united in this world, the body and soul are *potentially separate*. Such is the supposed "unity" of the missing person.

In a person-based view of human nature, soul and body are so united that they are not even potentially separate. So, death looks significantly different than it did before.

Instead of the soul separating from the body, the organic-physical body ceases to function. Then the physical matter of the body separates from the metaphysical body.

After death, the remains are similar to the placenta that departs from the child at birth. Both of these remains are no longer alive, and therefore, are destined for burial. But when they were living, *both were a part of a* person.

As part of the fetal child, the placenta connects the child with the intra-uterine environment. And as a part of the person after birth, the physically functioning body connects the person to a much more expansive and intensive environment. Because of an ongoing process of development, our present "placental" connection with our earthly environment is much more complex than our previous embryonic-fetal connection with our maternal environment once was.

Death is, then, similar to birth. It is our second birth. It is our entrance into another stage of development in a still more expansive and intensive environment.

Entering the final stage of our development at death, our second birth leaves our "placental" matter behind for burial. We become post-physical. But we remain metaphysically complete.

After death, we will be complete human persons in a way that is similar to our being complete human persons at conception. In our beginning, we were almost completely pre-physical. After death, we will be totally post-physical, but only in the quantitative, not in the qualitative, sense.

In heaven with the saints and angels, we will be metaphysically human, luminously sensient, perfectly rational, and powerfully intuitive, persons. Our whole being will see, not just our eyes. Our whole being will hear, not just our ears.

But in the everlasting torment of the demons, if that is a person's final decision, he or she will nevertheless remain metaphysically complete, though totally distorted, as a human person.

Before we become accustomed to thinking of death as the second birth of an ontologically complete person, we will have to go through a period of intellectual reorientation. This shift in our mentality will be similar to that experienced by the people who first heard that the earth is not as flat as it looks, and that the sun does not move according to what their eyes see.

At the time of Kepler and Galileo, for instance, some learned scholars refused to look into the telescope to see the evidence that the sun is the center of our planetary system. They found the inner move beyond eyesight to insight too much to take. But everyone today has adapted to, and takes for granted, a truer view of the solar heavens.

Both the solar and the "soular" turnarounds in awareness call for a new way of seeing what meets the eye.

What about Evolution?

We know about the creation of the world as revealed in *Genesis*. We have heard, also, about the theory of evolution. But we must admit that we do not know the details of our origin in the cosmos.

Genesis does not reveal an all-at-once creation of the universe. Whether there were six twenty-four-hour days or six huge spans of time, there were several *stages* of creation. These "days" represent a temporal process.

Whether or not, or to what extent, the creation of the cosmos was an evolutionary process is open to an ontological interpretation. Such an analysis would have both theological and scientific implications, and would remain necessarily *theoretical*. The physical sciences alone could never yield decisive evidence, especially of *human* evolution. The nature of the issue is basically metaphysical.

We can readily acknowledge an evolutionary process in the stellar universe. It seems reasonable that there was a gradual expression of physical energy in a multitude of elements, and long epochs in the formation of galaxies composed of these elements. Likewise understandable is an evolutionary shift into another kind of energy: organic energy. This second kind of energy gradually would have expressed itself in a vast variety of living creatures.

But the existence of immortal persons cannot be explained by energy of any kind. *Power* can be the source of persons, but *not energy*.

The beginning of human persons on the planet earth is not a physical or an organic matter. It is ontologically metaphysical. And an effort to understand this kind of event requires an adequate way of thinking. In other words, our ordinary way of thinking is plainly inadequate. We erroneously think that evolution involves a soul *entering* some kind of pre-human body.

In a person-based context, the appearance of human persons is quite similar to the soul-centered ontology of conception described earlier in this chapter. In an evolutionary setting, the soul does not *enter* some kind of highly evolved organism. Instead, the soul *receives and transforms* organically developed matter into its own bodily expression of itself. This explanation would be as true about the first human persons who existed in the cosmos as it is true about all the rest.

The difference, however, is in the parental context, that is, in pre-human (transitory hominid) versus human parents. In both cases, the new person does not come *from* the parents, but *through* the parents. The first two human persons (Adam and Eve) to exist on earth, in an evolutionary context, would have come into existence not *from* but *through* a pre-human source.

Theoretically, the receptive-transformative power of the soul in a soul-based human being could make the *coming-through* kind of event metaphysically possible.

Our Feminine-Masculine Personhood

Eve is deep in our personhood. She represents our substantial receptivity and its transforming power. Adam is just as deep within us. He represents the expressive power of our being. Without it, we could not even be. Obviously, then, both Eve and Adam are necessary within us.

Individuality is Adam's base. That is why, at conception, the male is the individuator. That is also why, according to *Genesis*, Eve proceeds from Adam.

Taken literally, the account in *Genesis* seems to reveal a physical procession of woman from man. A better understanding would be that Revelation gives a physical depiction of a metaphysical reality. Eve proceeds from Adam primarily in a metaphysical manner, and secondarily, physically. The physical is always an *expression* of the metaphysical.

Eve's individuality as a person originates *metaphysically* from the Adam within her own being. The individuality of every being, as a being, is its masculine principle of self-expression expressing itself.

Within each individual person, man or woman, Eve represents substantial receptivity; Adam represents expressive individuation. Eve and Adam also represent the distinctive powers of personhood: the powers to know and to love. Our power to know is both receptive and expressive. It is receptively intuitive and expressively rational. Similarly, our power to love is responsive and responsible (feminine and masculine). Manhood emphasizes the inner Adam; womanhood, the inner Eve.

So, in the light of our person-based nature, a cultural shift can begin to take place. The "soular" sun of our feminine-masculine personhood can begin to emerge from ancient clouds and fog. The cast-out shortsights that resulted from the catastrophe in Eden can begin to pass away into history. We who are living in the culture of the alienated Adam finally will be able to recover a warm and luminous sense of our being in the true center of the universe.

Chapter 7

Finding Our Power for Wisdom

The sun in the sky radiates energy, light, and warmth for all living things on earth.

Similarly, the center of our personhood, when liberated within us, radiates the power of life, the light of wisdom, and the warmth of love. *Power, wisdom, and love.*

These gifts of our being are so interpermeating that the power of life is radiant, the light of wisdom is warming, and the warmth of love is luminous. Some understanding about our power for the warming light of wisdom is essential for helping us to recover our personhood.

Beginning in the *power* of our personhood for knowing the *is* of things, wisdom causes us to wonder why there is anything at all rather than nothing. Wondering *why* anything exists depends on first knowing *that* something exists. As mentioned in the Preface, animals cannot know that anything exists, not even themselves. They are incapable of connecting with the *being* of the things they see, hear, smell, taste, and feel. Thus, they cannot wonder *why* anything exists.

Wondering and searching for answers begins in the *intuitive power* of the human mind that connects us immediately—through and beyond our senses—with the *real being* of that which we know. This immediate cognition—the light of *is*—is natural in every one of us. It is the preconscious source of consciousness. But we do not recognize it. History tells us why.

The Bridge That Adam Built

When Eve abandoned her active receptivity and Adam collapsed with her, a dark chasm between matter and spirit followed. To a great extent, body and soul fell apart. Adam's philosophers tried to put them together again. They wondered, "How is it possible for physical senses and spiritual powers to connect with each other?" They called the gap between the senses and the intellect the "bridge problem" in human knowledge.

At first, they called the bridge a "light." This was similar to God starting to create the world by filling the darkness and emptiness of the "void" with light (*Genesis* 1:1-3). As the creation of many creatures followed the first of them—the light—many concepts follow our own inner light shining on our senses. As Adam named the creatures, we name things through the creatures of our mind—our concepts of the natures of things.

Naming, however, is not the beginning of the process. The source of Adam's words is the light at the dawn of awareness first abandoned by Eve. She never told Adam how the power of this light unites the senses and the intellect. So he still does not recognize it. For him, the light is just there. Then onward he goes into concepts and reasons. Adam's philosophers never recovered the active receptivity that Eve, and then he, lost in the beginning.

For Adam's philosophers, the light is active, but not actively receptive. For them, the light makes sense-impressions intelligible, and that is as far as it goes. Actually, however, the power of the light receives, integrates, and spiritually transforms the power of the senses from within the senses. According to Adam, the light illuminates the *results* of the senses; it does not transform the *senses* themselves. Adam's leap toward results is a hurried shortcut that leaves the bridge unfinished.

As long as Adam thinks his soul is in his body behind his senses, he is sense-bound. His personhood is enclosed in a biological closet. He cannot bridge the gap between his spiritual intellect and the objects of his senses. He is simply out of touch with the world, as many of his philosophers came to think.

Adam needs to realize that his physical metaphor of a spiritual light is a good beginning, but a tragic end. The light between the senses and the intellect is spiritual. Physical sunlight makes it possible for physical eyes to see objects without the light itself seeing anything. But the radiance of the spirit actually *sees*. It

Finding Our Power for Wisdom

actually knows what eyes cannot know. Before, through, and beyond the eyes and the other senses, this finite spiritual power sees the being of both the world and God at once. Before Eve and Adam lost, within us, the consciousness of their consciousness, the light of the spirit knows the *is* of all that is. And still does: unconsciously and preconsciously.

The power of this spiritual light is actively receptive. It is an act of knowingly receiving the being of another that exists in its own reality and has a nature of its own. Simultaneously, this active reception by the light assimilates and transforms the senses and their impressions, and causes, in *this* way, abstractive knowledge of the other being's nature. As a result, matter and spirit are as united as a continuum. No gap, or chasm, or need for a bridge is there at all.

Without recognizing the light that actually sees, Adam's bridge is an artifice of his struggle with the matter-spirit connection. The chasm persisted throughout his history. Bridge-substitutes surfaced all along the way, such as a univocal concept of being (Scotus), the pineal gland (Descartes), innate categories (Kant), and dialectic logic (Hegel).

Because Adam and Eve "threw themselves away," they "were cast out" of their original selves. And because God sent them out of their original world (*Genesis* 3:23), they experienced themselves in bodies looking backward at their souls. Their previously glowing consciousness plunged into the darkest dimensions of themselves. Paradoxically, therefore, our most conscious act (knowing *being*) is, also, unconscious and preconscious. We are unaware of our most powerful awareness in which there is no chasm and no bridge possible. We only need to recover the unity that fell apart when we lost our original personhood.

Adam and Eve within us cannot do this alone. Since ancient times, God, the Creator of light, has been involved. And the Redeemer continues the process today.

From Moses to Maritain

When Moses heard God speaking to him from a burning bush (*Exodus* 3:1-14), something in the human nature of his mind made possible the tremendous revelation he received. "I am who am" revealed a being whose very essence is *to be*. "I am" is the reason why there is something rather than nothing.

Without the intuitive light of personhood, Moses would not have been able to hear such a simple, yet infinitely profound, revelation. For him, "I am who am" would have been merely the sound of words. He was unaware, however, of the light in his own nature that made it possible for him to *receive* the meaning of what he heard.

Many centuries later, some pagan philosophers began to wonder how we know the natures of things. As a result of their inquiry, the power of what they called "light" became significant. But the absence of Eve within their various interpretations kept the light basically dim and cool.

Plato (429-348 B.C.), originally a poet, thought there is a light for knowing reality. But, for him, that reality exists in another world. He thought we lived there before we were born. He interpreted the light as the radiance of the ultimate object of knowledge which he called the Good. This supreme Form or essence—the Good—supposedly illuminates all other Forms. Without this illumination we could not even know the essence of a frog. Plato supposed that the light of the Good enables us now, in this world, to *remember* what we once knew before we were born, including the essences of frogs, spiders, and dandelions.

His student, Aristotle, originally a biologist, stayed with this physical world. For him, the light is here and now.

Actually, two analysts of human intellection were seeing opposite sides of the same truth. Plato knew truthfully that our intellectual power connects *immediately* with its object. His interpretation of this immediacy sent him into a dimension of reality beyond the senses into a pre-cosmic world. Aristotle knew truthfully that our intellectual power is *mediated* by the senses. His view of this mediation kept him in this world. Significantly, Plato left the immortality of the soul unquestionable, while Aristotle left us wondering.

The spiritual light between the intellect and the senses is shining *immediately* on both the other being and on the senses within the knower. Simultaneously, the light of knowing is *mediated* by the

Finding Our Power for Wisdom

senses. Paradoxically, this light is both immanent (within) and transcendent (beyond). It is both within the senses and beyond them at once. It is the *transcendental* (immanent-transcendent) light of *being*.

Some philosophers, noticing the transcendent aspect of the light, wondered whether the light is divine (Averroes, an Arabian, 1126-1198) and Malebranche (1638-1715). After Averroes, Thomas Aquinas insisted, *"Hic homo intelligit"* (this human individual knows). In other words, the light is part of our human nature; it is neither some kind of general agent beyond, yet connected to, our nature, nor is it God.

Thomas, however, had an Aristotelian view of the light as immanent to the knower and as lacking the noetic transcendence of immediacy with the world. Maritain, a Thomist with a special interest in intuition, failed to see intuition as the power of what he called the "Illuminating Intellect" to know *being*. His thinking was influenced by Henri Bergson (1859-1941), who did not see intuition as being intellectual. For Maritain, intuition is sourced in a complex of human powers having an intellective component. Still, for him, as for St. Thomas and Aristotle, the illuminating or agent intellect remained a cause of knowledge without itself knowing anything.[9]

Along with Etienne Gilson, Maritain realized that something was still missing. Influenced by the rise of European existentialism, both of these astute theological philosophers developed their ideas about an existential judgment following the initial concept of an object. They became known as Existential Thomists.

Other philosophers and theologians, among them Karl Rahner and Bernard Lonergan, realized that this existential advancement in Thomism is still an unfinished interpretation of the dynamics of human knowing. Aware that some kind of *pre-conceptual* dynamism is involved, they developed what is called, notably, Transcendental Thomism. Their interpretation, however, turned out to be more idealistic than existential.[10]

The Shadow in the Light

Adam's idea about his own nature goes back to the time when he was alone with the animals. His power to name them (*Genesis* 2: 19-

20) revealed his difference from them as being a person. Then Eve arrived on the scene. Her presence in his life secured and heightened his awareness of himself as being a person. But when the two of them lost their active receptivity, Adam thought less of himself than before. His mind had fallen onto the passivity of the *tabula rasa* where rational animality became a figment of the "blank tablet's" linear logic.

What a dimming and cooling of the light that was. Severely, for centuries, Adam's animal-based concept of himself has limited his power for wisdom about love.

History did not have to continue that way. The same Aristotle who rationalized animality gave Eve a chance to improve the situation had she been alert. Beginning with what he called an "induction into first principles," Aristotle identified the first intuitions that make possible the reasoning process. His recognition of these intuitions was an invitation to Eve to speak up for wisdom. But she was distracted and said nothing. So Aristotle left these transcendental lights in the dark. He simply named them, took them for granted, and turned his philosophical attention to a masculine way of explaining the rational acts of the human mind.

A more receptive lover of wisdom would have noticed the intuition of *being*, and how the *is* of things is neither *sensed* nor *abstracted*, but is immediately and intellectively intuited.

Aristotle never said how we know *is*. He seemed uninterested. He did not appreciate the intuition of being as the pure *light* of the agent intellect *actually knowing* immediately the reality of things.

If, as Aristotle explained, the active intellect causes knowledge of universals without knowing anything, where would he say that our intuition of *being* originates? In the passive intellect? Then *being* would be more like a concept or category of logic, just as it was for Scotus. Sadly, that is exactly what many of Adam's philosophers regarded *being* to be.

The intuition of *being* is, in no way, passive. It is the actively-receptive causal power of human intellection. It is knowingly active throughout the mind and the senses, and is immediately in "touch" with the world, and even with God.

The real being of anything is the emphatic actuality that makes that being radically other than nothing. We know this even if we do not know that we know it.

Adam's philosophers, not seeing our nature as person-based (as body *within* soul and senses *within* intellect) were unable to see what the intuition of *being* actually is. This pristine cognition is our superlative pre-conceptual act of *knowing* the *is* of everything we know, finite and infinite. This act is vitally concrete, not abstract or logical. It is our intellectual union with the here-and-now reality of whatever we know through and beyond the senses.

Even when we are sleeping, the light of the agent intellect is knowing *being*. This act of knowing never sleeps or becomes passive. This light is the power of the soul—within and beyond the body and the senses—that receives and transforms the senses in such a way that, *beyond* and *through* the senses simultaneously, we know other beings. We humans never experience "pure sense knowledge." Only animals do.

Through the actively receptive light of *being*, Eve within us knows *immediately* the *being* of other beings, and that these beings have their own essences. Spontaneously, even subconsciously, the Adam within us wonders *what* these essences *are*, but only because we first know intellectively *that* they are. Abstraction, mediated by the senses, spontaneously results. Concepts, judgments, and the process of reasoning follow.

Intuitively Rational

Our nearest neighbors in the community of all beings are not animals, but are other persons—human, angelic, and divine. All of these persons are intuitively immediate with reality. Only human persons are both intuitively immediate and intuitively rational. Not having bodily senses, other beings in the community of personhood do not have to wonder "who, when, why, how, and where," nor explicate (reason out) implications carried within intuitions. Only human beings are *intuitively rational* persons.

Our hands, for example, have implications about our mind. We know this intuitively, and we can clarify the intuition. Hands can feel an object, then hold, grasp, take apart, and put it together.

Similarly, our intellect intuitively knows (like hands touching and feeling), receives (holds), abstracts a concept (grasps), analyzes (takes apart), and synthesizes (puts together) what it knows about an object.

But Adam tends to forget the feminine "feeling and holding" that keeps the mind in touch with reality throughout the reasoning process. His grasping at essences before Eve consciously "touches and holds" the *is* of their being short-circuits his thinking. He becomes fascinated with the grasping and the analyzing, while he becomes numb to the "feel." Easily abandoning the integrative synthesis, he prefers to work on the logical base of the passive intellect, there to thrive on mathematics and technology. This passive part of his mind has so much "gravitational pull" that his reasoning tends to fall into its grasp far from the intellect's pristine immediacy with reality.

This fall into logic for its own sake—not unlike the psychic phenomenon of "falling in love"—is inevitable, especially when the light of being is unrecognized or misunderstood or buried alive under Adam's "rational animal" frame of reference.

One of the best examples of captivation by logic is Descartes at the starting gate of modern philosophy. In seeking for philosophy a mathematical kind of certitude, his clear and distinct ideas became clearly and distinctly separate from actual beings in the world. The subsequent Enlightenment period in history began to work its way in the cold darkness of the chasm between subject and object where there was no recognition of the intuition of *being*. Adam's culture, already falling, plunged into the chasm, and has yet to see the light.

Since Adam's philosophers have not *explicitly* recognized their own intellectual immediacy with the world and God, they have not been able to withstand the attacks of sense-based empiricists on one side, and logic-based rationalists on the other. Nor have they been able to hold faith and reason together. In both of these situations, the integrating power is the actively receptive intuition of *being*—the preconscious insight of the luminous agent intellect that makes human consciousness possible. Without an explicit and sustained awareness of our intuition of *being*, we cannot see the continuity (actually a transcendental continuum with differentiations) between

Finding Our Power for Wisdom

the senses and reason, and between faith and reason. We opt for separations on all levels of the inscape. Adam seems satisfied with himself. Eve, when she awakens, wants something better.

She wants *intellectual*, not just emotional, *immediacy* with both self and others. She sees both herself and Adam as intuitively rational persons, not as rational animals. She notices how Adam's "rational animal" definition of himself prevents in him a conscious intellectual immediacy with himself and the world. By thinking that his being is based in biology, and that his awareness is confined behind the senses like a man behind bars, he fails to become aware of his intuitive immediacy with all that is, including God. He remains alienated from reality, still cast out of Eden, and still wandering in a wilderness of short-sights and misinterpretations.

Our power for wisdom is, therefore, the intuitively rational power of our personhood for knowing and loving the truth of being. Wisdom, the power of the light, is a loving way of knowing, and a knowing way of loving all that *is*.

Chapter 8

Turning Up the Light

"Everything you know about sex, but did not know you knew" was the title of my lecture at a college campus in the late 1970s. After the presentation, a woman approached me and said, "You are right; I knew all of that about sex before, but now I know that I know it." She could have asked, "What else do I know like this?" The answer could have been "Much more than you know that you know."

Such is the nature of wisdom. We sometimes call it "common sense." Simply by being a person, we have this intuitive kind of everyday insight. But few people are able to express it in words. As soon as someone asks "What, why, or how"?" the other person generally does not know the answer. Finding out what, why, and how requires a reflective process of "turning up the light."

Reflection, turning up the light, is Adam's gift in his relationship with Eve's gift of receptive intuition. Eve's intuition *connects*. Adam's reflection *differentiates*. Intuition is receptive presence. Reflection is expressive articulation. Intuition *knows* that something *is,* and that it has an essence to be understood to some degree or other by means of concepts and words. Reflection brings into the clearing what intuition sees in a fog; it *actualizes* conceptually and verbally what intuition "senses" intellectually.

Further yet, Eve, as a person, discovers that her mind is not just intuitive (though primarily so), but is also reflective. Turning up the light within herself, she sees that her intuition and reflection are, in no way, separate; they interpermeate. She discovers that she is reflectively intuitive and intuitively reflective.

The same, though oppositely, is true about Adam.

Both Eve and Adam have spontaneously intuitive *connections* and make reflective *differentiations*. As these inner opposites become more integrated within each person, these persons become more able to integrate with each other.

The integrating principle of this transcendental kind of man-woman intercourse is *active receptivity*. The awakening of Eve within both the woman and the man empowers both to become integrated *within* themselves and *with* each other.

The awakened Eve within Adam realizes that she preconsciously knows more than she consciously knows, thus calling for his expressive reflection. At the same time, she wants his reflection to stay within the context of her intuitive union with reality. When he becomes fixed on the multiplicity of the sciences, she calls him home to the unity of wisdom. Paradoxically, this integration of the masculine with the feminine enhances, while moderating, each person's male or female emphasis.

Obviously, then, an integrative communion between the poles of the paradox by means of reflective *intuition and* intuitive *reflection* requires a proportionate way of seeing and thinking. In order to support this relational way of thinking, a paradoxical kind of logic is necessary. But a logic of paradox, and therefore of feminine-masculine integration, is not yet developed. Nor can it be developed while we remain unaware of the inner light of *being* that is actively receptive before, through, and beyond our senses.

Thinking with "Two Hands"

Similar to having two hands for doing our work, we have two sides of our brain for thinking. While equal in value, our hands are oriented in opposite directions in order to face each other in a mutually supportive way. With one hand alone, we could do some of our work. But no one would want to be so handicapped. Similarly, the two sides of our brain are equal, but differently oriented in order to relate with and support each other.

According to Dr. Caroline Leaf, "both sides of the brain take part in every activity, just from different perspectives." She says that the left side processes information "from detail to big picture" while the right side does this "from big picture to detail."[11]

The left side starts from details; these are its main interest. It moves toward the big picture because the right side attracts it there. The right side starts from its interest in the big picture, and is attracted to details by the left side. The left-side interest in details causes the mind to focus on the parts of things. The right-side interest in the big picture causes the mind to integrate the parts into their wholeness.

This left-right organization of the high brain in human persons beautifully supports, and co-operates with, the Adam-Eve powers of the mind. The right side assists Eve's intuitive and integrative power. The left side favors Adam's reflective and differentiative power.

Furthermore, each side of the brain supports both Eve's intuitive interest in the big picture and Adam's rational interest in details, but with an opposite emphasis. For example, the left side starts from details (Adam) but moves toward the big picture (Eve). And the right side oppositely does likewise.

More than these left-right differences, however, Adam and Eve also have a whole-brain difference in the *connection* between the two sides. The female brain has more connective tissue between the left and right sides of the brain. Her advantage is more brain integration, and thus better integrative perceiving and thinking. His brain has less connective tissue between its two sides. His advantage is more brain differentiation, and thus better objectifying perception and abstractive thinking.

The female brain, because of its integrative emphasis, is naturally supportive of intuitive intellection. And the male brain, because of its less connected left and right sides, is naturally disposed for making the distinctions that characterize reflective thinking about intuitions.

Less connective "wiring" in Adam's differentiated brain means a greater tendency toward analyzing a whole and reducing it to its parts. Consequently, he is more prone to separative thinking, especially when he is out of touch with Eve. More connective "wiring" in Eve's brain means a greater tendency toward synthesis, the integrative kind of thinking that sees parts within the whole.

Reflective analysis reduces whole things into their parts; intuitively integrative synthesis puts them together again.

The power of synthesis is supposed to be active throughout the analytic process. Otherwise, the parts become new wholes, and the original whole is not recovered. The analysis, therefore, needs to be active within the context of synthesis just as reflection needs to be active within the context of intuition.

Eve's inclination toward integrative synthesis means that she, especially, sees the connection between details and the big picture. She is interested in both concrete details and their context. Her generalized thinking tends to be contextual, global, and circular in style.

Adam is less aware of the connection between details and the big picture. He is more disposed for abstractions about details and how these matters can be formed into new arrangements. His generalized thinking tends to be object-oriented and linear.

Eve and Adam have opposite ways of being both near-sighted and far-sighted. In relation to transcendental meanings, Eve's intuitive and global tendency is far-sighted. In relation to practical matters, she tends to be near-sighted. If she wants to buy a house, she looks at colors, sizes, and placements of rooms. Adam, more far-sighted, walks over the floors and listens for creaking floor-boards to determine whether or not the house is well-built. Thus they process information differently.

Though intuitive-reflective thinking is not the same as processing information, these two levels of mental activity can have a cooperative relationship. The higher can assimilate the lower for its own enrichment and completion. The lower, if not assimilated by the higher, can go off into the darkness of details that finally have little or no ultimate significance.

Left and right brain, upper and lower activities: all tend toward the whole-brain future of Adam and Eve. Our way to this future is in learning how to think paradoxically, that is, with the two sides of the brain acting together like two hands relating. Both hands can touch and grasp. Intuition is more like touching and holding. Reflective reasoning is like grasping and analyzing. Then, a further depth of

Turning Up the Light

touching and holding integrates the results of analytic thinking. Otherwise, we tend to become mentally "one-handed."

In the initially intuitive act of the mind, opposites like giving and receiving interpermeate each other and, as such, are paradoxical. Intuitive reflection differentiates giving and receiving. But reflection that loses its intuitive quality tends to *separate* giving and receiving. Then, giving seems to be active, and receiving seems passive. The paradox is lost. It needs to be regained. Better yet, why lose it at all?

Unfortunately, we are not educated for a whole-brain way of turning up the light. The system is too interested in processing information and in rational (separational) thinking. For the sake of that interest, Adam's logic has been exquisitely effective.

What is Adam's Logic?

Logic is the art and science of correct thinking. Correct thinking can be either true or false, depending especially on whether its first judgment is true or false. Logical correctness is not the same as truth. Method is not the same as insight.

There are three kinds of logic. These are Adam's, Eve's, and Adam-Eve ways of thinking. The first two kinds are developed: Eve's in the East, and Adam's in the West. The Adam-Eve kind is not developed; it is missing. Its emergence into the light of day depends on the future of Adam and Eve.

Eve's logic is exemplified by the Oriental yin-yang way of thinking. Yin and yang are opposites that need to *balance* each other. The balancing of opposites on a passive base, however, is not their *interpermeation* on an actively receptive base. This yin-yang thinking is not genuinely paradoxical thinking, nor are the other logics of the East.

Adam's logic—the art and science of the reasoning process—is highly developed, and has been the aptly functional servant of Western philosophy, science, and technology. But Adam's logic of the grasping intellect, without Eve's actively receptive way of thinking, is the reason why experimental science is over-developed, self-absorbed by mathematics, and running wild in areas where it does not belong, and why wisdom is so weak and powerless in Western civilization.

Since the philosophers of both East and West have been doing their thinking without a developed transcendental, paradoxical, logic of wisdom, their philosophies have fallen short of wisdom while striving for it.

Adam's logic of left-brain thinking depends on the passive "blank slate" of the mind. The starting point of this logic is the principle of non-contradiction, which states that "a thing cannot be, and not be, at the same time in the same respect." This principle is a major clarifier that causes the either-or, separational, way of thinking. Either-or thinking clarifies by conceptually identifying things and separating them from each other.

For example, an "uncreated creature" is a contradiction. Every being is *either* uncreated *or* created. Either-or thinking cancels the contradiction. The cancelling is done by *identifying* each one of the contradicting terms, and then, by *separating* them from each other.

Adam's logic is an either-or logic of identity and separation. This logic helps Adam to grasp the natures of things and to "take them apart" to find out what their parts are. His "either-or" thinking facilitates his analytic grasp by which he clarifies the implications within his loaded intuitions. His kind of logic defines and specifies. Without it, the Western world, with all its institutional creativity and inventiveness, could not have developed the way it did.

In the framework of identity and separation, any attempt at synthesis tends to remain an implicit separation. Putting parts together after they have been separated leaves a whole that is no greater than the sum of its parts. Humpty Dumpty, once fallen, cannot be put together again.

The Eve-Adam Logic of Wisdom

The challenge is to keep the living whole from falling into its parts. Thinking with both sides of the brain at once (easier for Eve than for Adam) holds the parts together within the whole while studying the parts for the sake of better understanding the whole. This way of thinking starts in the intuitive light of wisdom, stays there, and assimilates and transforms Adam's clarifying logic.

The intuitive, "big picture," right side of the brain-mind union, together with its integrating right-left connection (Eve), receives and

Turning Up the Light

holds the mind's initial union with the *whole* being of whatever we are knowing. We immediately know the *is* of this being, and that it has an essence.

Within the context of this intuitive union between the knower and the known, the left side of the brain-mind union (Adam) wonders *what* this essence is, tries to grasp it and explicate its contents (its splendors). The wholesome (Eve-Adam) result is differentiation within integration, not merely identity and separation.

The power of the mind's active receptivity is what holds together whole and part in this way. Active receptivity, itself a paradoxical union of opposites, is the source of the paradoxical logic of wisdom. Whole and part are paradoxical opposites. Active receptivity has no problem holding these opposites together.

Paradoxical thinking, by holding opposites together, is a "both-and," not an "either-or," way of thinking. *Both* whole and parts are important together.

Not all "both-and" thinking, however, is paradoxical. "Both this and that" does not express an interpermeation of opposites, when "this" and "that" are opposites that happen to be separate identities. But the expression "both Adam and Eve," when understood as an inter-relational union of opposites, is a paradox.

Paradoxical "both-and" thinking can include "either-or" logic. But "either-or" logic cannot include paradoxical thinking. The whole-brain (Eve-Adam) mentality includes Adam's logic, but not the other way around. Within the boundaries of either-or logic, no part can include the whole of which it is a part.

When Eve-Adam paradoxical logic assimilates Adam's logic of identity and separation, and transforms it into the logic of clarifying differentiation, Adam's logic stays within the Eve-Adam light of wisdom. It does not fall into any of the possible alienations from wisdom.[12]

Warmth of the Light

The light that sees is paradoxically continuous with the warmth that affirms. Transcendentally, the light and warmth are within each other. The being-seeing (agent) intellect and the being-affirming (agent) will are within each other.[13]

The seeing is our most original, actively receptive, act of knowing. The affirming is our most original, our receptively responsive, act of loving. In other words, our agent intellect is a giving kind of receiving, and our agent will is a receiving kind of giving.

Our original knowing and loving fell into a coma after Eve and Adam lost their active receptivity. These powers collapsed into unconsciousness, while continuing to be the "underground" source of our conscious mind and will. Recovery means bringing both the light and the warmth into immediate awareness.

The light is an act of knowing that never sleeps, even if we do not recognize it as such. The warmth of the light is our loving response to the goodness of that which we see in the light.

The original light and warmth are the source of our freedom. That is why Eve and Adam could freely choose to "reach for" and "swallow" a different kind of likeness to God than the kind they were given.

As we become aware of our original story, and engage ourselves in the process of healing, we can release into our awareness both our immediacy with the truth of *being*, and the spontaneity of our response to the goodness of *being*. This immediacy and spontaneity are spiritual acts meant to assimilate and transform the *knowing* powers of our rational mind and senses, and the *responding* powers of our will and heart.

Conscious reasoning and deciding, however, are like the smallest part of an island above the surface of the surrounding sea. These "above the surface" actions need to remain *continuous* with the preconscious acts of our powers, and not become split-off and free-floating. In other words, reasoning needs to remain within our intuition of the truth, and willing needs to remain within our spontaneous response to the good. By becoming more aware of the preconscious life of our powers, we can assist their process of assimilating and retaining in themselves the conscious expressions of these powers.

Our daily decisions and actions either increase or decrease the healing process. The clouds that we form in our mind and heart can easily dim and cool the warming light and make life seem gloomy, chilly, and stormy.

Without awareness of the light and warmth in our spiritual powers, rationalism and voluntarism took over the scene. From Duns Scotus, to Martin Luther, to the Puritans, the intellect took a leap of faith and the will landed in voluntarism (will power without insight leading the way).

Wisdom and Her Lovers

The inner source of wisdom is the heart within the mind and the mind within the heart. Wisdom is a loving way of knowing, and a knowing way of loving. Adam's lovers of wisdom did not see wisdom in this way. But Eve and Adam together would be another story.

Socrates said wisdom is knowing that we do not know. He seemed to have no idea that the agent intellect knows *is* without which no other intellectual knowledge is possible. Ontologically, wisdom is realizing that we know what we do not know we know. Most of our knowledge is preconsciously intuitive.

Wisdom, to the extent that we live it, "sees a world in a grain of sand," and a person in a single cell at conception. Wisdom receives, touches, and holds with insight and affection.

Sons of Adam have been lovers of science more than they have been lovers of wisdom. The spirit of Adam within them, alienated from Eve, could only yearn for wisdom without really finding it.

Most of these lovers simply gave up on the search and settled for the wandering of science into a multitude of specialties. Repressed and buried alive, Eve remains ignored by Adam as he follows his fascinations and takes so-called feminists with him.

In the absence of wisdom, science goes down its own trail into the darkness of biological engineering, human cloning, techniques of abortion, and other such extreme manipulations. In the absence of wisdom, the "can do" of these depersonalizing techniques simply means "should do."

Before Eve can integrate with Adam, she needs to integrate her mind and heart within herself. Her receptive union with reality in the *light* of knowing inspires her response to the goodness of reality in the *warmth* of an affirming love. Her wisdom receives and affirms the transcendental truth, goodness, and radiant splendor of being.

Then Adam can become intuitive, responsive, and reflective within the warming light. He can explain the *true*, while staying with wisdom. His science and technology will remain important, but contained and restrained. He can also defend the *good* firmly, and express the *beautiful* creatively.

So, Eve is calling him to turn around from his alienated pursuits, and come home to wisdom. Adam has ears to hear.

Will he listen?

Chapter 9

Finding Our Power for Love

Nothing in the world interests us more than love. Heart-hunger is pervasive. Yet love is little understood in Puritan-playboy America.

We are naturally drawn to emotional warmth, but are slow to recognize the truth about love. Consequently, the absence of insight into this truth adversely affects the warmth that attracts us. In this way, disturbed minds and broken hearts result.

By recognizing the different kinds of love and the relationship between them, we can begin to develop the needed insight. Then the light will be able to deepen and strengthen the warmth. In this way, minds and hearts can be healed.

Thanks to Adam's ancient Greek philosophers, we can identify four major kinds of love that they called *eros, agape* (a ga'pae), *philia,* and *storge* (stor'gae). We know them, respectively, as desire, caring, friendship, and familial affection.

Desire (*eros*) is I-centered. Caring and giving (*agape*) are you-directed. Friendship (*philia*) is we-related. Familial affection and bonding (*storge*) constitute the spontaneous devotion between family members. All of these kinds of love are conducive to human happiness and well-being. But the most important kind of love is merely implied. It is the one that makes the others what they are really meant to be.

The main kind of love is simply the spontaneous response of the heart to goodness. The warming light of being within the heart reveals the goodness of being, and inspires the person to respond affirmingly. This spontaneous response to goodness is the essence of love.

We might not be aware that we are actually affirming something or someone in this way. But our personhood naturally responds to goodness. By increasing awareness of our affirming response, we can release more of its warmth in our relationships.

An example of the affirming kind of love—though not called by that name—appears in *Genesis*. There, God responded to the fresh, new being of all created things by repeatedly calling them *good*.

Later, in the gospel of the Lord Jesus, we see the affirmational love of God for us. The stories of the father welcoming his wayward son and of the shepherd leaving his sheep to find one that is lost are examples of God responding to the goodness of even the wayward and the lost. This is the warmly feminine aspect of affirming love.

The same gospel shows the masculine aspect of this kind of love by calling for the *moral* goodness that confirms and expresses the goodness of being. The commandments of God are revealed as the responsibilities of love. In other words, af-*firm*-ational love for the being of a person includes *firm*-ness in relation to that person's actions.

In America, Adam's loneliness has become extreme. Spontaneous warmth of heart has been culturally constrained. The original Puritan and subsequent playboy mentalities have little or no awareness of the essential light and warmth of personhood. Though most Americans are influenced by other social values, the coolness and hardness of the Puritan, and the cold rawness of the playboy, continue to affect the subconscious core of the American character.

New Warmth Emerges

The psychological problems of the Puritan-Victorian culture in America began in Europe. Sigmund Freud tried to understand and diagnose them. But he could not overcome the Puritan idea that human nature is depraved. He saw our nature as basically irrational and as controlled by an inner system of defense mechanisms. For him, our animal nature is more rationalizing than rational. Later, Adolph Hitler, in a consummation of irrationality, scourged the face of Western civilization with his own defense mechanisms driven by unresolved rage and hatred.

The Viennese psychiatrist, Viktor Frankl, vehemently blamed the social effectiveness of Hitler's madness on Sigmund Freud. Frankl had suffered concentration-camp imprisonment in Hitler's culture of

Finding Our Power for Love

death. He was strongly critical of Freud's demeaning view of human nature. In his enlightening book, *Man's Search for Meaning*, Frankl insisted that the human need for meaning trumped Freud's idea about the human need for pleasure. He believed that people would suffer anything if they had sufficient meaning for their endurance.

Fortunately, in the middle of the tortured 20th century, Anna Terruwe, a Dutch psychiatrist, noticed the emptiness in Western civilization that no Freudian treatment could heal. She identified its cause as an absence of the affirming kind of love. She saw this deprivation as the source of emotional problems even deeper and more culturally pervasive than repression.

Beyond Freud's "will to pleasure," Adler's "will to power," and Frankl's "will to meaning," Terruwe, in effect, discovered a kind of "will to love." She became insightful and articulate about our profound need to be affirmed and to affirm others.

Eventually, Terruwe was joined in her work by psychiatrist, Conrad Baars, also a native of the Netherlands, who spent three years in a German concentration camp, and who, after liberation, came to America. By means of his own books and those he co-authored with Terruwe, and numerous conferences, he did what he could to spread the message of affirmation in America. A new sense of warmth began to emerge in the midst of the creeping cultural chill.[14]

The Affirming Kind of Love

Like the air we breathe, this spontaneous kind of love is natural to our personhood. Without some of its tender affection, babies die. Or else they grow up to one degree or another emotionally ungrounded, uncentered, and unconnected. They do not know who they are. Thus, they are forced either to survive by creating a substitute self or to remain a "no one" trying to please "everyone" to get some appreciation. But children who are given to themselves by affirmation can just be themselves peacefully. They will not have to use their heads to "figure out" who they are in their hearts. Nor will anxiety and depression, to some degree or other, surface to torment them.

To the extent that affirmational warmth is absent in our own lives, we are all dying within ourselves. The "soular sun" of personhood remains. But the clouds can become too dense for the light and warmth to radiate through them.

We need to open our awareness to the inner transpsychic "sun." Then we can begin to appreciate its luminous warmth in the affirming kind of love. Luminous because we finally *know* what affirmation is. And warm because we let ourselves actually *feel* it.

Affirmational love is, first of all, feminine. It is spontaneously both receptive and responsive. In the heart of our personhood, we *receive* the goodness of another person, and *respond* spontaneously with some sign of enjoyment of that other person's presence. Experiencing our receptive response, the other person tends to feel personally and emotionally strengthened. Feminine warmth like this is the continuing source of love at its best. Without words, affirmational love says "You are good as you are."

Affirmation, however, does not imply that "anything you choose to *do* is good." Doing expresses being. So the goodness of a person's being requires goodness in that person's actions.

Thus affirmation strengthens people not only in their sense of *being* who they are, but also in their *doing* what is good. They are affirmed both emotionally and morally.

Affirmation is affection with firmness. As such, it is the feminine-masculine (Eve-Adam) essence of love. It has integrative power for both the affirming person and the one who is affirmed.

Affection with Firmness

The Terruwe-Baars psychology of affirmation is a remarkably sound addition to America's healing professions. But we can go deeper than the level of psychology. The origin of the affirming response is beyond, while including, our emotional-mental life. This source is the soular "sun" of our personhood: agent intellect and agent will together.

In this radiant core of our being, Eve's *receptive response* to goodness evokes Adam's *responsibility* for goodness in action. While Eve's affirmation of being extends into emotional affection,

Adam's affirmation extends into moral firmness. The result is the healing paradox of both emotional health and good character.

Contemporary "personalism," because it lacks an authentic sense of personhood, emphasizes a false kind of unconditional love that ignores guidance for behavioral impulses and decisions. Slogans such as "do your own thing," "follow your own conscience," and "if it feels good, do it," surface inevitably. This thoughtless version of unconditional love is disconnected from the intrinsic laws of the heart that enhance and protect love itself.

Without moral firmness, "unconditional love" is not affirmation, nor is it love. It is unbalanced, unintegrated, and unintegrating. The other person is not being affirmed in his or her powers for self-determination and moral responsibility. The result is not a recovery from the freezing emptiness and loneliness in the culture, but a reinforcement of the very malady this fraudulent "love" tries to heal.

True affirmational love is the masculine firmness of the will *within* the feminine warmth of the heart. Neither the excessively masculine willpower of the Puritan nor the self-centered willfullness of the playboy can express this love. Both compulsive willpower and impulsive willfulness exercise the will apart from the heart. Without the *receptivity of our personhood*, the will and the heart remain unintegrated.

Once again, receptivity is the integrating power. Lacking this power, cultures tend to swing between the rigidity of moralism and the flaccidity of permissiveness. Between these extremes is the integrative core that unites firmness of the will with affection of the heart, thus preventing the desperate oscillation between moralism and permissiveness.

Affirmation and the Other Kinds of Love

Without affirmation and its soular warmth of the agent will within the heart, the other kinds of love—family affection, desire, charity, and friendship—are incomplete and unstable. *Family* relationships can become controlling and competitive. Appetites can overwhelm the *self*. Compassion for the needs of *others* can treat them like objects. And relationships between *friends* can be only talk deep.

The affirming kind of love strengthens and deepens the other kinds, and has a healing effect.

For example, a nurse can care for patients by efficiently cleaning and bandaging wounds, administering medications, and fulfilling other duties. He or she can do so either coldly or with charity of heart. But if the nurse also affirms the other as a person, above and beyond just caring for a needy patient, the charity becomes even more healing.

The miracle of affirmation likewise increases the wholeness of the other kinds of love. It empowers them to rise above the level of their *objects* to the meeting and greeting of persons as persons.

By fulfilling in this way the potential of each of the other kinds of love, affirmation also empowers them to unite with one another. Romantic love, for instance, is not inclined to integrate with friendship in the same relationship, nor even with charity. Each kind of love tends to settle with its own object.

But affirmational love, not object-bound, can bring together the other kinds of love. This integration can happen especially between a man and woman in marriage. Warmly affirming each other as persons, they can become friends, lovers, parents, and caregivers all in one. Paradoxically, while thus integrated, each kind of love remains itself.

Familial Love

A mother holding her baby represents the essence of familial affection. Family bonds between her and her child are as physical as their genes, as emotional as their hearts, and as lasting as earthly life itself. In varying degrees, something similar is true of other family bonds, including relationships with relatives.

Motivated by familial affection, a mother naturally responds to her child's needs for food and clothing. But if she never, or rarely, hugs her children, nor spends time simply enjoying them in an endearing way, the best part of familial affection is not given. This best part is affirming love. Without it, children cannot feel warmth of heart from their own mother. Their very being is left out in the cold. They go into life suffering from emotional deprivation and insecurity.

Finding Our Power for Love

Warmth of heart coming from the affirming kind of love is essential to the wholeness of *storge*. Babies have been known to die without this warmth in the hands that touch and hold them. If they do not die physically, they still fail to develop in other ways, especially emotionally.

Familial affection that is also affirming strengthens children in who they are. They become intimately connected with their own inner life. They feel secure and open to others, especially when this love comes from both a manly father and a womanly mother who, within their family bonds of *storge love*, affirmingly love each other.

Both parents are important for developing in the child the paradox of receiving and giving. As a man and woman, they receive and give with a different and complementary emphasis. But feminism, by masculinizing women and by demeaning both motherhood and fatherhood, has become more than a problem for families. And deeper than this selfist kind of feminism, American individualism has a "dismembering" effect on family bonds.

So we need to let the culture warm up. Light on the affirming kind of love within the familial kind can show us the way. Then a mother can hold her baby not only with her natural affection and care for needs, but also with the endearing smile that feeds her happy child, heart to heart.

Possessive Love (Desire)

The many and various needs (physical, emotional, mental, and spiritual) of the human person cause desire (*eros*) for persons and things that fulfill these needs. Desire is a kind of love, and is basically a part of love for one's own self. Because we value our own being, we want what we need for our personal development and happiness.

Though *eros*-love is usually associated with romantic and sexual desire, it extends all the way from a baby's cry for comfort to a saint's intense longing for God. The holy person's yearning, however, is the result of *receiving* affirmation from God's infinite love, and responding by affirming the goodness of God.

Beyond and within possessive desire, affirmation *receives* the goodness of the other, and *gives* that being to itself. Affirmational love is the source of gratitude for the things that fulfill us, and is the reason why possessive love needs the affirming kind of love to complete and heal it.

Sacrificial Love (Charity)

Empathy and compassion for others inspire *agape*-love. This giving kind of love cares for persons in their needs. *Agape* can inspire the supreme sacrifice of offering one's life for the good of others. The greatest example of sacrificial love is God hanging from nails in hands and feet for our salvation.

Charity can sustain the other kinds of love. When family affection weakens under a load of responsibility and trials, sacrificial love offers the help that is needed. And when the romantic dream fades away, charity inspires the maturation of desire. Also, when friends hurt each other, charity forgives.

But giving oneself to and for another is incomplete unless the giver goes beyond the other person's needs to the other's goodness as a person. Differently from charity, the affirming kind of love gives by receiving and responding to goodness. This more basic kind of giving animates sacrificial love with nurturing warmth from the heart.

Friendship

Unlike the other kinds of love, *philia* (friendship) means liking someone based on likeness. Two or more people realize that they cherish something in common, that they are quite similar in some ways, and that they like each other. Sharing similar interests implies a basic equality.

Furthermore, their mutual regard for the meanings and values they share extends into a mutual esteem for each other. Then their feeling of liking and valuing each other develops into a deep and lasting affection between them.

Equality, esteem, affection, and value-sharing are the qualities of friendship. And the depth of what people share determines the character of their relationship. Women talking about recipes at a card party or men bowling together on Wednesday night could be considered companions or buddies. But they are not necessarily friends.

Friends can share their needs, such as helping each other to solve their problems. But that is secondary. Basically, they do not want a friend to take care of their needs, but rather to *be with* them. Because friendship goes beyond needs, its level of relating transcends *eros* and *agape*. In its essence, friendship is mutual independence that means shared autonomy.

Affirmation strengthens *philia* and its difference from *eros*. The self-centered character of *eros* is not apt for sharing, even as it is aimed at genuine fulfillment. A main reason why man-woman relationships so readily become involved in *eros* is the lack of friendship as their base. The physical and emotional attraction that causes people to "fall in love" creates so much dependency that it is anything but the mutual independence that characterizes friendship.

People often have difficulty imagining a man-woman relationship that does not head for the bedroom. But as each person develops an awareness of feelings, thoughts, and values (a friendship within one's own self), this problem is lessened. The person becomes able to receive *eros*-feelings as energy for sexual awareness and wisdom, and not primarily as energy for genital involvement.

By affirming the energy of *eros*, and by becoming firm with it at the same time, the person is able to develop an inner friendship with *eros*, as different from slavery to it. This inner friendship becomes the necessary condition for a true friendship between persons.

Affirmation and Friendship

Affirmation and friendship are the only two of the five kinds of love that do not *need* the others to be complete. Instead, the other three kinds of love (desire, caring, and familial affection) need affirmation and friendship to be complete. For example, desire can cause a man to say to a woman, "If you love me, you'll do it." But this erotic notion of love needs friendship and affirmation, as well as marital commitment, to be more than a passing smile without a face. *Eros* can be subsumed within the power of affirmation and *philia*. Both within and beyond the other three kinds of love, the affirming and sharing kinds are transcendental and immortal.

In eternal life, *desire* loses its self-oriented connection to needs, and becomes the pure ardor of fulfillment in affirming love of, and friendship with, God and all others. *Caring* loses its other-directed attention to needs and becomes ecstatic. *Familial bonding* loses its earthly boundaries and becomes the "marriage of the lamb" and the great family of the affirming friends of God.

Furthermore, between the three divine Persons, affirmation and friendship are infinite. In the image and likeness of this infinite love, we are most fully personal and interpersonal.

Here on earth, however, we have all five kinds of love for God. And God has all five kinds of love for us. God *desires* union with us, and we desire union with God. The *agape* of our redemption is God's response to our need of all needs. We, too, can give ourselves to God with *agape*. And familial love (*storge*) between God and us is basic.

Here on earth, also, we are called to respect each kind of love in its own integrity and in its relationships with the others. Affirmation and friendship are essential for keeping the other kinds of love both distinct and relational. For example, an affirming friendship between a husband and wife strengthens their bond, deepens their desire and caring for each other, and enhances their affection for their children.

What difference would the many-splendored love of affirmation make for a father and son going to a ballgame together? For that same son going to a dance with the attractive girl he just met? For a family getting involved in a social project? What difference would an affirming friendship make for men and women working together at the office? For groups of people trying to solve their problems together?

The loneliness and coldness involved in Adam's individualism would become dissipated by warmth that endures because it is luminous with wisdom about love.

Celebrational Love

As transcendental, the affirming and sharing kinds of love include all that is, not just persons. "Seeing a world in a grain of sand and a heaven in a wild flower" are examples of celebrational affirmation and friendship. Something about the *being* of these apparently insignificant beings responds in a sharing way to a *person's* loving presence.

Celebrational love happens in many ways. A child laughs at a drop of water making its wandering way down a window pane. An artist paints a picture of a soaring eagle. An orchestra sounds forth from the depths of the soul. A choir reaches for the songs of angels. Adam and Eve within us see each other as if they never saw anything else before. A poet sings about his beloved being the mountains, the solitary wooded valleys, the faraway islands, the sounding streams, and the whispering winds that wander.[15]

In the Adam-side of our nature, neither the work-driven Puritan nor the fun-driven playboy, have an open ear for the transcendental wisdom of love. If we could hear these two cultural characters voicing their propensities, we could realize more surely what they are missing.

Chapter 10

Emotional Health and the Puritan

Adam in America today has many problems with himself. He is addicted to performance in scientific technology and sex on demand. More critically, he is alienated from wisdom by his blind fascination with the technical wonders he produces. He even drives himself toward creating monsters in laboratories, just because he thinks he *can do* it. And, by substituting glitz and fleeting self-satisfactions, he cuts himself off from affirmational love.

Still deeper than *these symptoms* are their causes. Adam has problems with his emotional life and his character development. His Puritan attitude toward his feelings and emotions is the source of his addictions. And his playboy disinterest in the virtues of good character treats his abnormal fixations as if they were virtues.

Suppose the redeemed and awakening Eve goes to have a talk with the Puritan. She is interested in getting to the source: the Puritan's attitude toward his emotional life. She knows her feminine concern for feelings is crucial for anyone's healing and well-being.

When she approaches the Puritan's workshop and knocks on the door she wonders whether he will take out some time to talk about his feelings. When he opens the door and she lets him know she just wants to talk about something, he says that he is too busy trying to meet his deadline, and to come back tomorrow or the next day.

When Eve returns, he lets her in, thinking she wants to talk about his work and his Bible. She asks about his family, instead.

As they speak, his feelings begin to show in his eyes. But not for long. He signals that he wants to return to his work. But Eve had noticed the spontaneous, though quickly passing, warmth in his face.

Feelings and Emotions are Important

Eve: I can tell that you have feelings for your wife and children. But you don't like to talk about them, do you?

Puritan: Some things are personal.

Eve: I agree. But what do you think about feelings? Why do we have them?

Puritan: Because we are sinners.

Eve: You don't think God created us to have feelings?

Puritan: Yes, but we are so depraved by sin, and our feelings are so out of control that we might be better off not to have them.

Eve: Is that how you see your children? So depraved by sin and so out of control that you don't want to feel anything about them?

Puritan: I have to admit that I have very strong feelings for every member of my family. But these are personal and private.

Eve: Are those feelings depraved by sin? Or are you glad you have them as gifts from God to give you strength to do your work and care for your family?

Puritan: Yes, my feelings for my wife and children do give me strength to take care of them.

Eve: So, how are those feelings depraved by sin?

Puritan: Well, there are other feelings that come along. Desires, fears, frustrations. On and on. You have to ignore them or they will take over. Then what?

Eve: Do you ignore your children when they have desires, fears, frustrations, and get upset and angry?

Puritan: No. I teach them how to ignore their own unruly nature. Reading the Bible and praying to God for help is the answer.

Eve: Good point about the Bible and prayer. About feelings, though. You seem to think there are good feelings and bad feelings. Isn't there anything good about desire, fear, and anger? Would you want to be without them?

Puritan: I can see that we need desire for some things. And fear can steer us away from more trouble. Anger can make us want to correct that trouble in the first place. But you have to *control yourself.*

Eve: Isn't there a question about *how*? If there is anything good about desire, fear, and anger, which you admit there is, do you really want to control them by ignoring them?

Puritan: If you don't ignore them, you would have to pay attention to your feelings, do some sorting, and that would take too much time and attention away from your work, family, and religion. There are better things to do than bothering with feelings.

Eve: You sound like a father who doesn't have time to bother with his children.

Puritan: Are you comparing feelings to children?

Eve: Yes. Little children live by feelings. I am sure you have noticed that. How you take care of your own feelings affects the way you take care of your children.

Puritan: You seem to be denying that our nature is depraved by sin.

Eve: Remember, I was the one who started it all. But I was redeemed by God, and so were you. With our restored ability to *receive* divine grace, we can now recover more of our original goodness. Hanging on to what you construe as depravity stops the process and only causes more problems.

Puritan: So, you think we should pay attention to our feelings. Does that mean going to a psychologist?

Eve: Not necessarily. It means learning something about the good in psychology, and avoiding the bad.

Puritan: What do you mean by the good and the bad?

Eve: The good never loses sight of the relationship between emotional health and good character. The bad avoids good character. The result becomes your cultural offspring.

Puritan: What do you mean?

Eve: The playboy.

Puritan: Disgusting.

Doing Some Sorting

Eve: You said you did not want to waste time sorting out your feelings. You don't want to give them that much attention.

Puritan: True.

Eve: Personally, I wouldn't want that kind of ignorance about myself. So I opened my inner eyes and was amazed at what I saw. You are right about sorting. It takes time and attention.

Puritan: What did you see?

Eve: Do you really want to take the time?

Puritan: Not really. But I would like to hear what you found out about sorting.

Eve: First of all, I could see that feelings and thoughts are two different things. We tend to confuse them, especially when we say, "I feel that such and such is true," instead of saying "I think..." Some of our thoughts are intuitive, and seem very much like feelings. Both are spontaneous. So sorting is necessary.

Puritan: Give me an example.

Eve: Would you say, "I think I am hungry?" No. You would say, "I feel hungry." You don't have to think about feelings in order to have them, especially physical feelings.

Puritan: I can think about dinner, and then feel hungry. It's like that with all of my feelings. That's why I ignore so many of them.

Eve: If you get wrapped up in your work and forget about dinner, will you ever feel hungry? You know you will. And there are other kinds of physical feelings such as thirst, pleasure, and pain. These are spontaneous responses to conditions within us and around us. Without these responses we could not survive, nor could we enjoy life. Without eating we would die. And notice, we can taste what we eat, and so, enjoy it.

Puritan: Some people eat and drink too much. They want pleasure, but end up with pain. What's so good about that?

Eve: This is where another kind of feelings is involved. These are psychological feelings called emotions. There are many different kinds. Some are happiness, sadness, fear, and anger.

Both physical and psychological feelings supply the energy we need for our actions. All are basically good for us. But, as you are so quick to bring out, things can get out of order. Too much sadness can make people want to eat and drink too much so they can feel better. That is how pleasure ends up in pain.

Puritan: Sadness is inevitable. How are we supposed to avoid its effect on us, except by ignoring it and just doing what we are supposed to do?

Eve: Ignoring again! Why can't we just feel sad when we are sad, and not have to eat and drink too much? Oh, I know what you would say to that. It would take too much time away from better things you could be doing.

Puritan: That is what I would say.

Eve: If you could accept a little more sorting, there is a way to understand why you are so reluctant to spend time with your feelings. And it has to do with your own dominant kind of emotional life—your masculine kind.

Puritan: This discussion has gone on long enough. I really need to get back to what I was doing before. Maybe some good will come of it, though. I might be able to do more sorting as I go along. And maybe I'll be more aware of the feelings that help me to do what I'm supposed to be doing. I hope it hasn't been a total waste of my time.

Affective and Effective

We can readily see that the Puritan is more concerned about being effective than affectionate. Eve would have clarified this difference for him. But he was not ready. Healing does take time.

The psychologists, Anna Terruwe and Conrad Baars, noticed the difference between what they called the affective and effective emotions. We might call them additionally, at their roots, feminine and masculine respectively.

Affective emotions *receptively* respond to whatever we perceive as good or bad. Effective emotions are *action-oriented* responses to needs, wants, obstacles, and dangers.

In our affective response to the good, we feel love, desire, and joy. We also respond affectively to the bad with hate, aversion, and sadness. There are many nuances and variations of these six basic responses. In one instance alone, joy can be nuanced as happiness, delight, gladness, pleasure, satisfaction, and so on.

In our effective responses to needs, wants, obstacles, and dangers, we feel hope and despair, fear and courage, and anger. These are motivating, protective, assertive, and defensive responses that move us to act, and supply the energy to do so. These effective (or masculine) emotions are meant to serve and protect the affective (or feminine) emotions.

For example, when I feel an affective response of love toward a beautiful flowering plant in a store, I might *desire* it for a table in my living room. Then I might effectively *hope* to go looking for an artful table for this plant. Hope supplies the motivation and energy to act toward that goal. The effective emotion of *courage* supplies the energy to overcome obstacles on the way, such as having to go shopping and not finding what I want. *Fear* might steer me away from rainy days or icy streets.

At a certain point in the process, a passing feeling of *despair* might cause me to wonder if my goal is achievable. *Anger* might cause a defensive reaction against one of the clerks who tries to sell me what I do not want. In needing and wanting to overcome these various difficulties, the *effective* emotions of hope and courage can keep me going. When the goal is finally achieved, I feel the *affective* emotion of *joy*.

Hope, courage, fear, and anger, then, are emotions for *outward action* that serve the *inner*, more receptive, emotions of love, desire, joy, and their opposites. In other words, the masculine, or operative, emotions protect and serve the feminine emotions.

But when fear and courage become too effective, they become overbearing, and can cripple or even bury our ability to feel love, desire, and joy. The Puritan's "must-do" kind of will power has this repressive effect. Then, love can only be willed, and barely or rarely *felt* (Terruwe-Baars).

Probably the most misunderstood of our emotions are hate, desire, and anger. These are the most readily repressed in the name of good character. We tend to think it is bad to feel hate, to feel some kinds of desire, and to feel anger. But all of these spontaneous feelings are good.

Take anger, for example. Many people are afraid of their spontaneous feelings of anger because these can cause aggressive thoughts. Some people, when asked why they do not get involved in social causes say they could not deal with their anger about injustice, and about others who do not seem to care. So they resort to apathy. But we need the energy of our anger for responsible action. Assertiveness is not aggression.

Only when we allow anger to fly into violence or mutate into resentment, or when we permit desire to become grandiose, lustful, gluttonous, greedy, envious, or indolent, or when we let hate harden into hatred, do good emotions fall into their dark side and become bad and unhealthy. So, how we relate with our spontaneous feelings determines our personality, our character, and our emotional health.

Compulsive and Impulsive

Anger flies into violence, desire becomes lustful, and hate becomes hatred because we do not know how to relate with our spontaneous feelings of anger, desire, and hate. If the feminine side of our personhood does not *receive* these feelings as good energy for a happy life, we cannot become authentically responsible for directing the tendency of this energy toward actions. The result becomes behavior that is either compulsive or impulsive.

Without a developed ability to relate well with our feelings, we think the feeling that can lead to a bad action is also bad. For example, in knowing that violence is wrong, we think it is wrong to feel angry. So, we say to ourselves, "Don't have angry feelings because you might act them out and get into trouble." In other words, "Don't feel because you might act." Like the Puritan, we become compulsive perfectionists who are so concerned about good behavior that we ignore our feelings, and even repress them.

The perfectionist also tries to manipulate feelings and *make* them perfect by saying, "Don't feel like that; feel like this." Or "Don't feel bad," implying "Be positive; feel good." The responsible person says, instead, "Feel what you spontaneously feel. But you don't have to act out what you feel."

If, however, we are concerned only about feelings and not about behavior, we swing to the opposite side of the perfectionist and become permissive. We say to ourselves, "Feel what you feel, and do what you feel." In other words, "If it feels good, do it." A misguided parent might say to a teenager, "If you feel like getting involved with drugs, alcohol, and sex, I can't stop you. You'll just do what you want anyway. That is probably the only way you will learn what life is all about."

Neither the compulsive perfectionist (the Puritan or Victorian) nor the impulsive permissivist (the playboy or playmate) is able to take care of feelings and behavior. The one is too concerned about behavior at the expense of feelings, and the other is too concerned about feelings at the expense of behavior. Both are unhealthy extremes.

Affirming our Feelings

Between the extremes of the Puritan and the playboy is the union of Adam and Eve within each one of us, and their care for their sons and daughters. Their care begins with affirmation. Eve receives and responds to our desires, fears, and all the rest. And Adam is firm with them at the same time.

The feminine side of our personhood wants to receive our feelings and emotions as energy for a good life. Receiving involves listening, understanding and responding positively. But that is not all.

The Eve within us also inspires the Adam within us to wake up and become actively involved in caring for the *expression* of our feelings in actions. Eve is responsive; Adam is responsible. Both emotional health and good character depend on both Eve and Adam together. But our emotional health depends especially on her, and our good character especially on him.

Chapter 11

Good Character and the Playboy

The Puritan values an individual's good character. The playboy, however, discounts its importance.

The Puritan Adam became compulsive about good character by ignoring his feelings in order to become and remain virtuous. "Don't feel because you might act," became his way of burying alive the "depraved" stirrings of his nature. But repressed feelings make a person unhappy, somber, and even depressed. In short, unbalanced.

Freud's bad news about repression eventually reached the ears of the culture. Before long, impulsive expression seemed like the only remedy. The Puritan problem had begotten the playboy reaction.

In America, Adam has been suffering from both the Puritan and playboy versions of himself. But, inspired by the emerging Eve within his bones, he is becoming aware of his need for healing.

Suppose then that he makes an appointment with a long-standing playboy who is now past his prime.

Adam: I'm concerned about what has been happening to the American character. The quality of our kind of individualism started out at the Massachusetts Bay Colony, as it were, went west to the Pacific, and recently has been looking like something from the ancient "flesh pots of Egypt."

Playboy: The nation's character had to go that way because it was much too rigid in the beginning.

Adam: All the way to a "free for all"?

Playboy: What was there to stop it?

Adam: Good question. A better idea of freedom could have made a difference.

Playboy: How can there be anything better than being able to do what you *want* to do?

Adam: Freedom is about developing your character, not so much about wanting and doing.

Playboy: You sound like a preacher from the so-called "Great Awakening."

Adam: It's true that the Puritans trumpeted good character. They were right, except that they forgot something.

Playboy: What they forgot was self-satisfaction. For me, it's enough to feel good, stay healthy, get richer, and have a good time.

Adam: Without limits? We have state and federal laws that not only limit our freedom, but protect it.

Playboy: The less laws, the better. We could repeal most of them, especially the laws that restrict our sexual choices.

Adam: There goes any chance of good character development. If we would stop to think about our need for limits, we could appreciate the value of having a good character. To keep ourselves fit, we don't eat and drink all we feel like eating and drinking, otherwise our size and weight get out of control. Of course, we need to eat and drink in order to live. But even there, we are faced with limits.

When you look in the mirror, you wouldn't want to see a face that is out of control: an eye in the place of an ear, and a nose where your mouth is supposed to be. A man's character can be like that: grotesquely out of control.

Playboy: I don't see anything ugly about enjoying life.

Adam: Mobsters and gangsters want to feel good, stay healthy, get richer, and have a good time. Apparently, they don't see anything ugly about enjoying life the way they do.

Playboy: But I'm not a mobster or a gangster. Twenty years ago when I met my third wife, I learned that she had connections with gangs and drugs. She changed because she didn't have my approval.

Good Character and the Playboy

Adam: That must mean that you have a better *character* than drug-dealing gangsters. You might have to admit that you have some interest in good behavior.

Playboy: Only to the extent that it keeps me out of trouble with the law.

Adam: If there were no laws, would you become a robber and a killer?

Playboy: Those behaviors just wouldn't be of interest to me.

Adam: What do you think about people who have your values and become thieves and/ or murderers besides?

Playboy: You are trying to paint me into a moralistic corner. All I have to say to them is that they are breaking the law and might have to pay the price. To the extent that we don't want to get in trouble with the police and the courts we need some kind of character. It's a matter of survival.

Adam: Do you really think that stealing and killing are OK if you can get away with them?

Playboy: I see that it's time for me to get ready for my next appointment.

Not *enjoying* his conversation with Adam, the playboy felt it to be an intrusion upon his way of life. Adam, however, grew in his understanding of the American character. Sometime later, he would try to talk with the playboy again.

Pleasure versus Principle

For the playboy, feeling good and enjoying life means seeking pleasure and *avoiding* the Puritan's principles of behavior. But like his Puritan forebear, the playboy does not know how to unite pleasure and principles in the depths of his personhood.

Both the Puritan and playboy are avoiders. One avoids pleasure as much as possible. The other does the same with principles. Both are basically unhappy people.

Pleasure is not the same as happiness and joy. People seek pleasure as a handy escape from emptiness. The void within them is an absence of the warmly spontaneous love called *affirmation*.

Neither Puritan nor playboy—masculine extremes—has a clue about the deep human need for this feminine-masculine kind of love.

In the absence of affirming love, the masculine individualist substitutes either principles or pleasure. The Puritan uses principles to distance himself from what he views as his depravity. The playboy uses pleasure to feel good about himself, no sin involved. Between and beyond these excessive opposites is the truth that would set both the individualist and the selfist free. The Puritan is not depraved, and the playboy is not sinless. Neither are we.

Though we are sinners, however, we are basically good and called to holiness. The affirming kind of love embraces this profoundly liberating truth.

Affirmation—affection with firmness—responds to the good (feminine) and is responsible for doing the good (masculine). The *good* includes our feelings. We receive them *as they are*. Then we become responsible for *discerning the impulses* that can result from feelings and lead to actions. We become firm in guiding our expression of received feelings in inward and outward behavior.

Pleasure is involved in feeling good. And principles are involved in doing the good. Both pleasure and principles (both *feeling good* and *doing good*) are involved in happiness.

So, happiness is much more than just seeking pleasure and feeling good. As many alcoholic folks can testify, the pleasure of drinking needs limits in order to result in happiness. A person can have too much pleasure, but no one ever has too much joy.

Feelings and Actions

Some of our feelings tell us what we *must* do to stay alive. Feelings of hunger need to be satisfied by eating, or else we will die. Feelings of thirst and tiredness need to be satisfied, too. But not all of these need-feelings have to be satisfied. Even our most basic biological needs are related to our freedom.

For example, we can choose to eat, drink, or sleep too little, too much, or just enough. If we change our diet to improve our health, we tend to experience feelings of hunger which we do not have to satisfy. Some people, through what is called biological feedback,

Good Character and the Playboy

can regulate even their involuntary processes. They know how to reduce their breathing and heartbeats well below the normal level of frequency.

While some of our physical feelings necessarily urge us to act, other feelings, such as physical sexual feelings, do not *necessarily* urge us to act. They leave us free. Basically, these sexual feelings supply the energy needed for our emotional and mental development as either a man or a woman. These feelings "want" us to affirm them, to think about their meaning, and to decide how we are going to respond. For example, two persons freely make the commitment of marriage before deciding to let these feelings go into action. This inner process integrates emotional health and good character.

Feelings and Freedom

Sexual feelings and angry feelings have much in common. They also differ since sexual feelings respond to something perceived as good, and angry feelings respond to something perceived as bad. Both seem directed, at first, toward physical action. Sexual feelings seem oriented toward genital sex. And angry feelings make us want to strike or knock down their object. But we do not get involved in sexual acts nor strike someone just because we might feel like doing so.

These feelings, then, are turned in another direction besides outward physical expression. They are turned inward where they need to be *received* into awareness. Therein they are mentally expressed in their deeper meaning for the development of our personhood and moral character before we express some of them in outward behavior.

For example, when we feel angry at someone and feel like getting verbally or physically aggressive, we can restrain our impulses. We can then receive our anger as energy for thinking about the problem. Finally, we can decide what would be a more effective way of expressing what we feel. This powerful emotion is a valuable source of creative energy, not only for figuring out the best way to express what we feel, but also for growing within as a person, and for relating well with other people.

Similarly, sexual feelings are a valuable source of energy, not primarily for acting out, but for *acting within* our awareness of them, and for developing the interiority of our manhood and womanhood within our personhood. Young people, especially, need to realize that their emerging hormones are moving them primarily toward new growth in their inner personhood. Secondarily, they are being moved toward heterosexual friendships and genital expression only in marriage. Otherwise their sexual development is shortcircuited, and can become fixated in narcissistic or adolescent stages of life.

The freedom that deeply and powerfully exists between feelings and actions is severely diminished when we think we are basically animals. We then suppose that the tendency of sexual and angry feelings toward physical or outward action is the only reason why we have these feelings, as it is in animals.

But a human person, though similar to animals in some ways, is, in no sense, an animal. For an animal, the expression of feelings is instinctual and not freely chosen. For the human person, *both genital and anger expressions can be freely chosen.*

We need to realize firmly that the primary purpose for our genital and angry feelings is not what seems to be their initial tendency toward physical action. The most basic reason why we have these feelings is to increase the awareness, sensitivity, thoughtfulness, and responsibility we need to grow in the kind of love for which the depths of our personhood exists.

So, some of our emotional and physical feelings, though they have very important functions, are still free to just *be*. Deeply connected to our freedom to decide, these particular feelings need not lead to their expressive functions.

Character is Responsible

We have the freedom we need to develop personal integrity in the natural virtues—the strengths of good character. This freedom exists in our awareness of the difference between feelings and actions.

As traditionally understood, the virtues are called prudence (good judgment), justice, temperance, and fortitude (courage). By growing in these and other relevant virtues such as humility and patience, we develop responsible limits for our actions.

Good Character and the Playboy

These limits are necessary for the development of order and beauty in our personhood. But if we are permissive and impulsive with our feelings, we are gross and badly deformed no matter how much and how skillfully we spin our rationale.

In working with individuals who have problems with impulsive behavior, a good psychologist or counselor manifests the feminine-masculine paradox of care for both feelings and behavior. The therapist affirms the other's feelings, and also helps to clarify that person's behavioral problem and its likely solution. An authentic love for both self and others makes possible this balance and integration.

The Love That Integrates

Adam needs to relate with Eve. They need to relate with each other, both within each person and between them. This need for their integrative relationship is urgent in a Puritan-playboy culture. Both the compulsive Puritan and the impulsive playboy display the unintegrated Adam. Both need the active receptivity that heals Adam within himself. Both need the original gift of Eve. Then Adam will be able to become himself—neither a Puritan nor a playboy any longer.

The Eve-Adam power of our nature for inner integration is our capacity for the affirming kind of love. This love is basically spiritual and extends from our depths into both the emotional and the self-determining areas of our personhood.

All of our emotions, including hate, exist for the sake of this love. If we could not hate the bad, we could not love the good, and the other way around. And since our emotions need the virtues to guide their expression, the virtues exist for the same ultimate purpose as the emotions, that is, for love.

In its spiritual origin, the affection with firmness that characterizes the affirming kind of love is able to unite the emotions with the virtues. We become able to *affirm* our feelings and emotions while being *firm* with them at the same time. This inner firmness is the restraint that prevents both impulsive and compulsive responses to our spontaneous feelings and emotions.

We can readily see how emotional problems affect a person's character, and also, how character-problems affect the emotional life. An emotionally impulsive person, for instance, will tend to be impatient. And an impatient character will tend to be emotionally impulsive.

This lack of emotional health and good character can be healed by the affirming kind of love that is deeper in our personhood than both our emotions and our moral character. Affirmation empowers integration. This affirming kind of love is the feminine-masculine paradox of affection with firmness that unites opposites such as emotional spontaneity and moral responsibility.

Our compulsive Puritan and impulsive playboy tendencies will be proportionately reduced when the Eve and Adam within us awaken and relate harmoniously in the grace of God. Then the warmth of affirmation in our emotional life, and the firmness of affirmation in our character—like the outstanding example observed by the whole world, Pope John Paul II—will be able to balance and integrate our unique personhood.

Chapter 12

The Healing of Human Sexuality

Human sexuality is trapped in Adam's "rational animal" idea of himself. Congested in this closet, his heterosexual being is restless and crying for healing.

A reasoning "animal" too easily rationalizes his animality. He either rejects it as sinful or welcomes it as sinless. He splits himself into either a Puritan or a playboy, and has nowhere to go but to one extreme or the other and back again.

Neither the Puritan nor the playboy understands the relationship between the warmth of affection and the heat of desire. Both think emotional warmth necessarily gets passionately hot. So the Puritan fears warmth and tries to stay cool. And the playboy ignores his heart the better to be emotionally cold and erotically hot at the same time.

A lonely and desperate culture results from the combination of these characters. Teachers don't dare to touch their students, nor parents their children, lest someone might think this warmth is sure to get hot, if not already so. Pastors are afraid to show affection toward anyone because it might look suspicious and end up in court. Two men or two women keep their distance for fear that the warmth they feel toward each other might turn up the thermostat. Women are often reluctant about letting their husbands touch them because mutual warmth automatically leaps into a blaze. Young people alone together for the first time might as well be nothing more than their hormones.

People find it difficult to feel and discern the ample *difference* between affection and passion. The culture's sexual incompetence has reached nearly comatose proportions. This condition will persist, in one way or another, as long as we continue to think that our manhood and womanhood originate in biology, and that there is no sexuality within the soul. Our personhood remains buried alive beneath the animal-based shortsight about our nature. Until this changes, the healing of our sexuality *will not be possible.*

Though Adam, at first, was alone with the animals, he was not one of them. God did not take some kind of mammal and breathe into it a human soul. According to *Genesis,* God used something much less developed than that. Dust. Scripture nowhere implies that we are basically animals.

We need a true sexual revolution. Soul-based personhood implies a soul-based sexuality. All of us, from theologians to prostitutes, need this good news.

Our manhood and womanhood originate in our personhood, not in our anatomy and physiology. Though we are *like* animals in some obvious ways, we are basically much more *like* God. And since likeness is not the same as identity, we are neither animals nor God. We are totally and radically human persons.

Our sexuality is *not* just a few biological appendages. Maleness and femaleness are soul deep. Personhood exists for the sake of love. Love is the reason why we are men and women. The male is oriented toward the female substantially, not superficially; and the female toward the male.

What is Sexuality?

"There is no sexuality in the soul, only in the body." That has been the conviction of the ages. But in the healing light of the turnaround, we can see that sexuality in the body of a person expresses sexuality in the soul. Insight into the meaning of man and woman begins with the soul and extends from there into the body, not the other way around. Therefore, a person-based definition of sexuality is required.

Sexuality can be defined as the relationship between the actively receptive (feminine) and receptively active (masculine) powers of personhood for intimacy and co-active creativity. This definition applies to the feminine-masculine relationship both *within* oneself and *with* another. It bases sexuality in the receiving-giving essence of personhood, not in biology. Thus, this view of sexuality includes *analogously* all persons: human, angelic, and divine. All are capable of intimacy and co-active creativity. Relating specifically to human persons, this definition necessarily *includes* biological maleness and femaleness.

Man and Woman

In relation to man and woman, the transcendental definition of sexuality bases their maleness and femaleness in their substantial *being*.

The being of a woman accents the inward and integrating qualities of being itself: receiving, responsiveness, relationship, withinness, immanence, intimacy, inclusion. The being of a man emphasizes the expressive and differentiating attributes of being itself: giving, responsibility, uniqueness, otherness, transcendence, self-identity, individuality.

In both a woman and a man the *emphasis* is inclusive of its opposite (correlative) qualities. In each one, the different emphasis and inclusion are integrally spiritual, psychological, and physical. Sexual development calls for an inner balance and integration of these correlatives *within* each of the three dimensions of our personhood (spiritual, psychological, and physical) as well as *between* them.

A man need not fear his feminine-like, or actively receptive, qualities. Receptivity is different in a man than it is in a woman. His predominant masculinity has a masculinizing effect on his feminine-like, or balancing, qualities. For a similar reason, women can welcome their masculine-like characteristics.

A woman becomes more developed as an unique woman when she integrates her emphatically feminine qualities with her correlative masculine qualities. For instance, a woman notices her feminine tendency to be a follower and decides to find something in which she can become a leader. This inner balancing enables her to "stand on her own two feet." Otherwise, by standing only on her dominant "foot," she tends to fall into co-dependency with a man who is likewise standing on one foot: his unbalanced masculinity. Both a man and a woman, in different ways, need inner integration.

This call of our personhood for the union of the Adam and Eve within us does not mean that we are androgynous or unisex beings. We remain profoundly heterosexual in emphasis.

Within the biology-based frame of the "rational animal," we are constrained to think that heterosexuality is basically physical. But in the liberating perspective of a person-based body, we are able to see the splendor of heterosexuality. The masculine-feminine correlatives of personhood are basically spiritual. Our spiritual heterosexuality expresses itself psychologically and physically.

Male and Female

The main organ of our personhood, the brain, is also the main organ of our sexuality. All the nerves in the body extend from the brain. In that sense, all of our organs down to our toes are virtually within the brain. This should not be startling to realize, since our entire body was present *in our being* as a single cell at conception, though not yet fully differentiated or expressed.

Every cell of the male body, including the brain, contains within it Xy chromosomes (configurations of genes that are physically shaped like an X and a smaller y). Every cell of the female body carries XX chromosomes. So, the whole human body is a *sexual organ*. And since the body expresses the soul within the soul, sexuality originates in the most spiritual depths of the soul.

Within the sexuality of the body, however, there are primary, secondary, and tertiary sexual organs. These are, respectively, the brain, the heart, and the genital system, with the heart and genital system functionally sourced in the brain.

Having two *interrelating* hemispheric lobes, the brain itself is heterosexual: this intra-cerebral intercourse is different in a man than it is in a woman. By having less connective tissue in the *corpus collosum* between its halves, the male brain is more differentiated (like Xy itself). The female (XX) brain has more connective tissue, and functions with more intimacy, between its predominant lobes. Between men and women, brain similarity is fundamental, but the difference in emphasis is decisive.

Feminists who opt for *sameness* are up against the human brain. For example, the human male is generally far more inventive in machinery and technology than the female. The female is generally more person-directed and interpersonally connected. Missing this difference by blanking out so much reality is astounding. Individual personalities might seem like "exceptions," *but deeper levels of personhood remain sexually different.*

Brain Levels

Left and right sides of the brain, with more connective interaction in the female, and with more differentiation in the male, are different, also, in three levels of the brain. Just as our body has high, middle, and low levels (brain, heart, and genital system), our brain, the source of all the nerves in the body, has high, middle, and low levels of function. There are no sharp lines of demarcation between these functional levels, only a uniquely definite emphasis in each.

The high brain (the cerebrum, especially the frontal lobes) serves the distinctive powers of personhood: the agent intellect and the agent will, and their intuitive-rational and responsive-volitional acts. The consummation of these acts is *power for wisdom about love*, which is the future of Adam and Eve.

The middle or mediating brain is more psychological (emotional-mental-motivational) than intellectual and spiritual in orientation.

Judging by its physical and emotional functions, the low brain includes the limbic system (amygdala, hypocampus, hypothalamus, thalamus) enclosed within the cerebrum. Also included is the cerebellum in the low back area of the cerebrum (that coordinates muscle movement), and the brain stem below the limbic system with its physiological functions. Sexually, this complex low area of the brain is the energy source of the human genital system.

These brain levels are logically vertical like the up and down steps of a ladder. But the physical way in which the limbic system is enclosed within the cerebrum indicates that these levels are functionally more like a telescope than like a ladder.

The high, mediating, and low functions of the brain are ontologically concentric. Adam sees them in a linear manner as based in the low brain and rising upward to the high brain: thus, the rational animal. Eve and Adam together see them contextually as the low brain within the mediating brain, and both within the high brain.

As persons, not as rational animals, we are called to the kind of human development that integrates the lower within the higher. This is our future.

The high brain is our source of power. The low and mid brain are our sources of energy. Our power is meant (by our personhood) to *actively receive* our energy and thus to actually integrate the reflexes and impulses of the low brain into the feelings, emotions, and motives of the mid-brain, and these into the power of the high brain. This integrative process assimilates or subsumes the lower within the higher.

Subsumation is not sublimation. To subsume the lower into the higher is not the same as *substituting* the higher for the lower, such as a young man getting involved in a productive social project instead of joining a gang. Subsuming low brain impulses *integrates* the lower within the higher. Substitution is not integration, though it can have a partially integrative effect.

Subsuming the lower within the higher is a conscious act by a person who knows the meaning of personhood. Sublimation is a subconscious act of one who thinks a human being is animal-based. A person develops by subsumation; a rational animal develops by sublimation. The difference is the result of an individual's self-concept. Our future is in our commitment to our personhood, and thus to our progress beyond the irrationality of the "rational animal."

Whole Brain Sexuality

Having more connection between the left and right sides of the high brain, the female has, also, more connection between high-brain intuition and the mid-brain heart. She has more left-brain verbal ability in relation to personal and interpersonal feelings and emotions.

The male brain, by contrast, is organized for more differentiation between its two sides and between its levels. His brain, more outward-than-inner-directed, and more oriented toward conquests of all kinds, is also more *directly* connected with the genital system than with the heart.[16]

Female and male differences in brain organization are evident in their initial sexual reflexes. The female's initial reflex shows up in the heart. She wants emotional feelings of "love" through verbal intercourse. He wants physical feelings of "love" through genital intercourse. So the male tends to *use* words (not real feelings) of love in order to get sex. And the female tends to *use* sex in order to get emotional feelings of love.

These reflexes and impulses are valuable sources of *energy* that need high-brain *power* for their own human fulfillment. Low brain reflexes are inner calls for high brain reception and reflection. Both male and female persons need to realize that their *initial* tendencies are not directives toward outward action, but energy for inward action.

Instead of depending on the male for emotional support, the female needs to receive her emotional reflex into her awareness. She needs to activate the subdominant masculinity of her personhood. In this way, she affirms her feelings and becomes firm with them at the same time. A similar process with the opposite emphasis is required for the male.

Instead of blindly and impulsively *falling* into each others arms, the two become able to relate as friends. Their mutual feelings of warmth do not get hot. Then they can freely and knowingly choose, or not choose, marriage and parenthood.

Co-creation and Procreation

The man-woman relationship is primarily co-creative in relation to the affirming, caring, and sharing kinds of love; it is not necessarily marital and procreative. So, the best preparation for marriage and parenthood includes a developed ability to see that the co-creative meaning of our sexuality is the basis and context for its procreative meaning.

God told the man and woman of *Genesis*, almost in the same breath, both to beget others of their kind and to become masters of the earth and its creatures" (*Genesis* 1:28). In the image and likeness of God, and together with God, they were to have both a procreative and a co-creative purpose.

Procreation is one of the various kinds of co-creative sharing between a man and a woman. But it is difficult to see and experience our sexuality in this way. It will not happen without a growing insight into the person-base of heterosexuality. Sex without an adequate development in sexuality becomes a smile without much of a face.

Sexual Orientation

Manhood cannot be understood in itself except as a substantial relationship to womanhood, and the other way around. Like our two hands, male and female are essentially oriented one toward the other.

A person with one hand could bake bread and play the piano, but no one would actually want just one hand. Neither would they want both hands turned in the same direction. They would lack the mutual cooperation and support afforded by opposite orientations.

Similarly, no one would want a world of androgynes who are neither men nor women. The transcendental structure of *being itself* is expressed in the orientation of two persons substantially turned toward each other. Being is transcendental by including all beings that *are*, in their withinness and otherness, in their immanence and transcendence, and in their uniqueness and relatedness. One side of these pairs is feminine and the other side is masculine. Withinness, immanence, and relatedness are feminine. Otherness, transcendence, and uniqueness are masculine. In this qualitative sense, sexuality is transcendental. The high brain knows it; the low brain has no clue.

Sexual orientation, therefore, is significant ontologically, not only biologically and psychologically. But a definition of human nature such as "rational animal" is profoundly disorienting right within our heterosexual orientation itself. It gives us the idea that sex is a part of our supposed animal base, and that rationality is other than sexual. The result has been the traditional idea that there is no sexuality in the soul, and that manhood and womanhood end where they are visible in the organs of the body.

This eyeball way of thinking is like recognizing that our hands are oriented toward each other, but falsely assuming that our arms and their functional sources in the brain are not so oriented. It surely looks and feels as if only the end organs (the hands) are opposites. But an eyeball-reflex mentality about human sexuality, similar to the lack of insight about the connection of the hands to the arms and

The Healing of Human Sexuality

the brain, results in many sexual problems. Both acting by reflexes, and repressing reflexes to prevent action, are forms of disorientation caused by the supposed animal-base of human sexual personhood. The troublesome fallout from this ancient and archaic perspective is profuse.

Examples are internal separations of various kinds. Pornography is an eyeball-reflex of the first degree. It *separates* sex, not only from its origin in the human soul, but also from its *specific* purpose. Contraception and sterilization, in different ways, *separate* sex from its specific purpose. Abortion, like murder, *separates* a newly conceived person from life itself. Fornication *separates* sex from marriage. In a different way, adultery does the same. Divorce *separates* a marriage from itself. Homogenital behavior *separates* sex from its substantially heterosexual structures.

These multiple schizoid actions have their "rational animal" rationalizations. But if we change the animal-base of our reasoning power to a person-base, these self-justifications lose their eyeball frame of reference.

Immediately, however, the idea of a person-based point of view is likely to be misinterpreted by contemporary personalists who are Cartesian in the way they treat the body as an object. Unable to see the body as an *internal* expression of our personhood, Cartesian-like personalists continue the same schizoid rationalizations.

According to their interpretation, the body is just as simplistically biological as it is in the animal-based view. The main difference is that the spins of the "personalists" are much more sophisticated and elaborate. For example, they view abortion as a matter of choice and reproductive "health care." Noticeably, many of those who are not "personalists," but who see themselves as basically animals are still able to think rationally about abortion as killing the innocent.

Schizoid sexual behaviors can develop as a result of early family conditioning and cultural influences, and are difficult to change. But the first step toward wholeness is recognizing and acknowledging the disoriented frame of reference we use for our sometimes highly elaborate self-justifications.

Homosexuality

A healthy heterosexuality includes same-sex relationships such as those between sisters, brothers, mothers and daughters, fathers and sons, and same-sex friends. In fact, children cannot develop well without learning how to relate, boys with boys and girls with girls. Women enjoy being together with other women, and men with men. They talk differently between themselves than they do with other-sex persons. Women are more interested in the subjectivity of family and friends, and men are more interested in the objectivity of projects and goals.

Paradoxically, this kind of same-sex interest is part of the meaning of heterosexuality. A same-sex interest, however, that is actually a persistent erotic attraction is inconsistent with a person's substantial heterosexuality. This condition of disorientation is better called homoeroticism.

Many are challenged by this and other anomalies. These persons are just as human as everyone else, and should be treated with civility, as well as with clarity and firmness about the reality of their condition. The playboy-feminist culture, however, does not support this clarity and firmness. The playboy views sex as a necessity for virtually everyone. The feminist ardently believes that women and men are practically the same. So, for them, the difference between hetero- and homo- sexuality necessarily seems insignificant.

Before the playboy revolution began, psychologists regarded homoeroticism as an aberration. When the idea took hold that "you have to have sex to be normal," the push to normalize contraception and homo*genital* sex began. Now, insisting that they are normal and natural, some individuals who have a homoerotic orientation want everything that heterosexuals have, including marriage and children. Along with radical feminists, they wrongly think that equality means sameness.

Chastity is unthinkable for both the playboy and the playmate-feminist. In such a cultural drift away from the higher regions of *eros* into the lower, coupled with an exaggeration of the self and hatred of common sense, what is there to restrain the downward momentum?

Possible Causes of Homoeroticism

We know that maleness or femaleness of a newly conceived child is genetically caused by either the X or the y chromosomes of the father. Disorientation, however, does not appear to be genetic. Whether or not it is hormonal or developmental remains a matter of research and speculation.[17]

Furthermore, whether stress between the child's parents can affect hormonal and emotional factors in the child's prenatal development seems to be a relevant question. An overload of female hormones entering the environment through waste disposal from so many women taking the anti-conception pill is known to be affecting wildlife adversely. What else is this hormonal imbalance affecting? In any event, it is likely that there is more than one cause of human sexual disorientation.

We do know that a father who does not want responsibility for a child can affect the mother so deeply that she goes to an abortionist. Her relationship with the father can be that significant for the new little person. The mother's relationship with the father always affects *emotionally* her bond with the child growing within her.

From the moment of conception, a human being is much more than a "genetic package" or a merely biological entity. Interpersonal relationships and their quality are part of the child's development from the very beginning of life.

Basic to these relationships are the child's needs for intimacy and identity. Intimacy is required by the feminine aspect of personhood. Identity is required by its masculine opposite. In the very moment of conception, *identity* as an individual person and as either male or female is provided by the father. Then a prolonged intimacy with the mother begins.

The father's formation of the new person's identity starts the process. Intimacy with the mother sustains it. But the process moves through many different stages of human life. Anywhere along the line, especially early in life, parental responses to the child's needs for intimacy and identity will be either beneficial or detrimental.

Consistent with his role in conception, the father remains significant for the child's personal and sexual identity. His loving firmness is especially effective in validating the gender-identity of both sons and daughters. The mother is also involved in the identity-formation of her children, especially through her obvious-to-the-child affirmation of the father. But intimacy is meant to be her natural emphasis. This mother-emphasis on the side of intimacy is a strong point for her daughter, but can be a weak point for her son, especially if her relationship with the father is weak.

If the father is weak or absent, and if the mother over-compensates by super-charging the masculine qualities of *her* personhood, her children inevitably will be adversely affected. Both their intimacy with her and their sense of identity from their father could become severely disoriented. Also, degrees and qualities of sensitivity in individual children are other factors involved.

Some boys, for instance, are naturally and normally more sensitive than others. If the father fails to respect this characteristic in his son, and demeans him instead, both his son's personal and sexual identity are weakened. Something similar happens if a father demeans his daughter's sexuality, or abuses her in any way.

The mother that emotionally substitutes her son for a husband, or seduces him in this way, is a profoundly disorienting agent. But the mother that loves and honors her husband, though she has several young sons and loses her husband in death, nevertheless fosters their identity-relationship with their father. Thus, a healthy (not perfect) relationship between the father and mother supports the gender identity of their children.

This diagnosis of causes is neither a matter of scholarship, nor of scientific inquiry, nor of mere speculation. It is a result of *thoughtful* common sense. Multitudes of parents have resorted to the intuitive power of what is recognized as common sense in relating with their children. They did not have to know consciously that they were doing so. But even more so, if they reflect and explicitly know *that* they know *what* they know, they can surely strengthen the warming light and luminous warmth of intuitive common sense.[18]

How Intimacy (Eve) and Identity (Adam) Interrelate

Intimacy begins in the womb of the mother. If she puts her hand on the right side of her pregnant abdomen, the child moves toward her affirming hand. If she does this with her left hand, the child moves there to receive her intimate affirmation.[19]

After the child is born, the formation of identity begins as the mother responds to the child's needs and emotions by *giving* them back to the little boy or girl, not by taking them away with impatience or negation. In receiving intimate affirmation like this, the child knows intuitively and preconsciously that "these needs are mine; these feelings are mine; I exist." This initial sense of identity, this "I am," is so important because each person is created in the image and likeness of God who is "I am who am." The child's personhood says "I am" in the image and likeness of "I am who am." In an *intimate* mother-child way, the little one's sense of *identity* is initially formed. Deeply preconscious in a baby, "I am" subsequently becomes "I am a girl" or "I am a boy." Sexual identity forms within the context of the child's self-identity as a person.

The baby's need for an intimately affirming kind of love remains contextual throughout the duration of the parent-child relationship. As the child grows, a rudimentary need for friendship emerges with the parent of the same sex. In this way, a further stage of intimacy develops a further stage of identity: both personal and sexual. While the father remains a father for the son, the son needs to *enjoy* male activities with him. Together with his father, he feels, knows, develops, and enjoys his maleness. They share, for example, games, sports, hunting, fishing, and building things of various kinds. They relate as male persons in both their face-to-face and side-by-side relationships.

Within this father-son context, a boy needs to relate, also, with other boys simply as friends in a side-by-side manner of sharing. He needs to be accepted by, and accepting of, them. Developmental activities, especially competitive sports, are examples.

Similarly, but uniquely, a girl needs to share and enjoy feminine activities with her mother and with other girls, and to develop her sense of "I am a girl" with them. Talking, telling stories, baking cookies, sewing, singing, dancing, and working on projects together are examples.

Side-by-side sharing between same-sex friends actually promotes the personal and sexual identity needed for the face-to-face intimacy of heterosexuality.

When a boy feels "cast out" by his Dad and by other boys his age, he lacks some degree of development in both his personal "I am" identity and his male-emphatic sexual identity. Consequently, he will find heterosexual intimacy difficult in two possible ways. He will be unable to develop and sustain friendship with a young woman without sex; *philia* will be shortcircuited by *eros*. Or, feeling little or no *eros* for male-female relationships, he might feel a same-sex attraction instead. The latter will be a signal that an authentic need, required by the intimacy-identity paradox of personhood, has not been fulfilled. Something similar is true, also, for girls and young women.

In the early life process of same-sex sharing, a boy does not need intimacy with his mother, nor a girl with her father. He needs his Mom to affirm his identity by being his af-*firm*-ing mother, not his confidant. And she needs her Dad to be her affirming father, not her confidant.

When good intuitive judgments are confused by heterosexual problems between a child's parents, and when a son or daughter is consequently disoriented to a significant degree, the child's low-brain *eros* can turn inward and become a desire for "someone like me." This same-sex yearning *substitutes* for, while imitating, what is designed to be a heterosexual desire. Substituting and imitating are clearly disorienting. The person becomes either feminine submissive or masculine aggressive. "Someone like me" turns out to be a disoriented version of "me and the opposite sex."[20]

Homoerotic relationships might seem like love. But well-oriented same-sex relationships are meant to include all of the kinds of love except the emotional-genital aspect of eros which is *obviously* heterosexual because it structurally includes a social (procreative) purpose.

Is healing possible? Yes, but many do not want to change. For some, the condition is more deep-set than for others. Of course they *want* to feel natural and normal and assured that nature makes them that way. Especially the dominant one. The masculine side of human

The Healing of Human Sexuality

nature is the least likely to want healing. It is well known that men seek emotional healing far less than women. But, with the right kind of support, healing is possible, and a positive—not negative—kind of chastity is necessary for all.[21]

Chastity means the sexual integrity that permits genital expression only within a faithful heterosexual marriage. In the context of an animal-based view of human nature, this "soular" view of sexuality seems to be, for some, too idealistic. But many people, inspired by their religious faith and prayer life have lived it, and continue to do so. The effectiveness of their spiritual life in developing sexual integrity, however, could be facilitated by more high-brain *power for wisdom about love*. This "consummation devoutly to be wished" requires a paradoxical way of thinking for increasing insight into the depth of our heterosexual personhood.

From Eyesight to Insight

Because eyesight is so important to our everyday life, it is easy to become excessively empirical about truth. The result is a shortsight as debilitating as eyeball blindness.

For example, we readily see with our eyes our sexuality in its end organs. When a baby is born there is an obvious way to determine whether the new person is a boy or a girl. At that moment of recognition, as well as subsequently, insight could actually see far more than eyesight. But because insight is so often minimal or lacking, the cultural environment tends to be the major formative influence on the child's sexuality.

A culture that tries to tell us we are spiritually like God and sexually like animals only, and that our manhood and womanhood are mere attachments to our personhood, massively lacks insight. If our sexuality originates in our glands and generative organs, we are artificial composites like centaurs and mermaids. A sexual body having a neuter soul is like the body of a horse having the head of a man (a centaur), or like the tail of a fish having the body of a woman (a mermaid).

These images are constructs of the imagination. But constructs of reason, such as the "rational animal" definition of human nature, can be similarly fictional. Influenced by fantasies and a subconscious desire to identify with animals, we can use reason to combine incongruities.

Adam's usual way of thinking about our body-soul nature is a construct of reason that is too much influenced by the constructive power of the imagination to be left unquestioned. The momentous crisis in human sexuality that we are going through today calls for a revolution in our self-awareness. Without it, there is very little hope for healing.

Chapter 13

In the Likeness of God

When Eve awakens from the coma of the ages, she will realize that she needs to emerge, once again, from the rib of Adam. In his cultures, she has been asleep in the marrow of his bones. Even when Eve tried to break away and become herself, she did so only to identify with his ways. Deceptively thinking she was free at last, she has remained stranded in Adam.

But Eve has been redeemed by God, and still needs to realize what that means. If she were to wake up and start to wonder who her redeemed self really is, she might begin to speak to Adam in a way that would surprise him.

She might say, "The root of our problem is in our likeness to God. We were created originally to magnify the Lord. Then I lost it, and so did you. But my challenge turns out to be more intensive than yours. Justifiably so! God seems masculine, so you seem more readily like him. And I seem like God only through you. Do you really think that is the way it is meant to be between us?"

Adam would be likely to respond, "You were created from my rib to be my helper" (*Genesis* 2:18-22). But Eve would be quick to say, "Yes, your helper, but not your servant or slave."

As she awakens still further, and the light of dawn becomes brighter, Eve would be likely to continue. "I was created to end your aloneness with the animals lest you become more like them than like God. There was a danger that this loss of likeness would happen to you. So God wanted to strengthen your likeness to him by drawing me forth from you to help you remain like God. That is primarily how I am your helper.

"But if I am like God *only* through you, I am still imprisoned in your rib. I need to become the woman I was originally meant to be. You need to become the man you were meant to be. And we are faced with recovering our first relationship with each other in a shared and equal likeness to God.

"Something about our sexuality mirrors the divine. And I don't mean just our difference in qualities. I mean the man-and-woman difference in our personhood."

Adam might be astounded to hear such an assertion from Eve. Would he be courageous and curious enough to open at least a small place in his mind and heart, and ask, "How is that possible?"

Sensing at least a meager readiness in Adam for inquiry, Eve could begin to tell him about the thick wall that formed between them when their original receptivity became passive. It was a wall like stone. It kept her, especially, away from her direct likeness to God—a likeness truly shared with Adam. Would he be willing to forgive her and move on? If so, she would be able to open the door in the wall and lead him through this ancient, no longer relevant, barrier.

On This Side of the Wall

When Adam and Eve were expelled from Eden, they were in survival mode. To increase, multiply, and fill the earth (*Genesis* 1:28) became what seemed their reason for being. So Eve might say to Adam, "On this side of the wall, we have existed for centuries mainly to become parents. Your fatherhood has seemed especially important in patriarchal Western civilization. And you have readily related with the fatherhood of God. So, when our redeemer spoke about God, he revealed the Father and Son.

"On this side of the wall, God is masculine and paternal-filial. And you, Adam, seem content with your likeness to the divine paternity. But your relationship with me, though redeemed, is inadequately discerned as long as we remain on this side of the wall. We need to go through its door and find out how I can emerge from my captivity in you."

Adam might ask, "Where is this door?"

The Door in the Wall

Eve: There is an opening in the wall that exists in our minds since we were cast out of our originally gifted selves. You and I were expelled together. If we could see our way through this wall's door we could pass from *your* fatherly likeness to God on this side of the wall to *our* spousal likeness to God on the other side.

Adam: Wait a minute, now. How can I be sure you are not going to lead me astray *again*?

Eve: I wish you would have protested like that the first time around. You could have prevented the situation from which we are now struggling to recover. So, going through the door is now your decision to make. I want us to find together what we lost.

Adam: Back there in the beginning, I failed to ask even one question when you tempted me. Now I will firmly ask some careful questions. Are you suggesting that we have a likeness to God *other than* our shared spiritual nature and my direct resemblance to the Father?

Eve: You know that God created me to be your spouse, not primarily to be the mother of our children. In other words, you, Adam, are first of all a spouse, and only then, a father.

Adam: If you think we have a spousal likeness to God, you are upsetting all the philosophy and theology of my philosophers and theologians. They never saw in divine revelation what you are asserting.

Eve: So, you don't want to wonder how our spousal relationship magnifies the Lord.

Adam: Wonder? I can always wonder what is on your mind. I guess that's part of being a spouse.

Eve: I see significant hints in the pre-Christian scriptures that there is something like a spousal relationship in God. First of all, God says in the beginning, "Let us make man in our image" (*Genesis* 1). The words "us" and "our" seem to be signifying more than one divine Person. *Proverbs* 8:22-31 shows God creating all things through Wisdom. According to *Wisdom* 7:25, which refers to divine Wisdom, "She is a breath of the power of God, pure emanation of the glory of the Almighty."

Notably, wisdom is identified as "she." And she is an *emanation*, not a generation, of God's power. This divine emanation implies that feminine Wisdom proceeds from masculine Power. My original procession from you seems to be a spouse-like image and likeness of this divine procession by emanation.

Do you want, now, to wonder your way through this door? We can go through it only together.

Adam: Before that happens, Eve, you'll have to answer more questions. Why does the Christian Gospel seem to be exclusively about a Father-Son relationship? Where is the spousal relationship?

Eve: You know, Adam, that our spousal (two-in-one) relationship is the background of our parental relationship. In the Christian revelation, Jesus is the Father's Son in a parental, or foreground, kind of relationship. That is where meanings like *generating* and *begetting* are significant, that is, in the parental foreground.

Adam: The Son of the Father in the foreground: who is he in the background? The spouse of the Father? This leaves you, Eve, with a great amount of explaining to do. How can a son be also a spouse, and one you claim a woman is like? This surely seems impossible to me. I feel inclined to forget about this wall and its door.

Eve: Stay with me, Adam. We very much need to move in the direction of personhood, or we will never pass through this wall. It is now getting to be high noon for me, and I want to proceed in the light.

Adam: Personhood?

Eve: Yes. The answer to your question about Wisdom and the Son is deep in the mystery of divine Wisdom as one Person in two natures. Are you thinking that we should not be wondering our way into the mystery of the Trinity?

Adam: Many theologians have done so. But all have said that the mystery is far beyond our power to understand it.

Eve: The mystery is infinite. It is inexhaustible. It seems absurd to be afraid that we will ever explain the mystery by continuing to wonder and understand more about it.

Adam: I wonder what you see, then, in the mystery of personhood that would be relevant to feminine Wisdom and the masculine Son of the Father.

Divine Personhood

Eve: We cannot even be a person without the *ability* to love another person.

Adam: What about a person's ability to know and understand? Neither of us could possibly be a person without this power.

Eve: Knowledge can exist without love in the context of the rational animal. But in the context of personhood, knowing exists for the sake of loving. God is love. So are we.

Adam: What did you say?

Eve: I mean that we cannot *be* love infinitely the way God *is* love. But we can be love finitely the way we are called to *be*.

Adam: What kind of love?

Eve: Our kind of love that is most like God is *philia* (friendship). This will be important to remember as we continue to wonder along. A being for love, that is, a person relating with another person, is both giving and receiving. Not just giving, but equally receiving. Otherwise love could not be mutual.

Adam: I can think of love that is not mutual. A father can love a child who cannot return that love as it is given. A man can love a woman who does not know he loves her.

Eve: In both cases, the person does have the potential to love mutually. This potential might be undeveloped or injured, but it *is*. Each of us has the ability to give and receive as you and I are now doing. My being as a woman emphasizes receiving, and yours, giving.

In this dialog between the two of us I'm calling on my inner masculine potential in order to stand on my own two feet as a person distinct from you. But I could not do this if you did not allow me to do so by genuinely listening and responding firmly, yet carefully.

I'm grateful to you, Adam, and hopeful, too. As I am becoming myself, you are equally becoming yourself.

Adam: I'm feeling a little better now, but I still don't see where you are going. Are you implying that there is receptivity in God?

Eve: Yes, but *not* passivity. There is not the slightest shadow of passivity in God. Your philosophers, as well as theologians, thought receiving is being passive. Instead, it is a correlative of being active. For example, when a man and woman are dancing briskly and beautifully, and when he is leading and she is responding, she is just as active as he is, though differently.

Adam: I think I'm beginning to see how you are going to move through the door in the wall. But I still believe in the Father, Son, and Holy Spirit. That leaves me firmly on this side of things.

Eve: The Father, Son, and Holy Spirit are, and remain *forever*, in the parental foreground of divine revelation where we are now relating. But there is a spousal background on the other side of this wall.

Adam: Let's take a break. This is getting to be quite a stretch for my normal way of thinking.[22] …..

From the Foreground to the Background

Eve: We have been silent for awhile, Adam. You have been going about your affairs as usual, and I about mine while praying for light and guidance concerning our inward journey. I'm eager to be re-created from you in my wholeness that we might share more deeply our lives together.

Adam: I'm ready to continue our search. But I'm still uneasy about your claimed likeness to the second divine Person. How can you say that those sources you cited from *Proverbs* and *Wisdom* refer to a divine Person? Isn't the reference to a divine attribute instead?

Eve: The use of the word "she" in relation to wisdom suggests a person as well as an attribute: both. Each one of the divine Persons emphasizes the divine attributes differently from the others.

Adam: Well, then, are you implying there are sexual differences in God? I cannot agree.

In the Likeness of God

Eve: Adam, you know that "Father" and "Son" are masculine names. You know also that you are an emphatically masculine person, not only in your body, but also in your soul, spirit, and very *being*. So, the meanings of the words "masculine" and "feminine" relate to *being itself*; as such, these meanings are transcendental, and thus relevant to God. Your philosophers and theologians cannot recognize sexuality (or hetero-mutuality) in their own souls as long as they base their nature in the animal kingdom. But, you, Adam, now base our nature in personhood. So, you are able to see, on the other side of the wall, how much our manhood and womanhood are like the mutual differences in the divine Persons.[23]

Adam: Let's go through the door, then. My first question will have to be this: how can feminine Wisdom possibly be, also, the Son of the Father?

Eve: You already know that the second divine Person *receives* personhood from the first divine Person. Notice the word: receives. Actively receives! Wisdom is primarily receptive, and thus can be qualified as feminine.

Now look at me, Adam. Here you see a person who is primarily feminine. But that is not all. I am also expressive. Obviously. That is how I am like the Wisdom Person of God. My being is primarily feminine and inclusively masculine.

At the very beginning of his gospel, John calls the Person of Jesus the Word. The name for the *expressivity* of Wisdom is Word, which is masculine in relation to the primary receptivity of Wisdom. In God, Wisdom is expressed in one Word, not many. So, the second divine Person is the Wisdom-Word of God. And the masculine Word-of-Wisdom consistently became male flesh as the Son of the Father.

But we are getting ahead of ourselves. Let's begin at the very beginning: the first divine Person. You are his special image and likeness, not only as a father, but also as my source and spouse.

Adam: Amazing! Amazing! Let me think about this Wisdom-Word idea for awhile. It's quite intense.

Eve: This way of thinking about our likeness to God is very intense for me, also. Let's be receptive in silence for awhile.

....

Adam, let's look to your own personhood for a clue about the first divine Person. As a man, you are predominantly a giver. As a woman, I need you to give me to myself. But you cannot do this well until you receive *yourself*. As a man, you are a *receiver within a giver*.

Adam: A receiver within a giver. Yes. The silence we just now shared seemed quite receptive. It was somewhat unusual for me, but possible.

Eve: As a man, then, you are a receiving *giver*. I am a giving *receiver*. We need to think paradoxically like this. Our usual way of identifying giving and receiving, and separating them from each other for the sake of a "blank tablet" clarity, will not help us to think transcendentally.

Adam: Clarity is clarity. But I suppose there are different kinds. We know that the Gospel teaches in paradoxes such as dying that we might live, and being both wise as a serpent and simple as a dove. So there must be a way, other than our usual kind of logic, for thinking through paradoxes. If I am a receiving kind of giver, this must mean that there are different ways of giving. Of course there are. Giving in order to get something from it is different from giving while receiving the dignity and response of the other.

Eve: Yes, and there is giving simply to be helpful; this is the nobly masculine kind. Giving in a receiving way is basically masculine, but also feminine: paradoxical. If we begin to think paradoxically about the first divine Person, we will see him as a receiving kind of giver. You, especially, are his image and likeness. Traditionally, we believe that the Father *knows himself*. And in knowing himself he begets the Son.

Adam: I suppose you would say this self-knowing is the Father's receptivity.

Eve: Not only in knowing himself, but in *loving himself* as well. "God is love" begins in the life of the first divine Person. Between us, love begins in you, Adam. If you don't receptively know and love your own being, not just your ego, you will not be able to let me *be*.

Adam: You are moving beyond my theologians when you describe a relationship within each person, not only relationships between them. If the divine Persons are, each one, integral in this way, you could be in danger of believing in three Gods.

Eve: There can be only one infinite nature. And each of the three Persons is infinite within one divine nature. There is only one God in three infinitely distinct Persons.

In their infinite life together, they are better identified by their most emphatic attributes of power, wisdom, and love. Though all three Persons are infinitely powerful, wise, and loving, the first Person emphasizes the infinite *power* of God *(Luke* 22:69). The second Person emphasizes the infinite *wisdom* of God (John 1:1-5). And the Holy Spirit personifies divine *love (Romans 5:5).*

If we see the emphatic attribute of each divine Person as a personal name, we can begin to see something about how they relate from within themselves. By receiving himself with infinite knowing and loving, Power *affirms* "I am who am" and *emanates* "you are." Power "emanates" Wisdom, his spouse (*Wisdom* 7:25). Wisdom infinitely *receives* the gift of personhood by knowing and loving self and *giving* love to the Giver. This *giving* is Wisdom's *expressive,* and thereby masculine, Word. Together, then, Wisdom and Power emanate "We are," the Holy Spirit.

The spousal relation between Power and Wisdom "emanates" the very Personhood of Love, who is co-equal with them, yet infinitely unique in one divine nature: one God.

Adam, why are you silent?

Adam: I'm trying to understand. So much paradoxical thinking is unusual for me. Since God is Love, we might say that the three divine Persons are the Power of Love, the Wisdom of Love, and the Mutuality of Love. If I am a likeness of the Power of Love, then *being* and *doing* this likeness must be my future. Your future is being and doing your likeness of the divine Wisdom of Love, which you are now being and doing between us. If I agree that this is, indeed, my future, then our original relationship can be restored in the likeness of the divine Mutuality of Love, the Holy Spirit.

I would welcome this future if I could better understand the feminine Wisdom of Love—the second divine Person—as, also, the masculine Son of God. Futhermore, our love is not another person between us as Spousal Love, the Holy Spirit, is another Person in God.

Eve: Both of these questions are involved in the way the spousal background of God relates with the parental foreground. For instance, if we were infinite, our two-in-oneness would *be* another person. The closest we can come to our spousal relationship being itself a third person is in our parenthood.

I'm so happy, Adam, that we have come this far together. The spousal background of the Father and Son is where I am like the Spousal Wisdom of God, and where you and I together are like the Spousal Trinity.

From Spousal to Parental

Adam: Let's see, then, how the Father-Son relationship emerges from the spousal background of God that we have been discovering. The creation of the world must be involved.

In creating the world, the first divine Person became expressively paternal. Following your suggestion about the spousal Trinity, this paternity of divine Power must mean that the Wisdom of God became expressively maternal. And the Person of Love between Power and Wisdom *inspired* them to become active together in causing so many creatures to be.

Eve: I'm with you Adam. What do you think about the Incarnation of the Word of Wisdom?

Adam: As you indicated earlier, the masculine Word of Wisdom became human and consistently male. Again, the Power of God became expressively paternal. Did the Wisdom of God become maternal? And the Word of Wisdom become filial? This sonship within Wisdom is still challenging for me to accept.

It seems too much like the second Person is really two Persons: one maternal, the other filial. Otherwise, you have the implication that, in his divinity, Jesus is his own mother.

Eve: That is the way you have to think, Adam, when you interpret sexuality as basically physical rather than basically spiritual. In your own body, it is absurd to say that you are your own mother. But when you realize that your body expresses your soul, and that your soul is primarily masculine and secondarily feminine (actively receptive), you can say you are, in that sense, your own mother, and even more so, your own father.

Adam: This reminds me of the analytic idea that we have within our psychological nature a *parent*, a *child*, and an *adult*. In that frame of reference, our inner parent can be both masculine and feminine according to the masculine or feminine *emphasis* in our personhood. Then, yes, the receptivity in my inner life as a man can have a maternal characteristic.

Eve: You began this part of our discussion by asking about the divine maternity within the Son of God as the Person of Wisdom. This is where we really need to see the *parental* foreground of God within the *spousal* background.

In the parental foreground, Jesus is clearly the Son of the Father. In the spousal background, he is the masculine Word of feminine Wisdom and is, as such, the eternal Son of the Father. Paradoxically the Son is *both* eternal and *not eternal*, in different (background and foreground) respects. Thus, in Jesus, feminine Wisdom *receives* the masculine humanization of the masculine Word by the Holy Spirit. This third Person, the Love between the other two, humanizes the Word of Wisdom as the Son of the Father within the Person of Wisdom.

But you cannot see this Spousal-Parental truth about the Trinity as long as you are standing in the foreground of God. You can see this only if you are standing in the background after you have passed through the door in the wall. From that glorious point of view, the wall actually disappears as if it never existed. What a return to our original paradise that is! Sorrowfully for me, I led you away. Now, I am hoping to lead you back. Not backward, however, but forward. Not outward, but deeply within.

Adam: What do you think my philosophers and theologians would say about your view of the Incarnation? They think that the Word became flesh by coming down here to earth and entering into a single cell in the womb of Mary by the power of the Holy Spirit. You say just the opposite: that divine Wisdom received a single cell in Mary's womb in such a way that Wisdom's Word became flesh *within* the Wisdom Person of God, and also within Mary.

Eve: Only when you see the foreground *within* the background can you see the Incarnation in this opposite way. Furthermore, your philosophers and theologians think the soul enters the body at conception. No, the soul actively receives the gametic causes of the body, thus expressing itself in a bodily manner. Until they begin to think ontologically, they will not be able to see the Incarnation as the divine Person of Wisdom actively receiving the single cell in Mary's womb that incarnates Wisdom's Word.

Adam: Will they want to change their perspective like that? My theologians say, also, that the Son is eternal with the Father. If you say that the Word of Wisdom became the Son of the Father at the time of the Incarnation, the Son, according to your view, is not eternal, even though you say he is.

Eve: In the sense that the Trinity, as *parental*, is immanent within the Trinity, as *spousal*, Fatherhood and Sonship are eternal. The Son (as the Word of Wisdom) is co-eternal with the Father (as divine Power). Paradoxically, also, divine Fatherhood begins with creation, and divine Sonship begins with the Incarnation.

Adam: I wonder whether my theologians will be ready to think that paradoxically.

Another question. They say that the Son is *generated* or *begotten* by the Father. You say that the second divine Person is *emanated* by the first. What would you say to them?

Eve: All are true from different perspectives. Within the Trinity as spousal, the two processions are *emanations*. In the Trinity as parental, the first emanation becomes *generation* of the Son by the Father. And the second emanation becomes the paternal-filial *spiration* of the Spirit by the Father and Son. Similarly, the spousal love between a man and woman becomes parental love between them when they have children. These are two different aspects of the same love between them.

In the Likeness of God

Adam: I see how the recognition of active receptivity (having no passivity at all) shifts traditional theology into a transcendental dimension. Without a transcendental ontology of personhood, we cannot see much beyond what you call a wall.

Eve: Active receptivity opens the door. Then the wall disappears.

Adam: Then we see the active receptivity of Mary in a new light.

Eve: Actually, everything in the foreground shines in a new light. Mary, in the foreground of God is the perfect icon of actively receptive Wisdom in the background. Pregnant with the Wisdom-Word incarnate, she mirrors divine Wisdom "pregnant" forever with the incarnate Word.

Adam: But look at the difference. Jesus is the very personhood of the Wisdom-Word. Mary is a human person; he is a divine Person.

Eve: True. Comparisons always have that kind of inadequacy along with their light on the subject.

Adam: The Son went through a terrible scourging and crucifixion. It is so difficult to think of the Person of Wisdom suffering like this.

Eve: Wisdom was *giving* birth. Childbirth is an arduous *expression* for a woman. But as Jesus said, she is so happy when the child is born that she forgets the ordeal (*John* 16:21). The crucified Son— Wisdom's Word Incarnate—was Wisdom giving redemptive birth to us and our children.

Adam: Hearing this about feminine Wisdom, some theologians would wonder why the Word became incarnate as male rather than female. They would wonder how a feminine Person can have a male humanity.

Eve: How would *you* respond to them?

Adam: They need more insight into the paradoxical structure of personhood. They would have to realize how feminine *Wisdom's* masculine *Word* would become incarnate consistently as man. God is infinitely consistent.

I can see, then, why Jesus called himself the Son of *Man.* He is the masculine Word of feminine Wisdom expressed in human manhood.

"Son of Man" *is* the Word *expressed* to us. "Son of God" *is* the Word *expressed* within God.

Eve: Notice, Adam, how all three divine Persons, not just the Wisdom-Word, are masculine in the foreground *otherness* of God in relation to the created world. The Father is emphatically masculine, the incarnate Son is masculine, and the Holy Spirit, as the Spouse of Mary, reveals masculine expressivity.

In the background, however, each of the three divine Persons is both masculine and feminine. The first Person is *inclusively* receptive (feminine); Wisdom is *emphatically* receptive (feminine), and divine Love, the Holy Spirit, in receiving Personhood from the other two Persons is *doubly receptive* (feminine).

Adam: Doubly receptive? This means that the other two Persons are expressive in what my theologians call the spiration of the Holy Spirit. Power and Wisdom are expressive according to the different emphases in their Personhood.

Eve: Would you say, then, that the Spirit receives Personhood from the first Person differently than from the other? Because their emphasis is different?

Adam: Well, we give love to each other differently, according to the emphasis in *our* personhood. I'm wondering, though, how the Spirit is expressive. Love is spontaneously expressive, especially *within* the Trinity. And the Person of Love expressively inspires both the creation and the Incarnation. Creation: "…the Spirit of God moved over the waters" (*Genesis* 1:2). Incarnation: "the Holy Spirit shall come upon thee" (*Luke* 1:35).

Eve: We can see, then, that God's foreground relationship with the world in creation and redemption is first to come into our awareness, and first to be proclaimed in divine revelation. That is why all of the divine Persons appear to us as masculine. In the background, however, all are both masculine and feminine with a different emphasis in each, and *women are directly like God in a way that, at first, seems hidden from view.*

Adam: Just as real though, if not more real. Our man-woman likeness to God is actually primary in being, though secondary in our awareness. First in our awareness is the Son of Man whose purpose was so sacrificial as to involve suffering and death by cruel violence. How repentant I feel! I am especially *responsible* for our need for redemption.

Eve: Wisdom suffered, too, in giving birth. I repent also. Oh, how God loves us!

Adam: We could never be grateful enough.

Eve: And that includes gratitude for the sacrificial priesthood of Christ. Yes, sacrificial and sacramental. Secondarily, ministerial. We need to emphasize that the priesthood is not just a ministry; it is a sacrament. And its sacramental character is masculine.

The Son of Man saying "This is my body," can be represented only by a man ordained with the power to "do this in remembrance of me" (*Luke* 22:19). So, even though women *can do* everything a priest does, no woman can sacramentally *be* a priest.

Adam: Just because she is a woman? This makes manhood and womanhood profoundly significant in the sacramental order. Well, we just discovered how significant our sexual difference is in our likeness to God. Consistently, here too, our man-woman importance carries over into the sacraments. I see that marriage is a sacrament, also. Yes, gender really matters.

Eve: I certainly agree.

You, Adam, have a special care for the foreground of divine revelation where the Church and the sacraments are so important. And I, now that I am re-created from you, have a special care for the background. That is where we need to be re-created, both of us together.

We still need to call the divine Persons by their foreground names: Father, Son, and Holy Spirit. We can relate with them in their parental relationships to the universe and to us. But even as we recognize their relationships within the Trinity, their interpersonal life remains in the background of our faith.

Oh, Adam, now thanks to both God and to you, I am no longer buried alive in you, nor in your Puritan-playboy culture.[24]

A Blessing for Manhood and Womanhood

Human persons have an analogical relation of maleness and femaleness to God. Man and woman are *fully,* not just spiritually, created in the divine likeness. The common denial of a sexual likeness to God implies, also, and wrongly, that the spiritual aspect of our nature is separate from our sexuality and that heterosexuality is spiritually neuter.

The ancients offered us a soul-body dualism. And now we are confronted with the recent identification of sexual differences with biology alone. Both of these mentalities imply that sexuality and spirituality are separate. Both of these forms of spiritual asexualism are a kind of sexual impotence—a powerless and unresponsive comatose condition—right within the very personhood of man and woman.

The historically biological and currently superficial interpretations of human sexuality beg for deepening. We must begin to understand and live as man and woman in the light and warmth of the Triune God. Not only as spiritual beings, but also as *sexual* beings. Then what would happen to divorce, adultery, fornication, autoeroticism, pornography, contraception, homoeroticism, pedophilia, voyeurism, abortion, and other evils? *The common idea that heterosexuality is unrelated to the Trinity is probably the chief cause of the loneliness of Adam, the absence of Eve, and the sexual disorders that plague the human family.*

We need to go deeper into the mysteries of our faith. We must not write them off as totally beyond our understanding. We can grow in our likeness to God Who is Love. Both our personhood and our sexuality (much deeper than, but including genitality), exist for the sake of this love.

In realizing that man and woman are sexually, as well as spiritually, like God, we can begin to glimpse our likeness to the relationship between the Persons of Power and Wisdom in the Trinity, and to the Love between them. By growing in wholeness and holiness in this way, we can experience a redemptive healing in the loneliness of Adam and lostness of Eve. We can become who we really are.

Chapter 14

True Sexual Freedom

After Adam's reflection together with Eve about the spousal life of God, what would he say about the playboy character of his own culture in America today?

Adam: You boys think you have discovered sexual freedom. But you have found, instead, sexual impotence of heart, mind, and soul. Many of you depend on medical prescriptions for performance dysfunctions. In my opinion, the most important causes of your problem are deeper than your doctor suspects. If you subtly, or not so subtly, think of yourself as a rational animal, you are alienated from the deepest source of male potency.

Playboy: We *do* think that way. What we do know for sure is that sex is as necessary for health as eating, drinking, breathing, and sleeping. We have to be free from restrictions in order to be healthy. There is no connection between sex and morality.

Adam: I'm not talking about morality, but about your health. You are wasting your sexual energy instead of using it to develop from a kid having fun to a person with the character of a man. Fixation in development is not known to be healthy for anyone. A grownup man is able to hold an erection of the heart for a lifetime in marriage. But you don't seem interested in that kind of potency.

Playboy: Though you deny it, I hear you talking about morality. That's for Puritans. And I'm surely not interested in Puritan suppression and Victorian repression.

Adam: Neither am I; not since I learned something new about male potency. It is power for wisdom about love. That is what both you and the Puritans need in order to become healed and truly healthy.

Playboy: Something new about potency? How did you learn about that?

Adam: I was in a sincere and revealing discussion with a woman. I still hear her speaking in my heart. Instead of treating her voice like a nuisance for which I have no time, I finally started to listen. She was saying something about the man-woman relationship. That caught my attention, and I ended up with a different idea about sexual freedom and male potency.

Playboy: She wasn't talking about morality?

Adam: No. She was interested in our sexual personhood, and not just our sexual biology.

Playboy: Sounds like you got taken for a ride.

Adam: I learned about a man's likeness to the power of God, and about the receptivity in my own power for awareness about love. That is how a man can become the kind of lover a woman really wants.

Playboy: That's not my experience with women. A little love-talk from me, and they easily cave into my game. I don't need the power of God for that.

Adam: Don't you wonder how those women would be if they knew who they really are?

Playboy: They think they know. See how they dress and their body language.

Adam: They dress and act that way because they think they know you, and that the only way to get your attention is to speak your language. They are still in your bones, and you like it that way. And you are still alone with the animals, and you even think you are one of them.

Playboy: I don't see any other way to be healthy. Repression is not the answer.

Adam: There is another way. Eve and I are ready to show you a true sexual revolution that bypasses the Puritan-Victorian way you want to avoid.

True Sexual Freedom

Playboy: Since you are in this with a woman, I'll listen. But you two will lose me just as soon as I hear anything moralistic and repressive.

Beyond Necessity

Unlike eating and drinking, sex is not necessary for an individual person's survival, and not even for a person's well-being. But it is necessary for the purpose of generating others of our kind.

For this purpose, biopsychic and physical feelings and impulses attract the attention of our spiritual powers. We can realize that these expressions of our nature have more than a generative reason for being. They exist primarily to increase our freedom, and to do so in an interiorly receptive manner. This actively receptive response to our feelings and impulses moves us into the essential powers of our personhood, not carelessly outward through our biology.

But if the mind of our sexuality remains asleep and passive, instead of awake and active, sexual feelings seem no different from feelings of hunger and thirst. This mindlessness causes us to think falsely that sex is a biological necessity. We become hapless and hopeless. And we think that chastity is negative, and that celibacy is a supernatural grace based on an unnatural condition.

Human persons have feelings and impulses that stimulate actions unnecessary for individual survival and well-being. For example, we do not have to act-out surges of anger. These responses of our nature to inner and outer conditions of life are *necessary* only for the person's inner development as a responsibly spontaneous person. If this challenge of personhood is accepted, subsequent actions are insightfully and freely chosen, not impulsively or compulsively driven.

Even genital and erotic sexual feelings are critically important for the individual person's inner development as a man or woman. They supply energy, first of all, for turning up the light of awareness in the mind, and for radiating the warmth of love in the heart. Turned inward toward personhood, this low-brain energy is meant to be *actively received* by and within high-brain power, there to generate the insights that radiate an affirming kind of love.

Before this inner turnaround is realized, however, a *receptively active*, not a mentally passive, mind is required. The person becomes able to receive the energy of psycho-physical sexual feelings for inner sexual development. The freedom for *being* one's being awakens. This is not the same as freedom for action. *Being* one's sexuality without *necessarily doing* sex is the meaning of true sexual freedom.

Being and Doing

The shift in our self-awareness from a biology-based personhood to a person-based biology profoundly changes our thinking about sex. This turnaround gives us the insightful power we need for true sexual liberation and healing. In the light of our personhood, we discover that the ability to *be* our sexuality frees us from any kind of biopsychic *necessity* to *do* sex.

Therefore, learning how to *be* our manhood and womanhood develops our personhood. We become consciously able to receive our feelings and impulses in their *being, as* energy for becoming more fully our whole being, not just for doing a part of our being.

When turned toward our personhood, these spontaneous stirrings in our nature call us inward and upward to discover who we really are, and thus to develop our manhood and our womanhood toward sexual maturity. Otherwise, we remain sexually fixated at an infantile or adolescent stage, and we are constantly trying to fill a huge emptiness that no amount or kind of sex behavior can fill.

Freedom for *being* our sexuality is male potency and female responsiveness at their best. This true sexual freedom is a natural capacity of our *human personhood*. Neither the compulsive Puritan nor the impulsive playboy realizes that there is such a thing as the freedom to *be*.

The Puritan regards sexual feelings as suspect or even depraved, thereby frustrating his ability to let them be what they are. And the impulsive playboy tolerates no internal connection between sex and restraint, thereby missing the natural and healthy restraint that results from inner receptivity. Even religious celibates, who think their way of life is basically supernatural, do not realize, also, how deeply natural true sexual freedom really is.

Trapped by the deceptive "rational animal" definition of our nature, chastity cannot be other than negative. And celibacy cannot be other than unnatural. But in the light of our person-based nature, we can discover our positive capacity for chastity, our natural ability for celibacy, and our potential for sexual maturity in both celibacy and marriage.

Moreover, the power of divine grace can waken and strengthen these natural abilities. Thus, a turnaround in our self-concept can free our nature to become more receptive and responsive to grace.

Playboy: Excuse me for interrupting, but I don't have an ear for much of this. I'm getting the idea, though, that there is more to health than I thought. It wouldn't be so much bliss for me anymore to just go to bed. Being? You can go to sleep and do that.

Adam: Actually, we are doing our being just by being, even when we sleep. But we are doing it in a kind of coma. There is even a religion that tries to get out of this coma, but ends up returning to it in another way. This religion, called Buddhism, understands that our everyday unawareness involves following our desires without a sense of their inadequacy. The idea of this religion, however, is to turn off our desires and to go into *nirvana*, itself an enlightened, though coma-like, passivity.

But doing our being is the opposite of that. It does not turn off desire, but ennobles it. That means coming out of the coma of desire-for-its-own-sake. We do that by actively receiving the energy of the desire at the level of wholeness. Turning off desire by either repression or nirvana is not actively *doing* our being.

Playboy: Of course, I'm interested in desire. But why is your version of it so difficult to understand?

Adam: When you are in the dark for a long time, then come out into the sunlight, you can't see anything at first. But just hang in there, and things start coming into focus.

Playboy: Can you give me something physical to help me get a grip?

Adam: Can you get interested in your predominant sexual organ, your brain?

Playboy: A sexual organ? Are you sure?

Adam: Let's see. I need to think about your question for awhile.

Sexual Freedom and the Brain

The nerves (organic live wires) to all our organs, including our sex organs, originate in the brain. The human brain is, by far, the most potent sexual organ we have. Unfortunately, we have barely begun to actualize this potential. Scientists tell us that only about five to ten percent of our brain potential becomes active. A large part of the problem is that our ancient, still virulent, shortsights about our nature keep us grounded in an animal-based mentality about who we are.

The physical, psychological, and spiritual components of human sexuality have relevant connections in the three main functional areas of the brain. These are the physical-emotional low brain, the emotional-mental-motivational mediating brain, and the emotional-mental-intellectual-volitional-spiritual high brain. The low brain's hypothalamus is the pleasure center that relates to hunger, thirst, and sex. This, together with the amygdala in the low limbic, is the generator of what Sigmund Freud called the energy of the id.

Differences between the female and male brain are significant for understanding true sexual freedom. More nerve connections and less specialization between the two main lobes of the female cerebrum leave the emotional heart of the brain more emphatic in the female. As a result, the connection of the emotions with both the high-brain intuitive mind, the mid-brain heart, and the low-brain emotional amygdala (not hypothalamus) is generally more spontaneous in a woman.

Having less connection between its lobes, the male cerebrum is more adept at specialization. Its rational side is less fluent with its emotional-intuitive side, and seems generally less connected with the mental-emotional and limbic heart, and more "straight-line" connected, instead, with the limbic sex center: the hypothalamus.

Unless the male becomes more *actively receptive and reflective,* and less passive in relation to his urges, his rationally controlling mind will continue to serve his limbic impulses. Unmindful of his deeper heart, he will continue to say, "If you love me, you'll do it."

True Sexual Freedom

And unless the female wakens her intuitive mind and becomes more insightful about her emotional heart, she remains mentally passive, feels inferior to the male, and becomes vulnerable to his controlling mentality. Lacking the needed sexual insight, both are missing the true sexual freedom latent in their nature as male and female persons.

When the male person says to the female, "If you love me, you'll do it," the female might respond by asking, "What do you mean by love? And what do you mean by 'it'?" If he says, "You know what I mean," she might say, "If you know what you mean, you will be able to say what you know; I want to hear you say it." If he is honest, he will have to say, "Love is the strong desire we feel for each other, but talking doesn't help." Then she might respond, "I need the talking, so let's talk." In this way, the female is able to move the relationship from the low-brain mode of *eros* into the high- and mid-brain mode of *philia*. She begins to reveal to him his capacity for active receptivity. This is her best act of love for him, and there is no "*it*" about it.

Considering, then, our brain involvements in our sexuality, we can see that the playboy values the lower systems of his main sexual organ. His challenge is to develop a whole-brained sexuality. And that means developing power for wisdom about the five main kinds of love and their integration in the affirming kind of love.

Spontaneous and Responsible

Watching a small child, we can readily see how feelings lead to impulses, and how impulses lead to actions. Responsibility for guiding the child comes from the care-giver: the parent or parent-substitute.

As children develop, this relationship between spontaneity and responsibility becomes deeply internalized. Young people become responsible in relation to their spontaneous feelings and impulses. They develop, within themselves, a parent-child relationship.

Since the mother emphasizes emotional intimacy with the child, she is meant to be particularly receptive and listening toward the child's feelings. Her receptivity is necessary for the youngster's spontaneity.

Between feelings and actions, however, guidance is needed. This is where the emphasis of the father is especially effective. His firm guidance is necessary for helping the young person to develop responsibility.

Within the person, receiving feelings into an affirming awareness is the responsive or feminine side of responsibility. Guiding the expression of these feelings in actions is masculine. Both kinds of responsibility, when acting together in true sexual freedom, prevent spontaneity from becoming impulsive.

A man has both the genital and emotional kinds of spontaneity in his sexuality, but with a masculine emphasis toward outward action. His responsibility in relation to his feelings is also emphatically masculine, that is, prominent in the ability to *guide* the inward and outward *expression* of spontaneous feelings. Feminine responsibility is aware of, and receptive toward, feelings; masculine responsibility is firm in either restraining or directing their tendencies toward action.

A man's ability to *receive* the energy of feelings for his inward strengthening of character is the responsive and feminine, though not the foremost, power of his responsibility. And his ability to guide their inward and outward expression is the masculine, and therefore prominent, power of his responsibility.

A woman is structured similarly in her inner life, but with an opposite emphasis. Her responsibility is more responsive, in contrast to a man's emphasis on regulation of behavior. Together they "dance" well in everyday life.

Both our spontaneity and responsibility are misunderstood when we unreflectively assume a "rational animal" concept of our nature. Thinking, as a result, that sex is a biological necessity, we are incapable of understanding biological feelings as energy for inner sexual development. We are oblivious to our inner receptivity for feelings. Consequently, we interpret responsibility as a masculine-only kind of self-control. This attitude is overbearing; it ignores, manages, suppresses, and misinterprets feelings. Such a mindset causes all kinds of emotional and mental problems within and between persons.

Assimilating versus Sublimating Sexual Energy

Sigmund Freud tried to solve the huge psychological problems caused by the biology-based view of human sexuality. He did this by becoming more biology-based than ever in the tragic history of the "rational animal." He reduced all of human energy to physically sexual energy, and that to the level of living tissue.

In the context of tissue energy, Freud developed his ideas of the id (urges), the ego (self), and the superego (inner agent of social control). He thought that the superego causes either an unconscious *repression* of feelings and urges, or an unconscious *sublimation* of feelings and urges into other-than-sex forms of socially approvable activity. Though he was convinced that repression is unhealthy, Freud regarded sublimation as healthy. He recognized conscious suppression of urges by the ego as the restraint necessary for peace with the superego.

But the tissue-base of Freud's theory, and the Puritan-Victorian context of the Freudian superego were unable to sustain sublimation and suppression. His revolutionary discovery of repression as an unconscious denial of feelings that caused so much psychological misery in the culture of his time, resulted in such an overwhelming fear of repression that restraint became unthinkable. Consequently, several decades later, the ego collapsed into the urges of the id, and the superego vanished from the scene. The playboy's sexual revolution began.

Women, too, became obsessed with sex. Quicker than the playboy, however, women learned that this looseness does not lead to long-term happiness. Her bonding limbic hormone, oxytocin, fosters long-term commitment, and causes anger and unhappiness when not respected.

By contrast to the playboy's so-called "revolution," a true sexual revolution begins in the shift from the animal-base to the person-base of human sexuality. High-brain conscious assimilation (subsumation) of low-brain sexual energy replaces the unconscious sublimation that the playboy abandoned. *Awareness* of psycho-physical sexual feelings as energy for inner sexual development helps to alleviate both the fear of repression and the impulsive expression that defensively reacts to this fear.

A new, truer, and healthier self-concept gives the high-brain its starting power for assimilating lower-brain energies into the powers of personhood. The masculine tri-level structure (low-middle-high-brain ladder-image) of the rational animal supports sublimation from the lower to the higher. It is not, however, person-based. The feminine-masculine concentric, or telescope-image compatible with the concentric structure of the brain, is person-based. It calls for the process of subsuming the lower *within* the higher. Our personhood needs subsumation more than sublimation of our sexual energies.

The movement from an animal-based sublimation to a person-based assimilation profoundly changes our concept of human sexual energy. Sublimation is an unconscious process. Assimilation is conscious. Sublimation unconsciously directs sexual energy *outward* into other-than-sex kinds of socially accepted activity. Assimilation consciously receives this energy for an *inward* development of true sexual freedom. Before assimilation becomes relatively habitual, however, sublimation and suppression serve as supportive aspects of the developmental process.

Ways of Being Sexually Active

The term "sexually active" has, to this day, a primitive meaning. Sexual feelings are thought to exist only for having sex and having children. But in the person-based perspective, being sexually active is much more expansive and intensive in meaning.

Playboy: Attention, Adam! I hope you realize that my way of being sexually active has varieties, too. It includes oral, anal....

Adam: I mean something more *potent*. Do you have any idea what I might mean about being sexually active?

Playboy: Your use of the word "intensive" tells me that you are thinking about what you call the inward and upward assimilation of sexual energy. I suppose that is a kind of activity. But I wouldn't call it sexual.

Eve: Adam wants me to join in this conversation as one who is concerned about both you and your playmate. To the extent that you have not allowed her to connect with her own sexuality, you have not experienced anything beyond yourself and her surface. She is centered in her heart more than you are in yours. The heart is a higher and deeper sexual organ. That means she is spontaneously more inward and upward in her sexuality. And she has more receptivity for the assimilating process. But she buries it because you don't allow it. You are a major cause of her deeper frigidity.

Playboy: Are you saying that she is superior to me?

Eve: No, but remarkably different. Her emphasis serves to prevent you from identifying with the animals. She is meant to call you inward and upward in your own sexuality, though you might not be as spontaneously interested in that way. You are more challenged in the heart.

Playboy: Did I hear you say that the heart is a sexual organ? I don't see any difference between the hearts of a man and a woman. They are physically structured in the same way.

Adam: But the *brain connections* to the heart are significantly different. These connective variations between the brain and heart are physical as well as emotional and mental. That's why women tend to be more interested than men in matters of the heart. The same is true about the even less obvious, but more potent, high-brain difference between women and men.

Playboy: Potency again. To do what?

Adam: To turn on the light about your heart's power for the warmth of love. When you do so, you become sexually active inward and upward.

Eve: Instead of remaining cold and dead in your heart, you become alive and warm, and able to relate with a woman where she yearns to love and be loved. At first, you think this warmth has to become immediately hot. But women, when we are really true to ourselves, don't want the heat until we are sure of commitment to the warmth.

Adam: That calls upon another level of intensity in our sexual potency. Love requires wisdom. And wisdom calls for the sexual power of the brain in our primary way of being sexually active. Without the potency of wisdom about love, supposed acts of love are flaccid, no matter how hot they seem. The same will be true about the various kinds of love.

Playboy: What do you mean by other kinds of love? By now, I know that what I usually think you mean, you don't.

Eve: Before getting into the answer to this question, attend to wisdom. We realize that you and your playmate are not inclined to regard wisdom about love as a way of being sexually active. But it takes wisdom to be fully a *woman*, also fully a *man*, and to relate *as such*, one with the other. Without the needed insight, a man and woman tend to think, like you, that heterosexual warmth must always get hot.

Three Kinds of Sexual Life: Within, With, and For

Adam: Our sexual life begins in our main sexual organ, the brain. We awaken from passivity into the first, and most important, kind of sexual activity: affirming our sexual energy with firmness by *actively receiving* and assimilating this energy whenever we feel it, and by guiding its expression in our behavior. That is how we grow in insight, love, and freedom as a man or a woman. That's our first kind of sexual life. There are two more.

Playboy: It seems to me that my brain has only one connection.

Adam: The low brain does. But the mediating and upper powers of the brain call us to what I just now described about our first kind of sexual life.

Playboy: That leaves me out, and my playmates, too.

Adam: In the second kind of sexual life, male and female persons relate as friends. They may, or may not, choose the third kind of sexual life by becoming spouses and parents. The single life of celibacy is, for them, a significant option.

You, of course, have no ear for that. But you *are* trying to listen.

Eve: Did you ever experience friendship with a woman?

Playboy: One of them was super at tennis. We had good times that way. Nowadays women are into accomplishments that make them interesting beyond their shape, size, and appearance. But celibacy at any time? No way!

Adam: Why are you listening to us talk about more kinds of sexual life than just one?

True Sexual Freedom

Playboy: I won't be listening much longer. Your idea about sexual potency caught my attention. I figured that I might get another idea about how to preserve and increase what I already have.

Eve: Well, listen to this. You are a boy who does not want to become a man.

A boy becomes a man, and a girl becomes a woman, not only physically, but also emotionally, mentally, and spiritually. That means they need to become sexually active in more ways than physical so they can relate as persons, not just as entertainment functions.

Take your idea of friendship. Does it go beyond entertainment? Do you ever share thoughts, meanings, and transcendental values? This second kind of sexual life needs to be developed before people become men and women capable of making a decision about the third kind of sexual life.

Adam: First, a person gets to know who he or she is. Then the person gets to know who the other person is. If their sexuality is sufficiently developed within them, they are not inclined to end up in bed before knowing who they really are, and certainly not before they are married. They are able to relate with each other in the light and love of true sexual *freedom*, instead of in the enslaving drive of low-brain urges.

Eve: So the first kind of sexual life is *within*. The second is *with*, and the third is *for*: for the life of others. Within, with, and for.

Playboy: I suppose all of that is what you two mean by sexual potency.

Eve: Yes, including responsiveness.

Playboy: I need to take a break. The next time we talk, I'm either bringing along with me my current playmate or my Puritan parent. If I would bring her along, that will take some courage I do not yet have. If she likes what you call wisdom, I might have to like it, too. Or I might decide to go back where I was before and be alone with the animals, as you, Adam, said you once were. After this, though, it would never be quite the same again. I would always wonder what I'm missing. So long for now.

Sexual Freedom and the Affirming Kind of Love

Both the Puritan and playboy think that human sexuality is a way of functioning. It is that, of course, but not primarily. Our sexuality is first, continuously, and finally a way of being. It is our way of *being love*. And *being love* is giving by receiving the goodness of the beloved. Within this context, we function best.

More than any other kind of love, affirmational love or affection with firmness is *sexual* love. In the affirming way of *being love*, affection and firmness together have an integrating effect that is profoundly healing. Feminine affection and masculine firmness unite the poles of our personhood in our first kind of sexual life.

Sexual freedom results.

In our second kind of sexual life, *agape* and *philia* become forms of sexual love. And in our third kind of sexual life, *eros* and *storge* become marital and familial forms of sexual love. Affirming love is the integrator of them all.

Our sexuality becomes an interpersonal way of being, not just a way of functioning. Our sexual functions are no longer primary; no longer driven.

By realizing the inner difference between being and doing, we can liberate our inner life for the responsibility-within-spontaneity that is neither compulsive nor impulsive.

Both the Puritan and playboy-versions of Adam can then relinquish their power over our culture. As these dysfunctions lose their drive in the *light and warmth* of affirming love, the missing freedom of our manhood and womanhood will have a chance to be regained.

Chapter 15

The Friendship of Man and Woman

In the beginning, man, woman, and God were friends. In the end, they will be friends again. Between the beginning and the end is a very long and agonizing story called history. If the beginning were the end that it was meant to be, there would be no such passage through time.

Something happened in the depths of being that has been revealed to us as a sequence of events. According to the story, it began with a voice. "You can be more like God than you are. You can reach, grasp, and take more than you have?" In other words, "Your receptivity is not like God. There is none of that in divine perfection. So you need to become more active. How? Just decide for yourself. That's what God does."

Unfortunately, the woman of *Genesis* decided to reach, grasp, and take more than she had. Then something astonishing happened to her special gift of receptivity. She noticed how she felt more passive, and how everything in the world looked more "out there" and farther away. Instead of revealing themselves from within, these other beings closed themselves off and showed an outsideness she never saw before. No longer interpermeating each other like rays of light, all things became objects that could be grasped and taken.

Feeling alone and lonely, she tried to persuade the man to share in her "new likeness to God." He agreed. Immediately, they looked at each other and were amazed at how different they appeared and felt. They found themselves cast out of the world of radiant beings into a strange world of "out there" things. They could now grasp and take these things under their control.

But Adam's grasp turned out to be stronger and more far-reaching than Eve's. While she longed for his heart, he controlled her mind. For ages, the friendship they lost seemed impossible to regain.

From Eden to "Equality"

Since the time of *Genesis*, the man-woman relationship has been thought to exist for the sake of increasing, multiplying, and filling the earth with people. For this purpose, throughout the ages, parents chose their children's spouses. Both parents and children developed their relationships within the context of either the tribal or the extended family.

Following the Middle Ages, Adam's story began to move out of tribal associations toward what came to be Western individualism. The structure of the family began to change. Instead of parents choosing mates for their children, sons began to choose their own mates. But daughters could say to desirous men either yes, no, or maybe. So, a yes had to be won. Because of the woman's longing for the man's *heart*, he discovered that he had to approach her from his own heart before she would become his for life.

As a result, courtly love began to develop. The familial kind of love (*storge*) began to lose ground to the romantic kind of love (*eros*). In this way, individualism raised the base of the man-woman relationship from the generative to the psychological level of interest and motivation. Historically, this progression was the necessary transition from biology-based toward person-based marriage.

As male individualism moved into Puritanism, "Increase and multiply" (*Genesis* 1:28) became secondary to "It is not good for the man to be alone" (*Genesis* 2:18). The inherent loneliness of the individualist, coupled with romanticism, caused a shift from the primacy of children to the primacy of the spousal relationship itself.

Families became less inclusive of relatives and more limited to parents and their own children. To a greater extent, men lived for their discoveries, scientific conquests, creative achievements, and spectacular mechanical and political inventions. As daughters and wives, women remained the property of men, and the family remained the woman's predominant purpose.

Since the middle of the 20th century, the sexual revolution has been destroying many of these parent-child families by deviating wildly from the romantic *eros* of the heart into chaotic eroticism. Marriages have been breaking down into divorce, remarriage, mixed families, unmarried couples living together, infidelity, children having children, single mothers struggling in order to survive, and homosexuals wanting to take the vows.

By splitting sex from its procreative power, "liberated" Puritan-playboy feminists went to work with men by day, and had sex like men by night. Reacting against their former passivity, these women asserted their equality with men by identifying with them. But their interpretation of equality as sameness could only neuterize their womanhood. In this way, the male mentality is controlling the female mind more than ever. As a result, some contemporary women are even less advanced than the one who was expelled from Eden. Eve, at least, knew she was alienated from her true self. Recent feminists compulsively deny it.

The Romantic Transition

In the historical period of romanticism (from approximately the fourteenth to the twentieth century), individualism became more clearly defined as a cultural characteristic. In both sexes, a new stage of self-awareness emerged.

Maleness and femaleness became exaggerated. Women became excessively feminine; men, extremely masculine. Their lack of inner balance and integration caused each to idealize the other. An emphasis on psychological, not just physical, desire resulted.

Unconsciously, men were looking for someone to concretize the feminine side of their own male individuality. Dante had only to lay eyes on Beatrice, and she became his inspiration for one of the greatest works of poetry ever written, "The Divine Comedy."

In women, an exaggerated sense of femininity caused them to develop idealized masculine images for the same balancing purpose. Adolescent girls would talk for hours about their dream-boys.

Both males and females projected their image of perfection onto persons of the opposite gender. Both tended to *fall* in love with anyone who seemed to reflect this image back to them. The result became the culture of romantic individualism.

The love-sick male, captivated by his image of the kind of female he was unconsciously desiring to balance his maleness, "fell" for any female, whoever she was, that seemed to fit into the glory of the picture in his mind. And the love-stricken female wanted a male according to her dream of the perfect man who would balance and complete her femaleness. Both were really, though unconsciously, seeking a feminine-masculine balance and integration within their *own personhood*. This profound ambivalence in romanticism made the romantic marriage of individualists especially vulnerable to disillusionment, psychological trauma, and divorce.

Soon after the marriage ceremony and honeymoon, the dream-boy and dream-girl faded away, and two romantics were forced to face reality. The shock was often traumatic. Face to face, without the dream-image shimmering between them, the two wondered "Who am *I*, and who are *you*?" Had they been friends before marriage, this kind of transition, or at least its severity, would not have been necessary.

The Romantic Breakdown

As romanticism developed historically, the unconscious images hardened until they became repressive. Consequently, the romantic individualism of the Puritan lost its vitality and became Victorian. Women and men became so defined and isolated into separate roles that many became emotionally and sexually neurotic.

Beginning in 1900 with Sigmund Freud's sex-based psychology, the steady reaction against Victorian repression became the sexual revolution of the twentieth century. The romantic desires of the heart descended into the raw impulses of the urges. The fiber of the family began to yield to constant, ever-deeper rending. This progressive weakening of the transitional (individualist) family has been signaling the need for a whole new kind of man-woman awareness.

Realizing that the young needed more preparation for male-female relationships, our society introduced, of all things, sex education into the schools. But what is really needed is sexuality education— not sex education. Young people need to know how to *be* men and women, not how to *do* sex. They need to realize that their sexual energy is not as related to the survival of the human race as it once was, but is primarily directed toward their inner sexual development, their first kind of sexual life. In other words, sex education without character education is sexually naïve and profoundly abusive.

Equally necessary is education in friendship. Understanding male-female relationships needs to begin with the kind of emotional and mental sharing that receives genital energy for inner maturation, while naturally not including genital behavior. This second kind of sexual life—the friendship kind—can be easily shortcircuited by premature sex and, also, by premature marriage. If the young could see how physical intercourse belongs only to the third kind of sexual life, they could become more prepared for a person-based marriage of friends who know who they are and how to love each other and their children in a person-based way.

Friendship is Mutual Sharing

By willing the truest and best for everyone, we can love them all, including our enemies. But we cannot be genuine friends with everyone. Friendship (*philia*) depends on *liking* another person with whom we have something in common.

Liking involves *likeness*. And likeness involves a kind of *equality*. This first of the essential characteristics of friendship (equality) makes *philia* different from the other kinds of love, none of which require interests in common. But the commonality of friends does not mean sameness. True equality is adaptable to both individual and male-female differences.

Based on likeness (not sameness) equality can lead to the other *essential* characteristics of friendship: mutual esteem, affection, and value-sharing. Friends value and esteem each other. Their mutual liking can grow into affection. As their relationship develops, they can share feelings, thoughts, meanings, and values.

In the relationship between friends, sharing is mutual giving and receiving. It is not mutual grasping and taking, nor co-dependency based on needs. Though friends can and do depend on each other, friendship, as such, is shared independence. Other kinds of love (*agape*, *eros*, and *storge*) are inherently involved with needs.

Male-Female Relationships

The more people are alike, the easier it is for them to like each other and to become friends. Girls generally tend to become friends with other girls, and boys with boys. After experiencing friendship spontaneously, the young become ready for more *responsible* male-female relationships.

Because the heterosexual relationship tends so strongly to fall into the arms of *eros*, liking does not get the chance it needs to develop into affection without male-female desires interfering. Early gender differences make heterosexual friendship especially challenging. Impulsive males are more sex-hungry than females. And heart-hungry females tend to want to succumb. These tendencies form the common problem of psychosexually undeveloped persons.

When teenagers in a mixed group were asked to say in one word what they thought love is, the boys used words like sex, girls, and fun. The girls used words like caring, sharing, and tenderness.

One young woman described her relationship with a guy she called Eddie. "He's always so smart in class. We went out a few times, and I wondered what happened to his brilliance. You'd think he could talk about a lot of things, but he only wanted to talk about sex. I tried to get him interested in things I heard him get pretty involved in before. But he always seemed to know how to bring the conversation right back to what he had on his mind."

Having little in common, males and females at this stage of life are not yet capable of becoming friends. Liking based on likeness is missing. Boys tend to *like* boys while *desiring* girls, and the other way around. Older couples can still have these "teenage" problems.

Without insightful, affirming receptivity in relating to feelings and impulses within each person's inner life, friendship—as such—cannot be sustained. Male-female sharing requires true sexual freedom. A strong sense of one's own personhood supplies the energy, light, and warmth needed to grow in the inner freedom for friendship. *Inter-sexual* development presupposes *inner sexual* development.

Thus, the friendship between a man and woman depends on an inner sharing between the feminine and masculine poles of

The Friendship of Man and Woman

personhood *within each person*. A man needs to *like* the receptive qualities in himself, and integrate these with his predominant masculinity until both poles reach an interior integration-having-an-emphasis within him. A woman needs this same process from the opposite pole of her personhood. A person-based, not animal-based, sense of who we are is crucial for this kind of sexual maturation.

When animals are born, they get up and walk almost immediately. But humans, though they have a walking reflex, cannot walk for months. The reflex needs to be integrated by the brain into a human self-awareness before a child can manage upright movement. Something similar happens with other reflexes in human beings. Growth in awareness needs to become soul-deep before young men and women become free enough for true friendship.

Not Platonic

The platonic idea is that the human soul and body belong to separate worlds. So, the body is sexual and the soul is not. This separation is the source of the notion that friendship between a man and woman can be "platonic."

But the soul is *not* neuter. A man is a man in his whole being—soul and body—not just in his body. Likewise, a woman is a woman in her whole being. Her brain-organization emphasizes integration of soul and body, while his emphasizes their differentiation. This cerebral variance might partly explain why male philosophers of the past did not recognize sexuality in the soul.

The mental and emotional sharing between a man and a woman cannot be asexual or platonic. Their difference in the organization of their body and brain is one of the reasons. And in their soul-deep relationship, they share their heterosexually different ways of feeling, perceiving, thinking, loving, and acting. The feminine inclination toward inner activity, and the masculine tendency toward outward activity shine in all dimensions of our heterosexuality.

A man-woman friendship that remains true to the warmth of *philia* without the heat of *eros* is not, because of that difference, a platonic friendship. It is an "essential" friendship, though it is heterosexual in all that is shared. Romantic love is not *essential* to man-woman friendship. Beingful sharing is.

From Eden to True Equality

Historically, the relationship between man and woman moved from a family emphasis on *storge* to an individualist emphasis on the romantic *eros*, to a selfist emphasis on the orgasmic *eros*. Following this collapse of the ego into the id, there would seem to be nowhere else to go but toward an awakening of the interpersonal equality of *philia*. Tribalism and romanticism belong to past and passing ages. But *family bonding and romance, while meant to lose their emphasis, are not meant to lose their reality*. Subsumed within friendship, these kinds of love become more person-based, and not lost in blood-bonds and self-conscious individualism as in the past.

Clearly, then, the maturation of the Puritan-playboy American character will involve the development of a person-based friendship between man and woman. American culture will need to become supportive, not distortive, of healthy man-woman relationships. Otherwise, the long trip from Eden to true equality between Adam and Eve within us might not include America, or even the Western world. Their search for the lost gift might have to be realized elsewhere on the planet, and in other ages of space and time.

Chapter 16

The Spousal-Parental Heart of Society

"I was a leak in my Dad's condom," a young woman once said. She was obviously a disturbed person who did not feel good or think well about herself. How could she?

Children born in the playboy era of the wanted and unwanted child carry a negative load similar to that of the Puritan who felt haunted by the God of predestination. "Am I wanted or unwanted by God; am I one of the chosen or not?" This source of anxiety caused the Puritan to be a self-proving individualist. Either that or become depressed and just drift along.

Puritan individualists *wanted* children as workers on the farm or in the family business, and as future caregivers for aging parents. But when the invention of machines reduced the need for children to be workers, and for women to be confined to the home, the relation of women to children began to change. Because machines in the home freed women to work in factories and offices for the economic advancement of their families, having children became less essential for their meaning in life. So they wanted any means available for limiting their families to the desired size.

At the same time, the fragility of Puritan romanticism adversely affected the marital relationship. Coupled with the impetus of the playboy revolution, this weakening of marriage fueled and inflamed the contraception and abortion mentalities. The effect, like a vicious circle, further destabilized the family. Procreative sexuality was demeaned to the level of a manageable biological function. And the prebirth child was reduced to the level of biological tissue.

Such a dramatic breakdown in the value of the child signals the need for a significant breakthrough in the meaning of conception and its source in the man-woman relationship. Specifically needed is an interpersonal understanding of human nature.

A clear insight into the value of the child depends on the sexual life within the personhood of the man and the personhood of the woman. They need to consider the mutual impact of their own inner life on the inner life of their child from conception onward.

The Source Within

The three kinds of sexual life: inner integration, friendship, and marriage begin within each person, whether a man or a woman.

Our deepest need for marriage does *not* exist between a male and female person. Our deepest need exists *within* each person. The masculine and feminine poles of personhood are longing to become two in one. When this inner integration is conscious and sufficiently well-developed in the first and second kinds of sexual life, a person does not need an image of the other sex to compensate for a lack of inner sexual development.

Unconscious searching for another person to compensate for an unbalanced inner self was an immense weakness in romanticism. The individual, being unstable within, falls into infatuation and calls it "love." Dropping into sex and pregnancy without a thought about the momentous meaning involved is the frequent consequence of this so-called love.

The inner marriage is both the dynamic source of, and model for, interpersonal marriage. Essential qualities of the inner marriage are also essential qualities of the marital commitment between a man and a woman. Some of these are intimacy, creativity, permanence, fidelity, and integrity.

For example, the inner poles of personhood *cannot* get a divorce. So, if the inner masculine and feminine powers have a conflict of values, they must either continue their process toward harmony and peace or they will tend toward schizophrenia or another form of psychosis. The two sides of personhood are together, for better or for worse, for life and forever.

The *inner* feminine-masculine kind of marital commitment is the person-based source of friendship *between* a man and a woman. If and when their friendship leads to vowed commitment in the third kind of sexual life, their marriage is not *driven* by unenlightened tribal urges or by dreams of "falling in love." Consequently, the

The Spousal-Parental Heart of Society

child is *received as a person* from conception onward, and not produced as an object of thoughtless wanting and unwanting propensities.

Sexual Love in Marriage

Eve: The playboy is here again, Adam. This time he brought the Puritan with him. He says he wants you to talk to his problem parent.

Adam: Problem parent; problem child.

Puritan: I had nothing to do with this boy being the way he is. He is really no son of mine.

Adam: What kind of marriage did you have that a playboy showed up in your household as if from nowhere?

Puritan: If my household is anything, it is industrious, prayerful, and God-fearing. Both my wife and I promoted these virtues between us and with our children.

Adam: Is that all you share with her?

Puritan: We love each other. She completes me and I complete her, and that keeps us together for life.

Playboy: Ask him what he thinks about sex.

Puritan: We are more interested in love and our family.

Playboy: See, Adam! I told you how repressive he is. This makes me interested in sex and not caring about love.

Adam to the Puritan: Do you see your effect on your son?

Eve: The Puritan was not as repressive as the subsequent Victorian lady. She wouldn't allow any mention of, or even suggestion about, sex. In the opposite way, she did what the playboy does. Both separate sex from love. She wanted love without sex, and he wants sex without love.

If we could better understand sexual love, that could bring the extremes closer together.

Adam: I see, Eve, that you want these two characters, here, to become less alienated. So what is sexual love, and how will it bring together the interests of the playboy and the values of the Puritan?

Playboy: Here's how. You work by day and you play by night. Pray if you wish.

Eve: But where is love?

Puritan: It's a passion of the heart that becomes sexual only in marriage.

Eve: Do you think you are sexual only in marriage? Maybe that's why the playboy wants to be sexual without marriage. Something is missing.

Adam: Both of you fellows need to expand your view of human sexuality. A man is a man, not a woman, in everything he thinks, feels, and does whether married or not. He is expansively sexual in that way. He does not have to get involved in genital sex to *be* a man. And if he is a man who is not a playboy, he agrees with the Puritan that marriage is the context for genital sex. He disagrees, however, with the Puritan that marriage is the context for his sexuality.

Puritan to Playboy: I suppose you think this expansion opens sex to anyone who is attractive to you.

Playboy: Well, someone will have to explain to me why sex is limited to marriage if sexuality expands beyond marriage.

Adam: Our manhood is both expansive and intensive. Open and focused. Our potential for fatherhood makes our sexuality intensive because other persons are involved. A woman becomes pregnant with another person at the moment of conception. This new person cannot survive without the care of those who are responsible for the child's beginning.

Playboy: But there are ways of preventing pregnancy. You don't have to get married.

Eve: The inclusion of genital sex in sexual love calls for marriage. But sexual love in marriage is more than genital sex. It cares for the whole person, not just a part. It shares everything, not just

The Spousal-Parental Heart of Society

something. It bonds deeply, not just superficially. It is affectionate with firmness and authenticity, not with ulterior motives.

Playboy: What is sexual about all of that?

Puritan: Didn't you get it about how sexual we are? All of our ways of loving in marriage are sexual, not just one way.

Playboy: But I still don't see why sexual love needs marriage.

Puritan: Your problem is that you don't understand love. You are not even interested. You cannot even relate with a woman on the level where a man and woman want to become two-in-one.

Adam to the playboy: The Puritan understands sexual love better than you do probably because he is, to begin with, interested in romantic love and fidelity.

Playboy to Puritan: Do you agree with Eve that *sexual* love includes all of the kinds of love she thinks it does?

Puritan: Yes, if our sexuality is really as expansive and intensive as she and Adam interpret it to be. I tend to agree that there is more to genuine sexual love than just a passion of the heart and physical intercourse.

Playboy: When I hear you talking about anything sexual, I have better feelings toward you.

Eve: Toward love, too? In all of its meanings?

Playboy: The word "love," still has mostly one meaning for me. I don't know whether it will ever mean more. If so, I'll let you know.

....

When asked about the nature of sexual love, people in eroticized Western cultures generally describe it as *one* of the different kinds of love. Programmed by the "rational animal" mentality, they interpret sexual love as being predominantly, if not solely, a psycho-physical kind of *eros*. Failing to recognize other kinds of love as being intrinsically relevant to human sexuality, they tend to exclude the various kinds of love from the meaning of *sexual* love. But sexual love includes *affirmation* (affection with firmness), *philia* (mutual sharing or friendship), *agape* (caring), and *storge* (familial affection).

In the light of our person-based manhood and womanhood, sexual love is a many-splendored complex of all five kinds of love. Affirmational love provides a warm and nurturing support for the other kinds. Within this context of emotional warmth, friendship is the basic mutuality between persons. Caring is the nourishment. Desire is the seasoning. And familial affection is bonding and socializing. Between the masculine and feminine correlatives of personhood, as well as between a man and a woman, *all* of these ways of loving are *sexual*.

Heterosexual friendship is the ground in which sexual desire, sacrificial caring, and family affection thrive. More than any of the other ways of loving, friendship requires true sexual freedom. Friendship is the "ground" that can be either rich and deep, or arid and shallow. All depends on the quality of the first and second kinds of sexual life *within* each person and *between* them.

The family is now called to move toward the whole meaning of sexual love. The core of the culture needs to develop beyond the *storge* (familial affection and bonding) predominant in tribal and extended families, and beyond the romantic individualism that followed. Including the five kinds of love, the wholeness of sexual love in the family is supported by development in all three kinds of sexual life: within, with, and two-in-one for others.

Generative Sexuality

Some parts of the human body are specifically structured into our freedom. They are, in that way, different from the organs and functions of circulation, respiration, and digestion.

For example, the anatomy of the tongue, larynx, and trachea is part of a freely chosen act of verbal communication. Another example is our sexual biology. Our genital organs and functions are structured into our freedom for choosing or not choosing acts of genital expression.

Both our verbal and genital powers communicate *interpersonal* feelings and meanings. Both can also communicate deceptions and other evils. Speech can be loving or cunning or hateful. Genital acts can be loving or adulterous or violent. But hatred and violence, cunning and adultery, are not the purpose of these powers. Love is.

The Spousal-Parental Heart of Society

Speech and genital intercourse, however, express love differently. Every kind of capacity for freely chosen action has two interrelated purposes: general and specific. The *general* purpose of both verbal intercourse and genital intercourse is *common* to both of them: the communication of love and respect. The *specific* purpose of speech is to *conceive* meanings in the mind of another person. Differently, the *specific* purpose of genital sex is to *conceive* new human persons.

There are many ways of expressing love in marriage. Genital intercourse is just one of them. Talking and listening, and planning for tomorrow, are examples of the more common ways of sharing marital love. Whenever spouses talk with each other, they are sharing a sexual act; and, by being two-in-one, a marital act.

At the same time, the general purpose of genital intercourse—expressing love—is marital only, whereas the general purpose of speech is not marital only. This difference in the common purpose of the two different acts is due to their very different *specific* purposes, and to the inner relationship of the specific to the general purpose in each kind of human act.

The *specific* purpose of genital sex is its power to procreate new human persons. A child is obviously a two-in-one-flesh expression of a man and a woman together. The effect clearly implies the two-in-oneness of the parents, not just physically, but psychologically, spiritually, and socially as well. This call to wholeness requires the interpersonal commitment of marriage.

The specific purpose of genital union is life-giving even though only one or a few or none of these acts in a marriage actually conceives new life. Similarly, the general purpose of speech is love-giving, and its specific purpose is truth-giving, even though not all of a person's acts of speaking are comprehensively true. These purposes are designed by God, not invented by humans.

Personal preferences to the contrary, this is the structure of human personhood. In the relationship between the general and specific purposes of a person's freely chosen *single act* of either verbal or genital communication, the matter of integrity becomes involved.

"What God Has Joined Together......"

Adam and Eve were created for union and integrity between them, not for divorce. The same is true for the unitive and procreative powers of their genital sexuality. These powers were not created for contra-conceptive separation. They are distinct, not separate. Nor are they authentically separable. Likewise, the unitive and conceptive powers involved in all other kinds of communication, especially verbally, are distinct but not separate..

In well-ordered speech, the speaker expresses to another person the meaning within that speaker's mind. If this communicator means "yes," but verbally says "no," the speaker violates both the general and the specific purposes of speech. This communicative act is internally *separated* from both of its purposes. If the separation is motivated by a desire to maintain peace and harmony with the other person, this peace and harmony is being undermined by deception.

Similarly, *every* contra-conceptive *act* of genital communication separates this act from its specific purpose. The contraceptive intent *prevents* life-giving within the act that is *specifically* life-giving by its very nature. If the separation is motivated by a desire to maintain peace and harmony with, and love toward, the other person, this peace, harmony, and love is undermined by deception. This is why contraception, by being a kind of internal divorce, weakens the marital bond and tends to increase divorce between the persons involved. This possible trajectory proceeds *subconsciously* in spite of all conscious denials that such a tendency exists. Similarly, verbal deception between spouses can lead, also, to divorce.

Lying and contracepting, therefore, are similar violations of interpersonal communication. Both separate the specific purpose of a single act from its general purpose, and tend to undermine the relationship between the persons involved. The general and specific purposes of these two acts of communication are related like the palm of a hand to its fingers; different but inseparable. Separating the fingers and the palm violates both parts of the hand, and the whole hand as well.

There is also a deeper reason why a divorce within the purposes of a human act tends toward a divorce between the persons involved in the act. The Adam-Eve marriage within each person is deeply

The Spousal-Parental Heart of Society

affected by internally separative acts such as contraception and lying. When the inner marriage is disrupted, the *marriage between the two persons* is inevitably affected.

The inner marriage is a union between the feminine and masculine poles of human personhood—emphasized oppositely in a man and woman. Obviously, then, a distortedly masculine act—such as a separative, controlling, preventive act like contraception—militates against the inner feminine-masculine communion. There is nothing authentically feminine about a separative, controlling, preventive intrusion on an interpersonal act of communication.

Conception Regulation

Adam and Eve within us have a better way into their future. Their method of conception regulation calls for the man and woman to share it together. No kind of divorce or alienation is involved.

Conception *regulation* is essentially different from *contra*-conception, or conception prevention. Regulation begins in the receptive (feminine) attitude of both male and female persons toward their interpersonal power to give life. The couple wants to know how their generative power can be regulated *from within,* not by intrusion from without. Seeking and acting on this knowledge brings in the masculine side of the method. Husband and wife study together their generative power and cooperate daily with its natural fertile-infertile cycles. As natural conception requires both the man and the woman, so does natural regulation of conception.

As a deformed masculine method, contraception is individualistic. One person is required to use the contraceptive. Though the other person might consent to the use of a drug, or a device, or even to surgery, he or she is not essentially involved in the method. But *natural conception regulation* is, by its essence, interpersonal and cooperative.

Contraception is physicalistic. The natural methods are holistic. Contraception does not require inner sexual development; it serves, instead, manipulative attitudes and practices. Differently, conception regulation calls for the *active receptivity* (Eve) and *potency* (Adam) of true sexual freedom.

The natural methods of sexual regulation are like a musician relating with a composer's score. It takes love and discipline to follow the score and play it beautifully, instead of just impulsively blowing a horn or pounding a piano. The natural law of human personhood is the "score" written into the marital relationship. This human imperative requires much more than falling in love, doing what comes naturally, and getting "protected" from and for sex.

The fact that most acts of genital union in a marriage are not actually life-giving does not lessen the value of generative sexuality. Though love-giving and life-giving are not equal in *quantity*, they are equal in *quality*. These two purposes of genital sexuality need to be respected and valued equally and integrally.[25]

From Violation to Violence

Our cultural understanding of genital sexuality is so low-brained schizoid that it implicitly connects sex with violence. Then, the implications naturally tend to become explicit. Rationalizations for contraception can eventuate, ultimately, in the annihilation of civilization. Short of nuclear destruction, nothing can demolish everything in its path like the fire of sex once it leaves the spousal-parental fireplace at the heart of our social existence.

Young people hear that their parents need to be "spontaneous" with sex. The true word, not used by rationalizers, is "impulsive." Then the son or daughter wonders, "What about me? I'm younger than they are and have more of that kind of energy." If the young person then acts accordingly, the fire creeps out of its place, as unmarried daughters come home pregnant. Then parents get angry, abortion-violence follows, rapes and suicides increase, people fail to grow up, a demand for more rights arises while responsibilities vanish, the economy crashes, out come the guns and the worst forms of violence. What next?

Get sex back into the fireplace if it is not too late.

When we turn low-brain sexual energy away from life, it vectors toward death. To prevent this outcome, we need to turn on our high-brain power and consciously assimilate this energy in a way that keeps it warm and beautiful in our man-woman friendships, and hot

The Spousal-Parental Heart of Society

only in the spousal-parental fireplace where it vectors toward life, and not toward death.

A culture that rationalizes contraception takes a deadly turn away from the life-urge toward the death-urge. The rationalization begins so subtly as to seem true. People begin to think their generative power is merely biological, while their genital expression of love is personal and interpersonal.

But the specific (life-giving) purpose of genital sexuality is *just as interpersonal* as its general (love-giving) purpose. Two persons give life to another *person*. Without this explicit awareness, potential parents necessarily view the child as a simply biological *effect* of a largely biological *cause*. Since an effect can be no greater than its cause, unconsciously if not consciously, a supposed biological cause can have no more than a biological effect. Consequently, the child cannot be understood as initially anything more than biological tissue.

In a biology-based way of thinking, the rationale for contraception feeds directly into a rationalization for abortion. A simply biological effect cannot be a person. Abortion, then, is thought to remove a growth similar to a tumor. This way of thinking makes sex seem "carcinogenic."

No matter how consciously one denies that the contraceptive mentality provides a *logical setup* for an abortion mentality, logic subconsciously has its way. It works like a grinder. If you put into this setup the idea that contraceptives are good, and you deny that the use of them will lead to abortion, then the conscious mind might be convinced. But the subconscious mind grinds away. It says, "If you can separate sex contraceptively from its specific purpose for the sake of love, why not do so by abortion, also, and by the way same-sex persons do it who love each other? Sooner than seems possible, these subconscious workings come to the surface and become loudly conscious arguments.

The only way to stop the process is to feed the truth into the subconscious mind and let the subconscious "chewing" begin. Its power cannot be overcome by denial, but only by changing the starting point of the logic involved.

A vivid example of the power of straight-line logic "doing its thing" with the human mind is the way the U.S. Supreme Court proceeded from allowing contraceptives for the married in 1965, then for the unmarried in 1972, then for abortion until birth only one year later in 1973.

We have plainly seen the rapid progression of the contraceptive mentality from its first premise to its conclusion, not only in relation to abortion, assisted suicide, and euthanasia, but also in relation to homosexuality. Contraceptive and homoerotic sex both set aside the holistic design of human sexuality for the sake of what the partners consider to be love.

This logical progression from the first premise to the conclusion highlights the importance of the first premise. So, which will it be? The animalian design of our generative biology can be disconnected from our personhood for personal and private reasons. Or, the design of our generative biology is soul deep, and is, therefore, intrinsically inseparable from our personhood.[26]

The Child is a Person

A person-based man and woman know they cannot conceive a biological growth. It is impossible. They realize they can conceive only another person, even though the size of a single cell.

When people understand themselves *as persons*—from spiritual soul to fingertips—they have this insight beyond eyesight. They do not use eyesight based merely on microscopic "evidence" in an attempt to rationalize their lack of true sexual freedom.

Under a microscope, a one-celled person *appears to be* just a packet of genetic material. But with an insight into the wholeness of personhood, we can see that a one-celled person is much more than genetic information. As mentioned earlier, this single cell *has*, not *is*, genes and chromosomes.

As a person, the child is a *gift* to be received, not a *goal* to be achieved. The idea that children are a goal of marriage encourages the attitude of wanting and unwanting instead of developing insight and receptive affirmation. Understood as a person, the child could never be possessed as a thing.

The Spousal-Parental Heart of Society

A newly conceived boy or girl has, already at conception, a need for inner feminine-masculine balance and integration. Existing at the very beginning of life, this innate need begs for the *wholeness* of sexual love between a father and a mother. Internally integrated male and female parents encourage the emotional and sexual development of their child well before their son or daughter is born.

Anyone can see that an infant at birth is extremely sensitive emotionally, and is already responding to the attitudes of others. Depth psychologists know that the most hidden or subconscious feelings and attitudes of parents become part of the environment in which a child develops.

Sensitivity to feelings and attitudes does not begin magically at birth; it begins at conception. The embryonic and fetal person develops emotionally and mentally as well as physically in response to the emotional and attitudinal environment of the mother that is directly affected by her relationship with the new little person's father.

Attitudes about the beginning of human life either nurture or discourage the child *from conception onward*. Attitudes and feelings stimulated by parents cannot be hidden from the child's unconscious sensitivity to them. The young feel affirmed—mostly unconsciously, but no less really—when they sense that their personhood, from its very beginning in this world at conception, is held in sacred regard by their parents.

Children feel diminished and even demeaned when the beginning of their life is degraded as a merely biological object of their parents' wanting and unwanting.

An Affirming Father and Mother

Affirmational love is the most important kind of love for feminine-masculine integration. This basic kind of love is *responsive affection* (feminine) together with *responsible firmness* (masculine). Father, mother, and children thrive joyfully when loved in this way.

A child's needs for emotional intimacy and personal identity are most readily and adequately fulfilled by an affirming mother and father. An affirming mother emphasizes emotional intimacy while including care for identity needs. An affirming father emphasizes personal identity while including emotional warmth and support.

A father can nurture a child, but he cannot replace the nurturing given by a mother. The same is true about the firmness, guidance, strengthening, and sense of identity that a child needs from a father. A mother can be a firm and strengthening guide. But she cannot replace a father.

The importance of heterosexuality is irreducible all the way into the ontological depths of our human personhood. The masculine-feminine paradox of personhood, and the need for this paradox throughout the family, is well beyond the reach of any ideology or dysfunctional mentality that attempts to obscure it.

Children cannot think abstractly about their need for the *vivid concreteness* of both an affirming father and an affirming mother. The child needs them to emphasize *differently* and *oppositely* in their relationship. This outward polarity dramatizes the development of the inner marriage within the child. When children do not see, feel, live, and absorb the authentic nature of marriage within their parents, they remain handicapped in developing their own inner marriage. No explanation can step in and supply what is missing in concretely spontaneous family relationships.

Developing both the emphasis and the integration implied in the sexual paradox of personhood requires a strong sense of paradoxical reality. The challenge is profound. It is also an exquisite source of emotional-mental-spiritual happiness and joy in the spousal-parental heart of society.

Chapter 17

No Family Is an Island

Barren women once felt humiliated, and even cursed. In the tribal families of ancient times their condition was pitied. But at one point in their history, a barren woman became the mother of a new kind of family.

Sarah, the wife of Abraham, could not conceive for many years. God had promised her husband that he would have descendants far beyond tribal limits. When she was ninety years old and Abraham one hundred, Isaac, their only child, was born. Obviously, God made a singular point of Isaac's conception and birth.

Hundreds of years later, the Savior was born. Shortly beforehand, Zachariah's Elizabeth could not conceive, except by an answer to ardent prayer. Soon after, she became pregnant with her son. Then, more miraculously, Elizabeth's cousin, Mary, conceived without a man.

Jesus, conceived within Mary's active receptivity, became the source of the "family of God" destined ultimately for the "marriage of the Lamb" in heaven (*Rev.* 19:7-8). His effect on the culture of the time initiated ages of movement from the tribal family toward the family of nations (not a world government) that is now in the process of developing on earth.

Like the Nucleus of a Cell

From the ancient tribe into the future, the nucleus of the family—father, mother, and children—has been, and remains, the social core. As time passed, this nuclear center of life became increasingly more defined. Eventually, instead of parents choosing spouses for their children, romantic individualists began to choose their own spouses. As a result, the nuclear family began to stand out within the context of the extended family of grandparents, uncles, aunts, and cousins.

Like the larger content of a cell surrounding its nucleus, the extended family remained a supportive and interactive context for the nuclear family well into the 20th century.

Especially in America, Adam's grand inventiveness in making ships, trains, automobiles, and airplanes steadily increased social mobility. A great scattering of nuclear families resulted. Sons and daughters began to move as far apart as the coasts of a vast nation. In a single lifespan, some moved and settled many times. When cremation became generally accepted, some went so far as to make arrangements to have their remains divided and buried in places where they had once lived.

Like the nuclear core of a cell within its larger body, the family of a married couple needs to be surrounded by a social environment wherever they live. Thus, the vows of marriage are meant to take place within the supportive context and moral standards of the larger community. Basically, the community is an extended family, not just an aggregate of cores like a heap of marbles.

An affirming, caring, and sharing relationship with others beyond the social nucleus strengthens the heterosexual commitment of marriage. This openness is important even before the mutual commitment is made. If a spouse-to-be wants to know whether the intended partner really loves him or her, the evidence is to be found in the intended person's attitude and behavior toward parents, relatives, friends, strangers, and even enemies.

Individualism is Transitory

A little girl was once playing a game of tea-party with her aunt. In the course of their conversation, the little one began talking about her imaginary family of 300 children. "Where are they," asked her aunt. "They all left home," was the surprising reply.

Perhaps this youngster was intuiting a relationship between two different kinds of families: the tribe of 300, and the family of individualists who left home to find their own unique way in the world.

Historically, the tribe existed mainly at the biological level of nose-to-the-ground survival. Then the extended family of near relatives became more central within the tribe. Finally, the nuclear

No Family Is an Island 173

family of father, mother, and children began to stand out like an island rising above the surface of humanity.

But this "island's" ascent into historical view is not as isolated as it seems. Below the surface, an island connects with the mainland. And the mainland is continuous with the ground of the whole earth.

Similarly, an individual family that seems to be alone in the world is really in a human continuum that surrounds the earth and includes all families that ever did, ever will, and now, exist. No family is the kind of "island" that appears to be separate from the rest of humanity.

The emergence of the individual meant the rising of the "I" into view. But this "I" represents a developmental transition toward the relationality of "I-You" personhood.

The person, as a person, has an "I am I, and you are an *other I*" kind of consciousness. A society of mere individuals is a lonely crowd.[27] Inevitably, loneliness has been increasing in Adam's America. People keeping company with television programs and with commercials, computers, video games and other electronic inventions are basically solitary like Adam in Eden when he was alone with the animals in the beginning. People talking constantly through technological mechanisms are basically alone. Superficial connections mitigate, but do not alleviate, loneliness.

Even so-called "intimacy" of bodies has become, for many, a superficial connection. A culture of outsideness gradually becomes estranged from withinness.

Individual autonomy characterizes masculine cultures that are inherently *on the move outward toward "something better."* Autonomy is a masculine differentiation that is adolescent in character. The mature adult is both masculine and feminine with a definite gender emphasis, and is an "I-you" person rather than a loner in the midst of surface connections.

Lone Egos

Throughout history, individualists became heroes. They emerged as conquerors, explorers, inventors, statesmen, and outstanding achievers of all kinds. The Greek epic poet, Homer (conjecturally placed in the 9th Century B.C.), told tales of individualist warriors. But a culture of individualism took centuries to form as such. Puritanism was its consummation. And Adam's America became "the cream of the cream."

Charles Lindbergh, flying alone across the Atlantic, making the flight for the first time in history, became known as the "lone eagle." He was a prominent symbol of America's individualism.

In Puritan-Victorian Europe, however, the *ego* of many was breaking down into neuroses and psychoses. Responding to the crisis, Sigmund Freud developed his *id-ego-superego* method of psychoanalysis. Analysts became known as "shrinks." They laid bare the unconscious *id* seething beneath the *ego* that became like a dark and ominous sinkhole for heroic individualists. *Id*-like selfism, the opposite of heroism, came to the surface. The lone ego became the naked *id*.

But not all in the cultures of Adam are selfists. A milder form of individualism still persists. The Puritan is still the father of the playboy. Puritanism is still the origin and context for American culture. The "I" continues to be the source of "me and my rights."

The Fellowship of Loners

In the various cultures of Adam, individualists relate through the masculine mode of fellowship. They are congenial and friendly, but not prone to *becoming friends*. Men readily talk and laugh about sports and politics, and share objective goals, but do not tend to share their inner selves. *Who they are* tends to be *what they do*. Fellowship is a way of sharing their outward interests. Friendship, however, includes a more inward way of sharing who they are, while not excluding their outward interests.

Friendship is more than the masculine compatibility of fellowship. It is also the feminine sharing of interpersonal warmth. Both men and women need to develop more balance between the compatibility of fellowship and the emotional sharing of friendship, while retaining their natural emphasis.

How can this development of friendship happen in a culture where values tend to be little more than surface deep? Friendship involves the affectionate sharing of transcendental values. In the true, the good, and the beautiful, people bond with each other in their hearts and souls.

When individualists become able to share these kinds of values, their propensity for the fellowship of loners will be able to open up to another dimension in their nature. Adam listens to Eve, and gives her an opportunity to emerge from his bones. Then his masculine autonomy and techo-mechanical slide into oblivion can yield to a turnaround in his mentality. Eve can then appreciate Adam, and encourage him to be himself.

More awareness of the human person's need for friendship could begin to change the loneliness of the crowd. Fellowship would remain meaningful, but would become less prominent. A shift in consciousness would begin to transform an aggregate of loners into a community dedicated from the heart to the common good.

Family, Friends, Community

Between parents and children, family bonding (*storge*) tends to expand into friendship (*philia*), especially as the children become mature adults. Carefully cultivated friendship within the social core of father, mother, and children would strengthen the family bond so that it could become the model for the community as a new form of the extended family.

As it is now, high rates of divorce signal a crisis in the core. Marriage based on the romantic *eros* is too unenlightened to survive. Marriages based on *philia-storge-agape*, imbued with affirmational love, are the promise of the future.

Greater awareness of the true meaning of love and sexual freedom would strengthen the soul-deep person for marriage, family, and community, well beyond the "I" and "me" aspects of the American character.

If a committed sense of interpersonal awareness would begin to warm the cultural chill, it would not be destined to stop at the borders of the nation, nor at the boundaries of earthly existence. All persons—human, angelic, and divine—are one family in the realm of personhood.

The Spousal and Parental God is the source of the ultimate family of all persons. From and toward this infinite reality all historical movements originate and profoundly tend.

From the Inner Marriage to the Ultimate Marriage

The two-in-oneness of the "Adam" and "Eve" within each of us is the only marriage we will bring with us from the earth into eternal life. In heaven, the "marriage of the Lamb" (*Rev.*19:7-8) will be the ultimate all-in-oneness.

Noticeably, both the inner and ultimate marriages are celibate (*Matt.22-30*). This means that marriages and families here on earth depend for their happiness on the inner and interpersonal conditions of each person.

These inner and ultimate meanings for the relationship between celibacy and marriage are high-powered intimations for the value of a commitment to celibacy, and even for rare commitments to a celibate marriage between a man and a woman. These ways of life are consummate expressions of the true sexual freedom of human personhood. Celibacy does not mean emotional coolness, nor does it mean emotional heat. Warmth of heart belongs to the very essence of affirming love and friendship in both the celibate and spousal ways of life.

But how are teenagers in our society supposed to get this message if not by way of parents, teachers, churches, and other affirming relationships? Young people today are beginning to run into a wall of emptiness, and many have become aware of it. The deluge of hyper-distractions that beset them are no longer satisfying, and they are beginning to realize it. Their hope for the future is in their young and growing awareness of the prospects for cultural healing.

The call beyond the wall can be heard only in silence, not in the latest version of sounding brass and crashing cymbals. There is a summons from within, from the personhood of each person. Even children and adolescents learning about themselves and others around them can understand that the relationship between Adam and Eve continues within them.

So, when these newly aware young people marry and have families of their own, they will be able to nurture within their children the celibate inner marriage, thus increasing in the young their capacity for true sexual freedom and friendship. Stronger and healthier families can result. Then the culture can become more *interpersonal* and less individualistic.

Celibacy in both the inner and ultimate marriages, therefore, is the background for conjugal love and children in the foreground. From the tribal Abraham to the communion of saints and angels with the Triune God in heaven, no person is a loner and no family is an island.

Chapter 18

When the Wandering Cultures Meet

The man and woman of *Genesis*, exiled from their original gift of being, were deeply estranged from each other. Culturally, they went their separate ways. Their diverse mentalities wandered in opposite directions over planet earth. Eve went inward to the East. Adam went outward to the West.

Centuries later, some people from the East migrated to the far north, where two land masses (far East and far West) reached out toward each other. Crossing over from one to the other, these migrants from the cultures of Eve eventually settled on two new continents, now known as North and South America, that comprise the other half of the planet.[28]

Then Adam, in one of his European sons, tried to reach the East by sailing West. After a long and venturesome ocean voyage, he landed on what he thought was India in the East. But his landing area was really in the center of the two far western continents. There, Adam's cultures met Eve's when Christopher Columbus and his crew faced what they thought were natives from India: Indians.

Next, pilgrims from Europe ventured across the Atlantic to the northeastern shore of what eventually became known as a "melting pot" for people from all directions.

The melting started when the pilgrims shared with the natives a meal of thanksgiving. But this tenuous union of cultures soon dissolved into war. Adam and Eve did not know how to integrate. So, Adam's culture forced Eve's onto reservations. To this day, the two cultures are separate.

But something is happening in the roots of human personhood on this planet. Something deep in the underground is trying to break free into the light of dawn. The feminine and masculine correlates of human personhood, because we are more aware of them now, might become more ready to return to the two-in-oneness that was lost in the beginning.

The prospect of moving a selfist culture of "me and my rights" toward responsive and responsible personhood seems like a dream as far as the inner eye can see. But by turning up the light on the latent meaning of Eve's East and Adam's West, we can begin to see where the major cultures of history have been, and are now, tending.

The Cultural Roots of East and West

In the heart of the sad event that started human history, the *active* receptivity of our original personhood fell into the darkness and pain of universal passivity. In different ways, every culture that ever was, and now is, expresses the human struggle to rise from the lethargy and emptiness of this passive condition toward the true receptivity where inner integration begins.

Like the fallen woman of *Genesis*, the mentality of the East succumbed to passivity in relation to God. The result became pantheism: an extreme sense of immanence between God and the world. But the mentality of the West, like the man of *Genesis*, reacted against passivity and developed a masculine sense of the ultimate being. The result became the transcendent sense of God found in theism.

Because the mentalities of Eve and Adam were so far apart from each other at first, the East failed to integrate a feminine sense of immanence (or withinness) with a masculine sense of transcendence (or otherness). And the West, especially before and outside of Christianity, simply failed to integrate masculine transcendence with feminine immanence.

Both mentalities are alienated from the paradox of personhood and its integration of opposites. Due to Christian revelation, however, personhood was explicitly, though inadequately, discovered in the West, and Christian theologians struggled with this revelation's call for paradoxical thinking.

In the warming light of *being*, we can see that God is both immanent (within everything else) and transcendent (other than everything else). Neither the feminine mentality alone, nor the masculine mentality alone, is true to this reality. Both need to deepen their roots into fresh new levels of reality's "ground" and find the paradox of the transcendently immanent God.

The distorted sense of withinness in the East resulted in the Hindu idea that the deepest part of the self *is* God. But this Self is not a person. As Deepak Chopra says in his book, *How to Know God*, "God, it turns out, isn't a person; God is a process."[29]

According to this author, we *are* the absolute impersonal Self becoming increasingly Self-conscious, without any real sense of otherness. In the structure of personhood, however, otherness is the masculine correlate of feminine withinness. Therefore, the absence of otherness keeps the unchangeable Eastern Self impersonal. As a consequence, everything that changes, such as material objects in space and time, is really illusory. *Withdrawal* from what appears to be other than self is, then, the way to the absolute Self within us.

In Buddhism, however, there is no God. No absolute. There is only the human self and its enlightenment in the ultimate bliss of passivity and emptiness. In Taoism, *nature* is the ultimate. Again, there is *no personal God*.

So, in Hinduism, the transitory self is really the absolute Self in process. But in Taoism, the self is submerged in nature. These mentalities of Eve, while bearing some truth, are deeply mired in the passivity and emptiness resulting from her loss of active receptivity.

As the feminine East has moved inward and away from objects, the masculine West has moved outward and toward objects. One tends to retreat away from objects; the other moves toward them. In the Eastern world, enlightenment means awareness that objects are illusions. In the West, enlightenment means that objects are real, scientifically knowable, and useable for practical and profitable purposes.

In Hinduism, the self is basically God. In almost all of the Hindu traditions, the self is absolute and impersonal. But in the West, according to the "rational animal" definition, the self is basically an animal. God-based pantheism and animal-based individualism became, at least philosophically and apart from the Judeo-Christian revelation, the feminine and masculine extremes that resulted from the loss of our original personhood before the history of East and West began.

The Middle Eastern Transition

The historic movement from the pantheism and polytheism of the East toward the theisms of the West began with Abraham. In the three Abrahamic religions—Judaism, Christianity, and Islam—God is transcendent and masculine. For Christians, the transcendent God became incarnately immanent while remaining transcendent.

In the ancient relationships of God with Abraham and Moses, divine personhood began to appear in human history. The "I am Who am" of Judaic monotheism led to the Incarnate Lord who dared to say to a monotheistic people, "Before Abraham came to be I am."

Emmanuel, God with us, the Savior, is the consummation of the *paradox* of being. He *is* both the transcendence and the immanence of God in one Person. In a place between East and West—in the Middle East—he was conceived, born, lived, died, rose from the dead, and ascended into heaven.

The Hope of the Wandering West

Adam's cultures, including incarnational theism, wandered from Jerusalem in the Middle East to Athens, to Rome, to England, to America, then onward to the moon, to Mars (and beyond?). His masculine journey still proceeds onward, upward, and outward.

But something else has been deepening in the ground of reality. An awareness of personhood has been developing gradually in the West, especially with the Christian revelation of the Incarnate God as one of three divine Persons.

This greatest of all divine revelations raised the greatest of all questions as to how this could be possible. How can God be Father, Son, and Holy Spirit without being three Gods instead of one?

Taking this question seriously, Christian theologians developed the concept of three divine Persons in one divine nature. For the first time in history, an awareness of personhood became explicit. In the light of the divine Persons, man and woman, known from *Genesis* to be like God, finally emerged in historical consciousness as persons.

In the Middle Ages, St. Thomas Aquinas, mainly influenced by both divine revelation and the pre-Christian philosophy of Aristotle, developed a further insight into human personhood. He did this by emphasizing the substantial unity of the human body and soul. Unfortunately, his understanding of this unity was substantially weakened by his acceptance of Aristotle's animal-based definition of human nature.

The strength of Aristotle's mentality accentuated its weakness. Its masculine individualism both aided and distorted the Christian vision of personhood. Aristotle's matter-form interpretation of the relationship between the body and the soul significantly mitigated the ancient and persisting tendency toward dualism. At the same time, his matter-form contribution was not developed enough to prevent this same problem from showing up again.

Culturally, the negative—not the positive—effect of Aristotelian individualism is now predominant in the soul-body dualism of the West. But a person-based turnaround is also possible. Our cultural roots, though profoundly weakened, are still alive. Their remaining vitality is our hope for their growing much deeper in the ground of reality.

Present Trends

The continuing immigration of people from Eve's cultures into Adam's world has been moderating the extreme masculinity of the American character. People have been moving to America from all parts of the planet. They include Chinese, Japanese, and Indians from the Far East; Muslims from the Middle East, Asia, and Africa; and Hispanics from the South.

Oriental influences are evident within the health-care professions. Chinese methods of cooperating with nature, such as acupuncture and herbal medicines, are gradually integrating with the much more aggressive drugs-and-surgery methods used in the West.

Under the banner of diversity, our nation assimilates people from other cultures that are not formed in Puritan individualism. A warming and thawing in the landscape and inscape is gradually happening. Hispanics, especially, possess a sense of the feminine derived from the Lady of Guadalupe, Patroness of the Americas.

Hispanics and some of the others are more likely than Muslims to be assimilated into the American character. Though both of their cultures are family-based, the Hispanic culture is more adaptable to individualism while remaining familial.

In some respects, the God of Islam, Allah, is more transcendent and masculine than the God of the Puritans. Furthermore, the sons and daughters of Allah are increasing, multiplying, and filling the earth, while the sons and daughters of the Puritan's voluntaristic (eventually choicist) God have been contracepting, sterilizing, and aborting themselves away. Only family-based cultures will inherit the earth.

So, what will happen if Allah, the extremely masculine God of Islam, takes over? The passivity of Eve and the loneliness of Adam would be likely to continue. But there is another possibility. In the writings of Islam, Miriam represents the presence of a uniquely feminine person. According to the tradition, she, like Mohammed, was visited by the angel Gabriel. This factor in Islam potentially raises the feminine to an honored status and could offer hope for something better.

This feminine presence became especially relevant in 1917 at Fatima, Portugal, a place with the same name as Mohammed's daughter. There, three shepherd children were visited by a beautiful Lady from heaven who showed them hell, asked for prayer and conversion, and promised a time of world peace. Known as the new Eve, she had lived in Israel, and had become the mother of the founder of Christianity. Her intentions for the lonely Adam and the three Abrahamic religions are intriguing to contemplate.

In the meantime, masculinized feminism is still unfeminine. It is, nevertheless, a hyperactive and distorted cry of Eve for liberation from the passivity into which she plummeted.

The extremity of the feminist reaction against Eve's passivity did little if anything to turn women toward Eve's original gift of active receptivity. Inward action, not outward reaction, transforms the passive into the receptive. Furthermore, *reacting against passivity is just another way of being passive.*

Instead of actively integrating with Adam, the reactive Eve identified with him. Identification obliterates the possibility for integration.

Underground Trends

While the wandering cultures are finding their way to meeting grounds on the planet, the serpentinian starter of their journey has been lurking in the shadows with a special eye on Eve. She must not find her lost gift. When she gets close to doing so, she must be diverted into the selfist, energy-conscious New Age Movement that identifies cosmic energy with God. Thus directed into subtle-energy interests, she will not regain her power for wisdom about love through her likeness to God. She will then be able to attract Adam's attention away from the transcendence of God into dreams about gaining power, wealth, and glory on earth.

In some of their children, the serpent's version of Adam and Eve trailed through history from its beginning to this day. Alive and active as ever, their ideology festers in the underground where they manipulate, plot, and plan. The serpent's Adam has been, and still is, interested in a utopian form of world government that practices deception as a way of controlling everything. The other children of Adam and Eve who are finding their lost gift need to stay alert to what's lurking.

Even if the Serpent's Adam succeeds as plotted and planned, the results will not last. The new Eve, the beautiful lady from heaven who appeared to the children at Fatima, will overcome. True to her promise, the children of the Redeemer's Adam and Eve will find the lost gift.

Personhood and Cultural Change

Becoming aware of the true meaning of history is a giant step in cultural development. Such awareness is required for our journey toward integrative personhood. Not until we can see where we are going can we find our way. And where we are going cannot be found on trips into outer space. These masculinized ventures are mechanized wanderings into the most impersonal world of all. In such escapades, Adam looks for Eve where she cannot be found.

And she cannot be found until *she* finds her own *person-based* self. Shortsighted feminism needs to become insightedly feminine at last.

So, when the impersonal cultures of the East and West open themselves to the personhood in their roots, they will be able, finally, to become friends. Instead of trying to federate all nations in a masculine mode, a feminine-masculine kind of friendship between nations can be realized.

The result could become a likeness of the bountiful goodness that the man and woman of *Genesis* never really forgot in all of their centuries and millennia of searching for each other.

Chapter 19

Adam's America and the Lost Gift

Can there ever be harmony between the compulsive willpower of the Puritan and the impulsive willfulness of the playboy? No.

Neither of these masculine extremes contains active receptivity in its cultural nature. Both lack this feminine power of integration. In opposite ways, both are symptoms of Adam estranged from Eve.

Currently, anything but harmony exists between the Puritan and playboy sides of the American character. The principles of the one and the preferences of the other are both disengaged from their integrating source. Neither principles nor preferences constitute the essence of personhood.

American defenders of principles tend to be individualists. Their Constitution supports the *rights* of individuals without mentioning their responsibilities. For them, these ethical matters are supposedly the concern of religion and the legislatures.

Defenders of preferences assert their comfort-and-pleasure rights without accepting corresponding responsibilities from religion and the legislatures, much less from the Constitution.

The problem began with the noble and heroic founders of the Republic. They were sons of the cultural Adam-among-the-animals, while the cultural Eve was still in Adam's rib and in the mind of God. Their powerful dedication to the principles of individualism became, in human history, like the summit of an exceptionally high, post-tribal hill. Such a masculine trajectory had nowhere to go but technologically into outer space, and at the same time down the slope into the darkness of the playboy valley below. Up and away, and down and out.

So, what went wrong in Adam's shining city on a hill?

Rights without Responsibilities

The designers of this Republic established a government of, by, and for, the people in order to protect the people from tyranny. They also realized that a democratic form of government would not survive without moral commitment in the people, and that those who cannot, or will not, control themselves cannot govern themselves.

Especially with their Puritan interpretation of human nature as being depraved, the originators of the American form of government were wary about the capacity of the people for self-control. This background suspicion might have been the reason why Benjamin Franklin responded to an inquiring woman, after the Constitutional Convention in Philadelphia in 1787, "You have a republic, Madam, if you can keep it."

Thirty years later, in 1817, John Adams said to Thomas Jefferson, "Our Constitution was made only for a moral and religious people. It is wholly inadequate for the government of any other."

The Declaration of Independence in 1776 recognized the rights to life, liberty, and the pursuit of happiness as gifts of God, not gifts of the Government.

The founders, therefore, depended on a culture of good moral character and Bible-based Christianity to support their Constitution. They did not anticipate yet another revolution that eventually would undermine the government's balance of legislative, executive, and judicial powers.

Unexpectedly, in the 1960s, perversities formerly hidden in the closet came out into the open. "Make love, not war" soon became a war against traditional values that targeted especially the woman, her prebirth child, and the integral structure of the family.

With that and other reactions, the culture moved from the moral principles of the individualist toward the me-centered feelings and preferences of the selfist. Feelings became so predominant that it became politically incorrect to hurt anyone's feelings, except those of conservatives who respect the role of principles. This seismic shift caused the cultural sense of responsibility to collapse into a demand for still more Constitutional rights that the founders never dreamed would ever come to the surface in a Bible-inspired nation.

That the Ten Commandments would seem one day so offensive as to be forced into the closet by being removed from the State and relegated to the Church was one of the farthest possibilities from the foresight of the founders.

By attacking the Declaration's right to life, the Courts began to take liberties with the Constitution. Executives and legislators are now taking genuine rights away from the people. Too much liberty at the top of the Republic is beginning to look like a takeover-makeover.

So, today our culture is ready to say, "No, thanks, Mr. Franklin, you can keep your republic with its dependence for survival on morality and religion. It is not politically correct; it is hurting the feelings of too many people."

Thus, the assumption of the founding fathers that the culture would remain morally and religiously stable left a weakness in the system. The Constitution remained vulnerable to the childish assault that has actually happened, and that continues to proceed down the slope of the shining city's hill into the darkness below.

The Culture and the Court

The Constitution—the backbone of America—has been shaken by out-of-control forces in the selfist culture. A major weakness in the supreme law of the land is due to its explicit emphasis on rights without an equally explicit emphasis on responsibilities. This imbalance not only destabilizes the Constitution in its relationship with the culture, but also threatens our survival as a democratic republic.

In spite of the creative vision of the founders, the more recent partisans of the selfist ideology have bypassed the legislative powers of the people, and appealed for their preferential rights to the high court farthest from the people. Supreme Court justices, influenced by the out-of-control playboy culture, began to sit on their benches like kings and queens on thrones. From there, some of them began to declare new so-called "rights" that they claimed were implicit in the darkest shadows of the Constitution.

Thomas Jefferson had noticed this judicial weak spot in the system, and had worried about its tyrannical possibilities. In a letter to William Jarvis, on September 28, 1820, he said, "It is a very dangerous doctrine to consider the judges as the ultimate arbiters of all constitutional questions. It is one which would place us under the despotism of an oligarchy."

Only infants have rights without responsibilities. Adolescents, while learning to become responsible, are generally more interested in their rights. But mature adults realize that an individual's rights cannot long endure without that individual's responsibility to respect and uphold the rights of others.

As the culture has regressed into childish demands for more and more rights, the judicial part of the system has moved into an excessively ruling position. Becoming overbearing, especially in the 1960s, the Supreme Court "rulers" started to see in the Constitution a whole train of privacy rights that were boldly demanded by the playboy's infantile philosophy of life.

Privacy, as such, has no inherent principle of limitation. Thus privacy for marital contraception promptly led to privacy for non-marital contraception, for a woman's right to kill a prebirth son or daughter, for her doctor's right to do the killing for her, and for homosexuals to practice sodomy and to demand equal rights for marriage. Nationally legalized privacy for doctor-assisted suicide and so-called mercy killing are immanent possibilities. Meanwhile, the right to privacy of the child in the womb is totally ignored.

No Wall of Separation

To secure their irresponsible privacy rights, partisans of the playboy reaction against Puritanism insist on separating church and state. They use Thomas Jefferson's "wall of separation," a passing phrase in his 1802 letter to the Baptist Association of Danbury, Connecticut. These separationists use this phrase *out of context* to impose their agenda on the Constitution's First Amendment. The image of a "wall" facilitates their process of isolating the right to life and traditional marriage by relegating these issues to the church so the state can better accommodate their selfist desires.

But the First Amendment simply states: "Congress shall make no law respecting an establishment of religion, or prohibiting the free exercise thereof." The words "congress" and "establishment" clearly indicate that the *federal* government shall not establish a state religion. The phrase "free exercise" means what it says, and

Adam's America and the Lost Gift

obviously protects religious expression from federal regulation. A difference—not a separation—of roles in the republic is all that is implied. Unfortunately, Jefferson used the raw masculine word "separation," rather than a more refined term such as "real and clear distinction."

Church and state are constitutionally meant to be friends, unique and different—not separate—and sharing basic morality in common. Either one of them dominating the other, or walled off from the other, is not friendship.

Church and state are suffering together the irresponsibility of selfism. So they need to work together to balance the Constitution with some basic amendments of responsibility on the irrevocably fundamental right to life and marriage issues. They can succeed by connecting human life—including sex—with morality, but with more insight this time around.

For instance, an adequate definition of *personhood*, capable of including all persons, from single-celled conception to unneglectful natural death, would be the fulfillment of a primary Constitutional need. And it would counteract the *functionalism* of both Puritan principles and playboy preferences. An example would be "a human person is an individual being with the *natural*, not necessarily *functional*, abililty to know and love in a self-reflective way."[30]

Without a firm affirmation of *natural* personhood, the reaction against permissiveness will become a pendulum's swing back to the previous extreme, and no healing of the Puritan-playboy Adam will be in view.

Back to Puritanism?

When moral strictness and willpower deteriorate into "me and my private choices," family bonds disintegrate, and prisons increase and multiply. Social stresses become so great that the next thoughtless reflex in the culture could become a return, not to a natural law and Biblical sense of morality, but to a compulsive sense of morality, which is moralism.

The difference between moralism and morality is like a dry-boned skeleton compared to one that is alive in a healthy human body. True morality is a loving respect for God, self, other persons, other creatures, and the good earth as our home in space and time. This morality is the *firmness* of affirmational love. It is not driven by fear of punishment, but is peaceful with hope and trust.

As the American people become aware that the claim to rights has gone too far, they are called to realize the need for a future and deeper return to true moral responsibility. This breakthrough is required to reverse the breakdown that threatens the survival of a government that is of, by, and for a *responding* and *responsible* people.

Our compulsively moralistic Puritan background could not be changed by any kind of reflexive reaction against it, such as playboyism. We, the American people, must face the Puritan origin of our national character, the better to understand it. Only then can we assimilate it into a broader and deeper insight into God, man, woman, and child. Then we will be on our way to the recovery that is our destiny.

Beyond Individualism and Selfism

The individualist Adam cannot hold rights and responsibilities together for long. He tried to do so in what has been called the natural law. Partly included in the Ten Commandments and in the philosophy of Aristotle and Thomas Aquinas, this law of our nature has remained masculine in the good sense, but unbalanced, in its interpretation.

The animal base of the Western world's view of the natural law left the law vulnerable to Puritan individualism and playboy selfism. Consequently, its meaning has gradually deteriorated and eventually disappeared. Influenced by the rationalistic Enlightenment and the empiricism of John Locke, the natural law context for the American Constitution is *anything but person-based*. It is much too weak to resist any kind of challenge from a me-obsessed shift in the culture.

Not until the sleeping Eve awakens in the cultural soul of Adam will Americans be able to integrate rights and responsibilities in the *natural law of human personhood*. This sense of law is not based simply on justice. It is based mainly on the feminine-masculine nature of the affirming kind of love that includes, within its firmness, justice and the other virtues.

Love has its laws. These demands not only respect, but also limit, the privacy of persons for the good of themselves and of other persons. Individualists and selfists sometimes talk about love from morning to night. But they are rarely interested in knowing what love really is and what its necessary virtues are. They are saturated with either moralistic or preferential meanings for "love."

Beyond the Rib of Adam

When a masculine culture like American individualism descends to ground zero, there is nowhere else to go but inward. But how can the Puritan-playboy Adam go within to find his missing personhood while the Puritan-playmate Eve, who is supposedly the keeper of withinness, does not know who *she* is?

Her recent feminist reaction against her passivity was masculine, as any *reaction* can only be. Consequently, she drove herself into the control of the Puritan-playboy Adam so thoroughly as to disapper into his rib and lose herself in his Puritan work-ethic and playboy sex-ideology.

In this condition, Adam cannot see Eve as other than one of his own bones. Therefore, American feminism leaves Eve nowhere to go but within. In her encounter with Adam, she must not "passive-out" in one way or another. She has much to ponder in her heart before she and Adam can become friends, and before she can call Adam to his own inner reality.

Going within, she needs to become aware of how *passive she has been*, and how *reactively hyperactive* she has become. Seeing herself in her historical background, she can realize that the Puritan's romantic view of marriage was meant to be her transition, not to playboy eroticism, but to the person-based marriage of man-woman friends. She will see how she misinterpreted her situation in history when she began to demean her home as a "comfortable concentration camp," then left it, only to fall still deeper into the hands of the Puritan-playboy culture that reigned.

After that, marriage itself began to sink into same-sex hands with nothing to stop the fall from continuing. Radical and mindless feminism, with its ideology of man-woman sameness, became the precedent for an alien intrusion such as same-sex marriage.

The present situation calls for a profound shift in American feminism. The alienated Eve needs to discover her *active receptivity* as *the* integrating principle within the feminine-masculine paradox of personhood. For this consummation, both her passivity and her reaction *against* her passivity are powerless.

So Eve, together with the re-creative power of God, needs to emerge, not only from Adam's cultural bones, but especially from the depths of his cultural soul. And the emerging Eve will be able to discover her own person as a woman. She will become a prayerful receiver of divine grace, and a co-liberator of Adam together with God. She will become Adam's friend and lover, a nurturing mother of children, an unique source of wisdom, thus transforming the culture together with him.

The woman of *Genesis* within us today can develop her uniquely gifted and redeemed personhood. If she does, she will be able to inspire Adam to reconsider his animal-based concept of himself and of his sexuality.

Adam likewise can discover his own receptivity and its integrative power within himself. Then he will be able to welcome Eve on the level of their personhood. He will become ready to share with her the freedom of friendship, without needs and desires driving them away from their original being. In friendship, they will be able to transform their various impersonal cultures into an integrative culture of persons.

Adam's history of Western individualism—a long and ardous, often violent endeavor—was meant to be a cultural transition from the tribal family of the ancients to the community of families in a new culture of affirmational wisdom and love. So when the redeemed Eve emerges from Adam's cultural heart, his Puritan individualism and playboy selfism will be faced with the next American revolution.

Chapter 20

The Future of Adam and Eve

The lonely crowd of individualists on one side and the melting pot on the other. Such is Adam's America. Realistically, is there a future for an Adam-Eve revolution here? The reader wants to know.

Adam: It seems to me that a "melting pot" culture that is also individualistic is potent with the promise of a revolutionary paradox. This paradox includes the uniqueness of the individual as much as it includes the relationships of the individual. Both. This nation is not there yet. "Melting" needs to soften the ruggedness of individualism. In other words, a culture of the "lone eagle" and the "lonely crowd" needs more depth in its soul.

Reader: Do you mean that "melting" will deepen us? As far as I know, things that melt lose their solidity and drop in height.

Adam: Stay with the paradox. You can become relational to the core while you remain strong and stand firmly in your individuality.

Reader: I need to learn how to unite opposites like this. How did you learn it?

Adam: With help from Eve. I learned how to share our unique ways of seeing things. I found her in myself, and she found me in herself. That gave us access to the paradox of personhood. Through her I found a better way of being Adam. She says that now I am "all man."

Reader: I suppose you would say that now she is ….

Eve: Adam and I are special friends. We discovered together the paradoxical meaning of friendship. This means that people are mutually independent. They are neither independent like the lone eagle nor co-dependent like two people who cannot exist without each other.

Adam: Our friendship is like the relationship between the divine Persons. They are mutually independent, though we tend to think of them as being co-dependent.

Reader: You must be seeing something in mutuality that I don't see yet.

Adam: Remember, we started out by talking about being unique and related at once. Mutual independence is just another way of saying the same thing.

Reader: So, let's say that America goes deeper than the "melting pot" on one side of our national character, and deeper than the "lone eagle" on the other. How is this idea about mutual independence supposed to affect the situation we have in this country today? We have so much divisiveness and conflict. People call it the "culture wars."

Adam: It's a battle between opposites that needs to be resolved by a paradoxical sense of rights and responsibilities. One side leans on rights; the other leans on responsibilities. In America today, the claim to rights is getting stronger, while the responsibilities are steadily weakening. As a result, the government is taking over the responsibilities that belong in the people. Instead of becoming stronger, the integrative paradox has become our vanishing promise.

Reader: Can we do anything to revive the promise?

Eve: We can, if we are willing to see how opposites become friends and share their part of the truth with each other.

An Example

Adam: First of all, the culture of the people needs to become strong enough to keep the government in its place so it does not become a tyranny. We had that kind of culture for awhile, but it was not balanced and mature enough to prevent its own weakening.

Reader: Balanced and mature. What do you mean?

Adam: Government "by the people" requires a culture of balanced and mature self-regulation in the people. This means that at least a majority of individual persons would have an upstanding (vertical) moral and religious character. They would be able to hold in its place, well above the power-hungry dark side of human nature, the horizontal management of human needs, wants, and supplies that are concerns of the government.

Eve: There must have been a weakness in the religious and moral values of the original culture. Otherwise, it would not have lost so quickly its ability to hold the government in its place.

Adam: The weakness was in the people's cultural concept of themselves. They were too individualistic and thus vulnerable to becoming selfists. They became too concerned about their privacy, and began to demand privacy "rights" that started to pull down the government from its place. Then, as the government bowed to their demands, its power over the people increased. The relationship between the people and the government went way out of balance. The weakness was really mine as a religious and moral *individualist*.

Adam's Progress

Reader: You were a Puritan, then. How has your religious and moral character changed?

Adam: I changed by listening to Eve, and sharing with her, the way we are doing now. My religion has become more aware of friendship with God. And my sense of morality is more rooted in the interpersonal natural law of human personhood. I no longer think of myself as being a rational animal, but an intellectually intuitive and rational *person*. The result is really a revolution in my character.

Reader: I suppose you would say that the American character needs to do likewise: develop more interpersonal friendship with God, between men and women, and between all persons, who are no longer thinking of themselves as being basically animals.

Eve: More friendship between men and women is the key. The burning sexual inferno in American culture today is putting the nation on a path to oblivion. The fire needs to return to the home-centered confines of the fireplace.

Adam: In spite of that problem, the people have been generous in helping others around the world with their needs. These people are quite spontaneous with *agape*, but pathetic with *eros*. I agree that more friendship between man and woman would bring out the power of *philia* to integrate *agape* and *eros*.

Reader: Interesting! One side is generous in giving; the other is ravenous in taking. Seems like a cry for something to bring about balance and integration.

Eve: America needs power for wisdom about love.

Reader: Not just these people; all people on earth.

If you don't mind my asking, why were you two so weak in the beginning that you lost your way? Did you become individualists; was that your problem?

Eve: Oh, oh! Did we? Adam, you became an individualist. But I became anonymous. We were anything but friends.

Going Deeper

Adam: We have to admit that we were weak and vulnerable to attack when we first appeared in Eden.

Reader: But why? You were created perfect. You were not created weak and vulnerable to attack. If you think you were created to be less than perfect, you give no credit to God who was supposedly your friend.

Eve: True. If you really want us to answer your question, you yourself will be involved. You think we are responsible for your weak and suffering condition on this earth.

Reader: True, also. I would really like to know why you were so susceptible to evil in the beginning because I, myself, am paying for what you did. Not only me, but everyone else.

Eve: This much I know. The gift of my being from God was perfectly given. If I became weak and vulnerable to evil, I alone am responsible. I did it to myself. I have no one else to blame, not even the serpent.

Adam: You are sounding like an individualist.

Eve: We must have been created to be uniquely individual *persons* of a perfect kind. And completely free to receive the gift of being with joy and gratitude!

The Future of Adam and Eve

Adam: According to that, we must have been free also to fail in receiving the gift. But why would we fail?

Reader: And when? After you, Eve, were created from one of Adam's ribs?

Eve: It must have been when God created me out of nothing.

Reader: That is not what *Genesis* says.

Eve: If we go by what *Genesis* says, Adam was created out of dust from the earth. His body was fully formed *before* God breathed life through his nostrils into his lungs. God appears to be a rather primitive kind of *maker*, not an infinite creator

A Turning-Point Question

Reader: What is the difference between a maker and an infinite creator?

Adam: That is an important question. Its not one that *Genesis* sets out to answer. Questions about the nature of an infinite creator involve us in our way of knowing *being as being,* and need to be considered philosophically in depth. Divine revelation rarely goes there. When God said to Moses, "I am who am," and when Jesus said to the Jews, "Before Abraham came to be, I am," you can hear something about *being as being.* Your question about the difference between a maker and an infinite creator moves us into that mode of seeing reality.

Reader: It seems to me that the creation story reveals a very powerful and good creator. But, yes, it sounds different when it describes God forming you, Adam, like someone creating a form out of clay, and you, Eve, like someone removing a bone and shaping it into a woman.

Eve: Well said! The creation story does reveal God as being powerful and good. But not as being infinite. An infinite creator would not form Adam like a maker working with clay. I think Adam and I were created originally out of nothing by the *infinite* creator.

Reader: If you are not getting that thought from *Genesis,* where are you getting it from?

Eve: Adam said it: from *being as being.*

Reader: But how do you know that?

Eve: Now you are asking about the lost gift that we are finding together. The *being* of every person knows *being as being* just by being a person. When *Genesis* says that I was created from Adam's rib, that is a maker's way of saying something much deeper about the infinite creator's way of creating me. I have to go to *being as being* to find out something about how Adam and I are related in our being, and how we were created together.

Reader: Was I created out of nothing, too? I think I'm one of your descendants, and my soul was created by God out of nothing when I was conceived in my mother's womb.

Adam: That sounds like the way a maker would do it. Almost like a mechanic putting parts together.

Reader: Man, you're right about that! No wonder people have such little respect for the beginning of human life in this world. They sense that something is wrong with the whole picture they have in their minds. I think you might be onto something when you talk about *being as being*.

The Search Continues

Adam: That makes me want to look again at what Eve said about her failure in receiving the gift of being out of nothing, as the cause of her moral weakness in Eden. It makes me wonder about my own lack of mental and moral nerve in those days. Maybe I, too, need to ponder myself in the light of *being as being*.

Reader: Be careful, Adam. Eve might be on the wrong road.

Adam: No doubt you have noticed that I was even more gullible in Eden than Eve was. If she didn't receive the gift, I surely did not.

Eve: I led you away from the light of being, and I need to lead you back again as you discern the way carefully in the light of divine revelation. We need to discover something about ourselves that, because we are responsible, only we can discover. It happened before Eden in a world that *Genesis* obviously omits, along with omitting the creation of the angels. There is a beginning before the so-called beginning. This leaves a wall between two beginnings. And I want to find the door in that wall, too.

The Future of Adam and Eve

Adam: We can see that the serpent, as a fallen angel, came into our world from the world of the angels not described by *Genesis*. That is clear enough. We know that the angels, who appear at various times and places in the pages of divine revelation, were God's first created persons.

Reader: But we are not angels. We are a different kind of person. We have a physical body, and they do not.

Adam: You might be implying that we were morally fragile in Eden because we were created as a body into which God breathed a soul.

Reader: I don't think your body was your problem. Something deeper.

Eve: Neither was the problem a moral one. It was deeper than that because it affected our whole being. We were not cast out of an earthly garden, literally. We were cast out of ourselves. We did not receive fully the perfect finite being that we were given when God gave us the gift of being. And that made us morally weak in the beginning.

Reader: Why doesn't the author of *Genesis* tell us this?

Eve: I don't think God would tell me how deeply I faltered in receiving the gift of my finite being from my infinite creator. I have to discover this myself because I alone am responsible. The serpent tested me on the moral level, not on the deeper level of my being.

Reader: You said you don't think you were cast out of an earthly garden. Where were you if not on earth?

Eve Passes Through the Door in the Wall

Eve: I was in the world of original being. In fact, I wonder whether paradise ever existed on this planet. Maybe it is a "place" somewhere between heaven and earth, and we were created to be perfect there. Maybe that is why Jesus on the cross said to the repentant fellow on a cross next to him that they would be in paradise that day. He didn't call the place Heaven. This seems to indicate that there is an "in between" world where we once were, and from which we were "cast out" into this lower world here.

Adam: You don't mean a kind of pre-existence, do you?

Eve: I know that my original failure-in-being pre-existed my moral failure in Eden. And I don't think we were originally created by a maker in Eden. If all finite persons were created out of nothing, they were created together by an infinite creator; not some now, and some later, by a maker. The difference between a maker and an infinite creator turns out to be the door in the wall between the two creations.

Adam: So you think all of us were created out of nothing together with the angels. But we are *not* angels.

Eve: We are a different kind of person from them, the kind that could live on earth. They could not.

Reader: According to your view, then, we were created together with the angels from nothing. We know that some of the angels received the gift, and that others did not. What about us? You must be thinking that I, too, failed to receive fully the gift of being in the beginning before the beginning. So, I don't have you to blame for my present condition?

Eve: You are the one who needs to say that, not me, nor God, nor anyone else. You can continue to blame us if you choose. Or you can follow us as we search for and find the lost gift of perfect finite being as a person in the image and likeness of God. Blaming someone else is our favorite escape from our relationship with the gift of being and the infinite Giver.

Adam Sees the Light

Reader: Why didn't we receive such a momentous gift?

Adam: Individualism must have been involved.

Eve: What do you mean?

Adam: We did not want to say "I am." We wanted to say "I am who am." Oh my Lord! Did I say that?

Eve: I think you discovered something, Adam. In knowing *being as being*, we knew that we were finite, God is infinite, and we wondered why we could not be infinite, too. We hesitated about being finite. And that is how we threw ourselves out of ourselves

The Future of Adam and Eve

into the darkness of passivity and waiting for redemption. We are here on earth to decide whether or not we will receive the gift of being, as given.

Adam: This is all quite a shock for me.

Reader: I don't know what to think about all of this, but I know I will have to decide what to think. Hamlet said, "To be or not to be." You, Eve, say, "To receive or not to receive."

Adam: I sense a deeper gratitude in myself for the Way, the Truth, and the Life, our Savior.

Facing the Future

Reader: How does all of this relate to the American character?

Adam: This nation's emphasis on individual freedom is surely highlighted by the depth of our story. I realize that American culture is low in power for wisdom. And where wisdom is dim, love is weak. But grassroots Americans have the everyday wisdom of good common sense. Many of the academics and politicians stray into intellectual dysfunctions and become alienated from their roots. But not basic good-hearted, mentally alert, people.

Reader: But America's culture and government are losing their founding impetus. Maybe your discovery about the relationship of individual freedom to *being as being* can strengthen the weakness in our national character.

Adam: I hope this will be so. But we just do not know what our descendents will do. We still have the great Biblical prophecies to live through about the time of tribulation to come. A unique time in the history of the world. The Lord even says, "If that time had not been shortened, no one would have survived (*Matt.* 24:22). Even the sun, moon, and stars will be involved.

Eve: There are many other prophecies, too, from the holy and urgently concerned, Virgin-Mother Mary. She has been telling us, through visionaries in various places around the globe, that those times described by Jesus, her Son, according to Matthew, are near. Very near. At Fatima, she proved to 70,000 people that she meant what she said about preparing for those times. Her proof involved the sun in the sky. It went into a huge spin and plummeted toward the terrified crowd before returning to its peaceful place. But she promised the three little shepherds to whom she spoke that, in the end, her Immaculate Heart would triumph and there would be peace on earth.

So, we do have these things in our future.

Adam: Yes, Eve, the prophecies turn our attention not so much toward the culture as toward our concern for the salvation of each individual person, our descendant, in whom we still live. Enough of them *opening the door in the wall*, letting in the kingdom of God, and turning up the light, could be a leaven in the culture.

Eve: Turning up the light. That is what you and I have been trying to do on this planet. In our beginning, we were created in the light of *being*. We knew the *is* of God, of ourselves, of everything else. But we pulled back to look at the light as an object out there. And that act threw *us* "out there," facing three major walls of darkness in our relationship. We saw beings as objects and even became objects of ourselves and of each other. We lost the opportunity to enjoy the glory of the warming light.

Now, together in our descendants, we can search for and find the lost gift. We are beginning to *receive, actively*, our true personhood, our perfect likeness to God, and our original being. In the grace of God, these are the long lost splendors of our interpersonal power for wisdom about love.

For a further explanation about the original creation and sources to be consulted, see Developmental Reflection C, "A Little less Than the Angels," p. 229.

Developmental Reflection A

The Meaning of Personhood in Trinitarian Theology

Jesus died a cruel death on a cross for merely suggesting to hard-core monotheists that he was one with "I am Who Am." After his Resurrection, and before he left the earth for heaven, he named the three divine Persons: Father, Son, and Holy Spirit. He left no explanation. Nevertheless, faith in the Great Mystery was so strong that many of his followers became martyrs for the Faith.

The new Christians, in their devotion and liturgy, worshipped the Three, and baptized in their names. They believed that "God is love" (1 *John* 4:8). They knew that "In the beginning was the Word, and the Word was with God, and the Word was God" (*John* 1:1).

With the passage of time, some of these Christians began to wonder about the Son of God. Is he divine, or is he just the Messiah sent by God? What did he mean when he said, "Before Abraham came to be, I am"? If he is divine, is there more than one God? That cannot be. So, how are the Father, Son, and Spirit one God?

Though the words "trinity" and "person" did not exist, at that time, in religious discourse, questions like this started the long history of theological discussion about the Trinity.

Various analogies of Father, Son, and Spirit, such as "lover, beloved, and love" were used. But the man-woman likeness to God revealed in *Genesis* did not surface, as such, in the history of Trinitarian theology. Three main causes seem to be involved.

First, the ability to see Adam and Eve as a model for relating to the three divine Persons was not possible without an adequate understanding of personhood. At the time of the earliest theologians, people had proper names such as Joseph, Sarah, and Nathaniel. Generalizations, such as "father" and "son," served to identify their relationships. Noticeably, the divine names, especially Father and

Son, signify relationships. They are not, though they imply, proper or personal names.

Furthermore, the paternal-filial relationship between the Father and Son is a mutual giving that is, as other-directed, masculine in emphasis. Giving, however, definitely implies receiving. And true receiving implies interiority. Inner-directed receiving is feminine in relation to other-directed giving. Since the interiority of the divine Persons was not sufficiently recognized and was thought by some of the theologians (such as the Cappadocians) to be unknowable, the likeness of Eve to God was not explicitly within the focal range of consideration.

Finally, the kind of logic needed for a transcendental way of thinking was, and still is, missing. This logic of ontological wisdom is a paradoxical, or *both-and*, kind of intuitive thinking that can remain true to the unity of opposites evident in reality. Paradoxical thinking results from a first-intention mentality that is able to carry within it the *either-or* (second intention) logic used for ordinary demonstration. Paradoxical thinking is, in this way, integrally *both* a first intention *and* a second intention manner of thinking. It is an integration of intuition and reason while remaining intuitive throughout the reasoning process.

The mind's immediate cognitive union with another reality is its first intention. The mind's subsequent focus on its own knowledge, for the sake of clarifying it, is its second intention.

The second intention science of consistent thinking, developed by Aristotle, identifies things and separates them for the sake of clarity. An example is separating man and woman by clearly identifying or defining them.

Paradoxical thinking, by contrast, neither identifies nor separates. Instead, it integrates for the sake of a deeper understanding. An example is a man and woman becoming two-in-one by their shared spirit of marital commitment: an integration of natural (not logical) opposites. Separating things by clearly defining them in their own identity is not a setup for integration. If the mind tries to bring together separated things taken as separate, it is likely to force the matter by reducing them to sameness. An example is trying to equalize man and woman by thinking they are the same, or virtually identical, in nature.

Because the theologians lacked an explicit awareness of the kind of logic required for thinking about the Trinity, they had to struggle mightily to rise above the second-intention logic of substance and accidents, univocal terms, and the abstracting process of identity and separation. Concepts formed on this passive base are not adequate for first-intention thinking about the *pure-act* of infinitely real being.

Not until the knowing power of the agent (actively receiving) intellect is recognized as intuitively in touch with the being of that-which-is-known will it be possible to explicate the implicit logic of transcendental wisdom.

In the scope of mainly univocal (single meaning) logic, the "three in one" of the Trinity tended to be *unconsciously* a mathematical problem to be solved, rather than a paradox with an infinite depth of meaning.

Trinitarian theologians have been limited in their thinking by the three obstacles described above. They are the absence of a sufficient understanding of personhood; the masculine character of other-directed relationships between the Persons without a recognition of their interiority; and the use of an inadequate logic. Nevertheless, they did the best they could with Adam's way of thinking.

Adam's Theologians

Beginning with the Son, identified by St. John, as the eternal Word (*logos*), Justin Martyr (d.165) distinguished between the immanent and expressed Word, that is, the Word *within* God, and the same Word as *expressed* in Christ. This difference between the *immanent* and the *expressed* Word became especially significant. After that, theologians distinguished between the immanent Trinity and the Trinity as expressed (or "economic") in relation to creatures.

In the early years of Christian reflection on divine unity, God's Word, *expressed* in the nature of a man, suggested a likeness to the Greek *persona*, which was a mask worn by an actor on stage, and through which the actor's voice sounded outward to the audience. Similarly, the divine Word sounds toward us through Christ. Somewhere along the line, the self-word "person," emerged from the mask-word *persona*. From there, the divine Word was called a Person, and so were the Father and Holy Spirit.

Next came the big question: "How are three divine Persons a Trinity in one God? There should have been an accompanying question, "How can the human mind meet the demands of such a momentous inquiry?" Accordingly, Adam's theologians might have developed the kind of logic they needed for responding to the challenge they faced. The three divine Persons are neither identical nor separate, as ordinary logic would interpret them to be. They are infinitely unique, yet integral, as an extraordinary kind of logic would help us to see.

Infinitely unique? The theologians saw the Father, Son, and Spirit as *identical* in the oneness of God, nevertheless different, not separate, in their identity. This "logical inconsistency" seems partly due to their intuition of the paradoxical nature of the subject they pondered. But by interpreting the oneness of God as the divine substance (*ousia*), they prevented themselves from seeing the complete paradox. In ordinary logic, a substance is that which underlies accidents such as an individual's powers for action. But the divine Persons are not accidental powers of a substance.

Origen (d. 254) taught that the Son is one in *substance* with the Father, and that the Father eternally *generates* the Son. His ideas of "substance" and "generation," set the stage for the subsequent history of Trinitarian theology. The Greek idea of substance (ousia) is cosmological in origin. The idea of generation is biological in origin. Without a transcendentally paradoxical way of thinking in Trinitarian theology, the strength of these concepts is, also, their weakness.

Arius (d. 336) seemed eager to feed off the weakness in Origen's theology. Too ready to harden the biological meaning of generation, he thought that the generation of the Son by the Father subordinates the Son to the Father. By radicalizing this perceived subordination into a separation, Arius taught that the Father *created* the Son in time as the greatest of all creatures. He denied that the Son is one substance with the Father, and eternally begotten by the Father. In a sense, Arius was being perfectly logical in his way of reasoning from Origen's shortsighted premises. Thus began the Arian heresy that rapidly spread like wildfire throughout Christianity, and is still characteristic of Islamic monotheism (no Trinity) to this day.[31]

In 325, the Council of Nicaea, especially through St. Athanasius, confronted Arianism by insisting that the Son is one in substance with the Father, and is begotten eternally by Him. Since then, theologians have struggled in various ways with the philosophical and non-biblical word "substance." The human mind cannot use the category of substance (as *that which stands under*) in relation to God without "second intention" logic affecting its conclusions.

After the Council of Nicaea, three Cappadocian theologians, Basil (d. 379), Gregory of Nyssa (d. 386), and Gregory of Nazianzus (d. 389) became more interested in the three divine Persons and their relationships than in their oneness of substance. They shifted their understanding of *ousia* toward the divine *nature*, which means a *substance* as the principle of action. The actions involved were the Father creating, the Son redeeming, and the Spirit sanctifying.

For these theologians, the first Person is the Father, not because of who he is in himself (I am Who am), but because of his relationship to the second Person as the Son of the Father. They insisted that the Persons in themselves are beyond our understanding, and that we can know them only in their other-directed evidence to us as Creator, Redeemer, and Sanctifier.

This otherness, both within God and in God's relation to us, is proportionate to the masculine emphasis of the Father and Son, and to both emanating together their masculine, or paternal-filial, Spirit of Love.

But personhood is impossible without interiority, that is, without a relationship within oneself.

Obviously, the Cappadocians closed the door on seeing anything like Adam and Eve behind the Father-Son relationship. Their model, called social, was three relating human beings sharing the same human nature. Other theologians wondered how this analogy did not imply three Gods.

St. Augustine (d. 430) was determined to avoid any three-Gods implication, so he abandoned the social analogy for one that has been called psychological. He thought that the soul in each human being is a better image and likeness of God than three human beings relating with one another. Within the self, each one is a trinity of lover, beloved, and love. Better yet, each one is a trinity of faculties: intellect, will, and memory. As a result, Augustine seemed to secure the oneness of God in a single divine substance. By doing so, however, he returned to the former problems of the substance-accident relationship and of unity by sameness. The implication is that three persons, like accidental manifestations of an individual substance, are identical in the oneness of their substance.

Augustine did use some of the logic of Aristotle and he did ponder the accident called "relation." He knew that the three divine Persons are not like accidents of a substance. So he said that relationship, besides being an accident, is also one of the transcendentals of being. As transcendental, relationship applies not only to substances in this world, but also to the divine substance. In God, according to this orientation, relationship and personhood seem to be virtually identical. The question remains: is a person a relation, or is a person relational?

The result of Augustine's thinking became the initial idea, developed many centuries later by St. Thomas Aquinas, that a divine Person *is* a *subsistent relation*. Besides being an idea so abstract that it tended to remove the Trinity from the interest of the people, it was a consummation of the logic of identity and separation. How can we relate, with the immediacy of love in our hearts, to a *subsistent relation*?

After St. Augustine, and well before St. Thomas, Boethius (d. 524) defined a person as an individual substance of a rational nature. This definition is such that it cannot apply to God. The divine Persons are not individual substances, nor is their nature *rational* in the formal sense. Rationality suggests the ability to proceed from the known to the unknown by means of connected judgments that are able to yield true and logically valid conclusions. In God, there is no unknown, and therefore no process of reasoning from the known to the unknown. God simply knows in an infinitely perfect way.

Six centuries after Boethius, Richard of St. Victor (d. 1173) moved away from substance-based theology to a social analogy similar to that of the fourth-century Cappadocians. He saw God as the *sharing* kind of love. Two Persons relating with each other and sharing a third Person as the "co-beloved" is, according to Richard, the perfection of love.

A little later, Thomas Aquinas (d. 1274) became Augustinian and Aristotelian, and returned to a substance-based view of the Trinity. Interpreting Richard's meaning for love as desire (*eros*), he did not accept Richard's theology. Desire implies need, he thought, and there is no need, or implication of something lacking, in God.

Richard, however, did not seem to mean the *eros* kind of love. He meant something more like *agape*, which is charity or the self-giving kind of love. Had he recognized that sharing implies receiving as well as giving, his notion about Trinitarian love could have meant *philia* or friendship, which actually means sharing: receiving and giving, not only giving.

In thinking about the divine Persons as subsistent relations, Thomas intensified the abstractness of Augustine's identification of personhood and relationality. Thomas also developed Augustine's intellect-will analogy of the Trinity. The Father generating the Word is like the divine intellect. And the Father and Son together spirating their paternal-filial love, as the Holy Spirit of Love, is like the divine will. Generation and spiration are, together, the circumincession (circle of processions) that constitute the interior life of God.

Still later, in the early 15th century, and probably trying to overcome the extremely abstract thinking of the Scholastics, Andrei Rublev, a Frenchman, created an icon of the Trinity showing three angels in human form like those who appeared to Abraham (*Genesis* 18). In the icon, these angels are seated around an altar-like table, and are relating with each other about the creation, Incarnation, and redemption. Beautifully depicted, each one turns toward another in a circular, outgoing, self-giving manner.

Once again, theological thinking about the Triune God returned to an other-directed social model similar to that of the fourth century theologians. Differently, however, Rublev used angels instead of men. Thought to be non-sexual beings of a purely spiritual nature, angels are seen as being more like God *than like sex-differentiated* humans. About this icon, critics would say that, like all social models, this one, too, depicts three Gods.

Genesis, however, does not mention directly the creation of the angels, but only the creation of a man and a woman as *the* image of God. Without a better understanding of the receptive interiority of personhood, the Adam-Eve analogy would have to remain outside the mindset of Trinitarian theologians.

Adam's Struggle through Modern Philosophy

Eventually, in the 17th century, the trajectory of philosophical thought began to move from the object of knowledge to the subject doing the knowing. It was then that modern subjectivist philosophy and psychology took hold. The first move in this direction happened with the French philosopher, Rene Descartes (d.1650), who turned away from the object to the subject by saying, "I think, therefore I am."

Strangely, this "I am" sounds somewhat similar to God saying to Moses, "I am who am." But the Cartesian "I am" was an isolated consciousness that could not relate immediately with anything in the world. It could relate only with the ideas that happened to show up in the subject's own mind. These ideas were the only objects of consciousness. The subject, therefore, remained object-oriented. Both the shallow inwardness and the minimal otherness of the Cartesian "I" offered little insight into the nature of *personhood*.

The Cartesian version of subjectivity, so disconnected from other beings in the world, separated reason from the senses so profoundly that subsequent philosophers could become only rationalists or empiricists, both stranded in the logic of identity and separation. That is what happened, thanks to Descartes' method, which he tried to make as rigorous and clear as mathematics.

Along the empirical trajectory of the Cartesian divide, modern clinical psychology became culturally influential especially with Sigmund Freud (d. 1939). This founder of psychoanalysis was so biology-based that he, too, missed the light of personhood. Though he discovered in the darkness some of the psychodynamics of the unconscious mind, he was an empirical extremist. His empiricism allowed no room for genuine human freedom, thereby distorting his insight into the unconscious capacity of the human mind for repression.

After Sigmund Freud, Carl Jung (d. 1961) discovered what he called "archetypes" in the unconscious mind, among which were the *animus* (a masculine image) and the *anima* (a feminine image). Jung cleared the way for a somewhat more holistic understanding of the psychological self.

In the world of the philosophers after Descartes, personhood was nowhere in sight. Immanuel Kant (d. 1804) tried to combine the extremes: rationalism and empiricism. George Hegel (d. 1831) tried to develop a logical method that would combine extremes by means of a thesis-antithesis process meant to terminate in a univocal absolute. His long journey from the antithetical "this" and "that" of the senses to the rationalist heights of the Absolute turned out to be a pseudo-dynamic version of the logic of identity and separation.

The move toward personalism began when Soren Kierkegaard (d. 1855) reacted vehemently against Hegel's rationalism. In doing so, he asserted the radical importance of the existing *individual*. But his theistic individualism did not survive the continuing presence of the Cartesian ego. Influenced by both Descartes and Kierkegaard, Jean Paul Sartre (d. 1980) developed his self-centered individualism in the form of atheistic existentialism. He saw the consciousness of the individual as a radical negator of every object in its path, and therefore, as free from all determination by anyone or anything else. This inauthentic freedom by negation is the desperate opposite of true freedom by affirmation. No wonder, then, that Sartre said, "Hell is other people."

Martin Buber (d. 1965), the author of *I and Thou*, and Gabriel Marcel (d. 1973), who expanded subjectivity into intersubjectivity, paved the way for the final emergence of what has been called personalism.

Theologians Karl Rahner (d. 1984), Yves Congar (d. 1995), and others wanted Trinitarian theology to become more interpersonal. But they could not overcome the "gravitational pull" of the traditional logic, and with language such as "axioms" and "modes" remained too abstract for the devotional life of the people. As a result, religion became more intellectual and liturgical while many customary devotions were demeaned and lost heart.

Finally, new life began when Hans Urs von Balthasar (d. 1988) recognized receptivity in God. In this contemporary context, Pope John Paul II, author of *The Theology of the Body*, became a heroic personalist. He saw marriage as a likeness of the relational inner life of the Trinity, but apparently did not see the *sexual* difference between man and woman within that likeness.

The Unfortunate Effects of "Substance" Thinking about the Trinity

The models used by Adam's theologians showed a significant uneasiness with "substance" thinking concerning the Trinity. These analogies oscillated between the social (three Persons relating) and the psychological (three faculties of one person). An example is the movement from the Cappadocian "social" model to the Augustinian "psychological" model.

The tension between the threeness of the Persons and the oneness of God kept this unfortunate alternation going. The cause of these two Trinitarian models reacting against each other was the logic of identity and separation fed by the abstract and impersonal concept of "substance" as the source of God's oneness.

This "substance" base of Adam's centuries-old theology was neither theologically biblical nor philosophically transcendental. It came out of the philosophy of nature and second-intention logic, and from there, was projected onto God. As such, "substance" was not appropriate for the paradoxical thinking needed for an ontological insight into the pure-act depth where the threeness of the Persons is *integral* with the oneness of the divine essence of being.

Adam's fourth century theologians prevented this deepening by deciding that any theological venturing into the Triune revelation beyond the paternal-filial evidence completely transcends the human capacity to know God. As a result, the infinite interiority of divine personhood was walled-off from insight, and the otherness of personhood was overemphasized. In the social model of the Trinity, the other-directed Persons seemed to imply three Gods. In the psychological model, the other-directed Persons became abstracted into "subsistent relations."

The Meaning of Personhood in Trinitarian Theology

If there had been any significant understanding of the interiority of any person as a person (finite or infinite), theology could have been freed to develop accordingly. Interiority in each of the divine Persons would mean that each Person knows and loves *within* self. That would mean a deepening of the social model. Instead, there was simply one God knowing and loving, as in the psychological model. In that frame of reference, a recognition of the withinness of each Person would seem to imply three Gods instead of one. Therefore, the idea seemed to be that the interiority of each Person *could not* be admitted.

Furthermore, each Person having an interior life would bring into the theology of the Trinity the idea of receptivity. Each would be able to give and receive love. But the idea of receptivity was thought to be incompatible with the pure act of God. According to secondary logic, the opposite of the active is the passive. Receiving, since it is not thought to be active, is passive. And there is no passivity in pure act.

Lacking a sense of withinness in each of the divine Persons, theologians (especially St. Thomas) saw divine knowing and loving as the Persons being, themselves, their relationships. The Father-Son relationship of generation within the Father is intellective. And the Father-Son relationship of spirating the Holy Spirit is volitional in the mode of love.

If, however, God is love as the Gospel says, each Person *is* (not has) the power to love. Without this loving *within* each Person, the Thomist "spiration" of loving *between* the Persons could not proceed. And since knowledge precedes love, the same is true about knowing. Each Person *is*, not has, the power to know. How could each Person be a *person* without *being* one who knows and loves?

For anyone whose thinking is based in the second-intention logic that greatly oversimplifies reality, such seeming complexity within the Trinity is too much of a mental burden. For the intuitive mind that thinks paradoxically, however, the infinite simplicity of God is an inexhaustibly-splendored richness.

Lacking what they needed in insight about the paradoxical interiority of personhood, and about the way of thinking required by this kind of insight, Adam's theologians struggled brilliantly with

Trinitarian doctrine while the giving-receiving interiority of each divine Person went missing.

Returning to Biblical Sources

In Chapter 13 of this book, on the likeness of Adam and Eve to God, the divine Persons are named according to the emphasis in their attributes: Power, Wisdom, and Love respectively. These are not proper, or personal, names. Neither are they relational names: Father, Son, and Spirit. The only proper name that God revealed to us is "I am who am" or "Yahweh."

In the light of the Christian revelation shining on the pre-Christian revelation, "I am who am" may be understood to include *both* the oneness *and* the threeness of the Divine Persons.

Jesus led the way to this understanding when he said, "Before Abraham came to be, I am." The people who heard him say these words were shocked. Their strict monotheism would not tolerate a man identifying himself with Yahweh or implying that there is more than one God. For his Trinitarian implication Jesus was condemned to death. He did not *explain* what he meant. His hearers were in no mood to listen.

Furthermore, God reveals. God does not explain. Revelation is divine; explanation is human. Necessarily, we want to understand something about Revelation. We want to explain it to ourselves by turning up the light within our intuition-based divinely inspired faith. This act of elucidation requires a philosophy that is adequate for our theology. It requires an ontology based on our immediate intuition of *is*; not just a metaphysics that is beyond physics. And an adequate ontology requires a turnaround in our self-concept from being a rational animal to being a rational person in the ontological genus of persons together with the angels and the three divine Persons.

When we consciously enter into our true setting in being, we can ask, "How do the three divine Persons of the Christian revelation relate to the one God of the pre-Christian revelation? In other words, how are three Persons one God in "I am who am"?

The Meaning of Personhood in Trinitarian Theology

This is a theological question. It is both a biblical and a person-based starting point for Trinitarian theology. (The "I" and the "Who" are personal, not abstract.)

We know from Scripture that the first Person is *both* the Father of the Son (the Word), *and* the Father of creatures (their Creator). His implied name, therefore, is "I am who am, you *are.*"

We also know from Scripture that the Word became one of us as our Redeemer. He is both with the Father and with us. In both relationships, his implied name is "I am who am, *with* you."

The name of the third Person, both in relation to the other divine Persons and to us, is "I am who am, *within* you." This name identifies the Spirit as the Love-Person *within* the other two Persons, and, also, *within* us.

The three Persons together share the personal name: "I am who am." As "you are," "with you," and "within you," they are different whole Persons. Deeper yet, each of the three are "you are," "with you" and "within you," each emphasizing differently. The *emphasis* within a paradoxical integration is the key to some degree of understanding of the Great Mystery.

In relation to the world of finite beings, all three Persons are creative, redemptive, and sanctifying. But the first Person is, by emphasis, the Creator. The second Person is, by emphasis, the Redeemer, and the third Person is the Sanctifier.

Noticeably, these other-directed identifications (creator, redeemer, and sanctifier) are the same as those recognized by the fourth century theologians. These are names for the triune God's world-directed operations. They are not proper names for the Persons within the interior life of the Trinity.

The age-old conflict between what the theologians called "the immanent Trinity" and "the economic Trinity" (God within God and God in relation to us) disappears in the three divine names, each of which signifies the Persons in both their immanent and economic relationships.

This way of thinking about the Triune God is not loaded with logical abstractions that make God seem cold, objective, and far away. Instead, truly biblical thinking can make our hearts "burn within us" (*Luke* 24:32).

The Adam-Eve Likeness of "I am Who am"

My personal experience in pondering the mystery of the Trinity reached a high point on the Vigil of Pentecost in 1959. I began to see beyond the parental into the spousal depth of the divine Persons.

Passionately interested in the ontological significance of life, I had been struggling with the meaning of marriage. On that day, toward evening, it occurred to me that the biblical Eve from Adam seemed like an image and likeness of the second divine Person proceeding from the first. In *Genesis* 1: 26-27 and 2: 21-24, the human male and female are described as created in the image and likeness of God with the woman created from the man. Adam called Eve "bone of my bone, and flesh of my flesh." Therefore, "they shall be two in one flesh." This "two in one" seemed similar to the "three in one" of the Trinity. I saw the likeness of the Holy Spirit in the loving commitment (the inner spirit of union) that made a man and woman two-in-one.

The main problem with this spousal analogy is obviously the likeness of Eve to the second divine Person revealed as the Son of the Father. The unsatisfactory prospect of a likeness of Eve to the Son might have been the main reason why the spousal analogy escaped the attention of Adam's theologians. Very much involved, also, was the biological concept of human sexuality, and the less than fully positive attitude toward women that prevailed throughout the ages of theological reflection on the triune nature of God.

Before 1959, however, I had developed a view of sexuality quite different from that of the surrounding culture. I saw the man-woman relationship as a kind of friendship more than as a tendency toward mutual possession. In that context, I was ready to see a man-woman relationship as a likeness of the triune God.

As a result, God-Incarnate seemed like a marriage of the feminine in God with the masculine in humanity. The spousal analogy seemed complete. I was satisfied that marriage means something truly wonderful and spiritually fulfilling. On the radiant morning of August 12, 1961, Robert Joyce and I were married. Our joyfully shared insight into the spousal depth of the Trinity affected us profoundly.

In 1978, as one of the speakers at the first convention of the Fellowship of Catholic Scholars, I revealed my initial thoughts about the meaning of sexuality in relation to the Trinity. No one of the theologians or philosophers protested. One of the bishops stood up and thanked me for my presentation.

Slowly over the years, my thinking continued to develop concerning the psychological and ontological meaning of sexuality, especially as constituted within the essence of personhood. Every person—human, angelic, and divine—is, by way of emphasis, either receivingly *giving* (masculine) or givingly *receiving* (feminine).

Consequently, the Power-Person of God imaged by Adam is receivingly giving. He is masculine in emphasis. "I am who am, you are" *receives* his own being within himself and *gives* personhood to the second divine Person. The Wisdom-Word of God, "I am who am, with you" is imaged by Eve." The Love-Person of God, "I am who am, within you" is imaged by the two-in-oneness of Adam and Eve.

"I am who am" is far more than a substance, and *is* three Persons so *inner-united* in their difference as to be one God. We cannot relate well with a substance. But we can lift our minds and hearts with joyful awe to Yahweh as Lover, Beloved, and Love.

In the long history of Trinitarian theology, the other-directed relationships between the Persons, without an inner receptivity within each one of them, meant that Eve's emphatic receptivity had no basis for a likeness to God. Consequently, an Adam-Eve analogy could not be relevant.

Furthermore, the concept of receptivity that was available to the theologians was passivized by their univocal logic. Since they knew that there could be no passivity in God, they were unable to recognize purely active receptivity with a different emphasis in each of the divine Persons.

Seeing the interiority of personhood, as both receiving and giving, opens the way for the biblical image and likeness of God to emerge into awareness and devotion. The spousal-parental relationship between the man and woman of *Genesis* surely includes their *intra*-personal sexuality as the source of their *inter*-personal sexuality.

The receiving kind of *giving* within the man and the giving kind of *receiving* within the woman are not only psychological and physical, but primarily spiritual and transcendental. As such, and by way of Adam and Eve as an image and likeness of God, we can see the receivingly-giving emphasis within the first divine Person, the opposite emphasis in the second divine Person, and the richly-splendored unity of both in the third divine Person.

"I am Who am, you are" is the Person who is both emphatically giving (masculine) and correlatively receiving (feminine). "I am Who am, with you" is the emphatically receiving (feminine) and correlatively giving (masculine) Person. "I am Who am, within you" is emphatically both receiving and giving (feminine-masculine). Sexuality and personhood, therefore, are both transcendental. Thus, persons (human, angelic, and divine) are analogous. This analogy supports the correlation between Adam and Eve as (according to *Genesis*) *the* biblical image of the Trinity.[32]

The Spousal-Familial Meaning of Christianity

At the supreme source of Christianity, the spousal-parental God who *is* Love characterizes the whole religion as having a marital and familial meaning. The spousal-parental Trinity is the source of the covenantal design of divine revelation beginning with the people of Israel as the bride of Yahweh[33] and leading to the Church as the bride of Christ.[34]

Jesus performed his first miracle at a celebration of marriage in Cana of Galilee. His Kingdom of Heaven celebrates the Marriage of the Lamb (*Revelation* 19). Forever and ever, the saved will enjoy the beatific love of the spousal-familial Trinity in one glorious and joyful family of God.

The holy family at the heart of it all is the spousal union of Mary and Joseph like the union between Eve and Adam in the beginning. Their son, Jesus, conceived by the Holy Spirit, is the incarnational marriage of God and man. The celibacy of all three in this family points to the spousal-familial essence of each single person within their own personhood.

Culturally today, marriage has lost its moorings and its meaning. Once again, the world depends upon the Church to rescue and liberate civilization from an age of darkness. We will begin to see what the sacrament of marriage means to God when we receive into our minds and hearts the Most High Nuptial Celebration of affirmational love and friendship within the inner life of the three divine Persons.[35]

Developmental Reflection B

The Paradoxical Logic of Wisdom

In a world where computers are rapidly accumulating facts of every kind stored in their "brains," we tend to forget that we ourselves are far more than facts of any kind. Computers cannot even begin to compare with our transcendental power for actually knowing the *is* of anything.

To be is to be an essential unity of opposites. Every being is both unique and relational at once: paradoxical. The meaning of each opposite of the paradox is *inseparably within* the meaning of the other. For example, each person in the world is unique and is also related to every other person. Thus, a thing is unique only in the context of others in relation to which it is unique. And a relationship is at its best between things that are unique.

To separate these opposites is a) to lose their meaning, b) to lose the paradox, and c) to fall into the either-or logic of identity and separation.

Because every being, whether infinite or finite, is both unique and related (uniquely) with every other being that *is*, uniqueness and relatedness are transcendental. Our thinking about *being* requires, therefore, a method of transcendental reflection using a paradoxical logic.

This is not our usual way of thinking. Ordinarily, we do our thinking by means of grasping the whatness of things and forming concepts and judgments. But we cannot *grasp* the paradoxes of *being*. Paradoxical understanding is an intuitive insight, not a clear and distinct idea. *Being* requires a transcendental way of seeing and thinking by means of a logic of paradoxical reflection.

This logic is implicit in philosophical and theological reflection about divine revelation. By remaining implied, however, it tends to remain weak, and the mind easily falls into its either-or logic of identity and separation. The challenge is to strengthen our ability for paradoxical thinking, the better to understand our intuitive insights and to increase their light.

Metaphysics versus Ontology

Both metaphysics and ontology are about *being*, but differently. Metaphysics is the philosophical ultimate in the scientific way of thinking about *being*. It is preceded by the philosophy of physical nature, and is limited by its basically physical frame of reference. But ontology is transcendental wisdom about *being*. It is person-based, not cosmos-based. It begins with our *immediate* connection with *is*. Wisdom can *include* a scientific way of thinking, but it remains primarily and consistently intuitive.

Metaphysics, studied as it is after the philosophy of nature, takes a bow of recognition toward the intuition of being, then turns around and becomes an objective study of the ultimate causes of things. For this purpose, as the supreme science, metaphysics uses Adam's either-or logic.

Ontology (*ontos-logos* or being-logic) starts with the intuition of being, stays there, and ends there. That which is known is not just an object out there, but is another being *as being,* and is, in that sense, another subject. Ontology, therefore, is an intersubjective way of knowing, not just another objective way.

An orientation toward this intersubjective kind of ontology began in recent times with thinkers like Gabriel Marcel (d. 1973) and Martin Buber (d. 1955).

Metaphysics uses what is called "the judgment of separation" to distinguish between material and immaterial (spiritual) realities. Ontology recognizes the unique difference, that is not a separation, between material and immaterial being, and between infinite and finite being. Any kind of unity based on a judgment of separation remains an implicit, if not an explicit, separation. The way to understanding ontological or transcendental paradoxes requires no judgment of separation; rather it involves an intensification of an intuitive insight.

Recognizing that the agent intellect knows *being as being* is the difference between ontology as wisdom and metaphysics as a science. Metaphysicians who begin by abstractions and separations

The Paradoxical Logic of Wisdom

from material being have, and retain, a cosmological frame of reference. They do not fully realize that human eyes, as eyes, see things differently from animal eyes. This kind of realization requires a transcendental insight into the way in which human eyes are ontologically *within* the agent intellect, and the intellect is actively operative *within* the very seeing power of human eyes.

This intense ontological integration of senses and intellect not only intellectifies the senses but sensifies the intellect. Spiritual sensing means spiritually (not physically) seeing the splendor of truth, goodness and beauty, and the ugliness of evil. Spiritual sensing means, also, spiritually (not physically) hearing words and music; feeling joy and sorrow; tasting *being* (*sapientia*); and smelling fragrances. Insight can be a transcendental kind of sensing.

Because we, by being persons, have this spiritually sensing power, we know ontologically from the moment of conception that God *is*. Far from conscious awareness, the intellect of a one-celled person is in the act of knowing God *is*.

How can anyone make such a claim? Certainly not by scientific investigation, nor by metaphysical analysis, but by *transcendental common sense*.

Ordinary common sense is the result of the agent intellect actually knowing—before, through, and especially beyond the senses—what we consciously know, but do not necessarily know we know, or how we know it. Transcendental common sense is the power by which we are able to recognize and appreciate ordinary common sense. We do not have to know consciously that we have transcendental common sense, but we have the power to become conscious of it, whether we want to do so or not.

Transcendental Paradoxes

First of all, there are different kinds of opposites. Some are paradoxical; others not. Some are transcendental; others not.

Opposites are not contradictions. Opposites have something in common; contradictories do not. Hot and cold have temperature in common. Tall and short have height in common. Giving and receiving have sharing in common. But these opposites are not paradoxes. The yin and yang of China, for example, is not a true paradox, but a balance of opposites like hot and cold, and tall and short.

A paradox is a mystery of opposites. It is an apparent, not an actual, contradiction. For example, dying in order to live seems contradictory, but is not, because the two terms, as used, do not have univocal and separate meanings. Opposites that mutually "cross over" into, or are within, each other, are not clearly definable. Examples are giving in a receiving way and receiving in a giving way.

Complimentary opposites balance the two ends of whatever they have in common. Paradoxical opposites are more than balances; their meanings *mutually* exist *within* each other. They do so in three different ways: naturally, supernaturally, and transcendentally.

Natural paradoxes such as gentle firmness and firm tenderness are qualities that describe some, not all, realities.

Supernatural paradoxes such as the Gospel's "dying to live," and "losing to find" are actions or ways of life that describe some, not all, realities. The infinite unity of God's justice and mercy is another example of a supernatural paradox.

Transcendental paradoxes are attributes of *being* that describe everything that is as *being*. The *power* for knowing these paradoxes is also paradoxical.

Transcendental opposites are not complementary. They are co-relative. Male and female, for example, because they necessarily include physical qualities, are complementary. Masculine and feminine qualities, because these are not *necessarily* physical, or even psychological, can be fully within each other as co-relative attributes, and can be transcendental in meaning.

Ontological intensification of pre-conceptual insight is needed especially for thinking about the transcendence-immanence of the supernatural both in the Incarnation and in the Trinity of God. Metaphysical thinking, because it retains its cosmological frame of reference, is less apt for theological elucidations. Metaphysics is more prone to either-or than to paradoxical thinking. Theological reflection on the co-relational divine Persons calls for the ultimate in transcendental thinking.

The Paradoxical Logic of Wisdom

Transcendental and supernatural paradoxes are called mysteries. Gabriel Marcel defines a mystery as "a problem that encroaches on its own data." As the words "problem," "encroaches," and "data" show, this definition uses scientific terms, and is not transcendental. Transcendentally, a mystery is a paradoxical unity of co-relatives that mutually exist *within* each other (they do not encroach upon each other), and which invite pre-conceptual insights that call for inexhaustible elucidation by means of paradoxical thinking. No clearly definable concepts are adequate for elucidating something about mysteries as mysteries.

Opposites remain paradoxes only as long as these opposites are understood as inseparable. This kind of understanding is insightful more than conceptual. Concepts are identifications that separate *this* from *that*. By trying to conceptualize a paradox, we tend to fall into the either-or kind of logic. Instead, we need to stay with the paradox and successfully integrate paradoxical logic with the either-or kind. This integration is insightful-conceptual: itself paradoxical.

Adam's philosophers struggled mightily to deal with the legacy of Descartes: his massive separation between the senses and reason. Some of them, Hegel especially, tried to solve Kant's post-Cartesian opposites ("antinomies") with a dialectical logic that began with *this* and *that*. Where a philosopher begins is where he ends. If he begins in logic, he ends in logic.

If you start out with a separation like "this and that" in order to surpass a separation, you end up with a univocal identity. For Hegel the terminus of his dialectical thesis-antithesis-synthesis became a univocal absolute far from the real meaning of being as *being*, where there is neither identity nor separation. Had Hegel begun with *this* and *this*, he would not have needed an antithesis in his logic, nor would he have proposed a dialectical method of thinking. He would have intensified, instead, his ontological insight into the co-relative *being* of *this and this*.

As transcendental, every being is both immanent and transcendent. Each being's withinness and otherness means that each is within every other, while being fully other than each one of them.

Thus, I am within the world and God, and the world and God are within me. Seeing being in this way is an intensity of insight (other than the spatial and the temporal) that requires a transcendentally paradoxical way of thinking.

Furthermore, the active receptivity of our *power* for thinking in this way is also transcendentally paradoxical. It is, itself, a unity of opposites that empowers us to think paradoxically. The active receptivity of the agent intellect is a giving kind of receiving. And the receptive activity of the agent will is a receiving kind of giving.

In knowing the being of anything, the actively-receptive agent intellect knows that this being *is* and *has* a nature. Knowing the *is* of a being is a pure-act of receptive insight. Simultaneously, knowing that this being *has* a nature activates the conceptualizing process. This *is-has* kind of knowing is the pre-conceptual source of both paradoxical and either-or ways of thinking.

The Adam-Eve Paradox

This book about the future of Adam and Eve and their power for wisdom about love is an ontological reflection. It is not scientifically metaphysical. Ontology is intuitive, reflective, paradoxical, poetic, descriptive, and declarative. While the philosophical Adam without Eve is a metaphysician, the philosophical Eve without Adam is a mystical pantheist. But together they are ontologists. Together they are interested in seeing how the light of *being* assimilates and transforms the way we know everything in human life from a speck of dust to the Trinity of God.

Active receptivity (opposites within each other) is the paradoxical power for wisdom about love. Adam's discovery of his own active receptivity (the Eve within him) raises his metaphysics from its demise in our time, and elevates it into the transforming light of being. The result can become a renewal in theology that forever deepens its roots, spreads its branches, and increases its fruits.

Developmental Reflection C

A Little Less Than the Angels

Why does the creation story of *Genesis* not include the creation of the angels? Why does *Genesis* start with us, not with them? Is it because we are sinners? Many of the angels were sinners, too. They, however, cannot be redeemed. We can.

The Bible is God's revelation about our redemption. It reveals very little about creation out of nothing. In order to be saved, there are many things we do not need to know. So why would we wonder about them? Are these things really none of our business?

Wondering why, and asking questions for answers that would deepen and enrich our faith, is part of our business as human persons. We are supposed to be rational for a reason. Much about us is sub-rational, irrational, and trans-rational. But rationality is the distinguishing characteristic of our nature as persons. Naturally, we want to know why.

As John Paul II tells us, faith and reason are like two wings that work together. *We can, and should, wonder about the creation that occurred before this world began.* Finding some of the answers could moderate the overbearing way in which theories of evolution have been promoted, and could challenge the simplistic way in which creationism, its adversary, has been presented. Also, more answers about origins could slow the surge of runaway atheism caused by intellectual problems with the existence of evil.

Facing the Gnostic Eve

Many who have tried to explain their intuitions about the origin of things have gone off into fables and "leaning towers" of the mind. They have not studied, first of all, how we know reality. Nor have they realized that an ontological question requires an ontological (deeper than imaginary, and deeper than metaphysical) way of thinking. They "sense" a light within themselves, but prematurely try to express it. Falling into their imagination, they project images and even wild and chaotic fictions of what they think they know. In this way, Gnostics and occultists go into what they regard as privileged, even "secret," knowledge. They search for enlightenment and an illuminating knowledge so unfamiliar that it is regarded as being unavailable to the masses.

Their *gnosis*, however, is pantheistic. It is really a passive-based, yet hyperactive, interpretation of human origins. They do not realize that the agent intellect of every human person is a *finite* pure act of preconsciously knowing the *being* of whatever is known, and that this knowing is actually the intuitive source of common sense. When not understood ontologically, the *light of the agent intellect* is prone to being misinterpreted in an extremely shortsighted manner. And the *finite*, pure act *freedom of the agent will* (see p. 72) is not even suspected to exist. That is partly why Gnostics think we are saved by knowledge alone. They are far from being authentic ontologists.

Furthermore, they obsess about the problem of evil, see the world, the body, and matter as evil, and use rituals and magic to escape. Their intellectual neurosis persists in a great variety of sects that thrive in underground movements that have surfaced and receded throughout Western history. Examples are the various schools of Gnosticism: Syrian, Hellenistic, Alexandrian, dualistic, and others. More recently, this affliction of the soul emerged in a new form called the Illuminati, that was founded in 1776 by Adam Weishaupt, an influence in Masonry and in other secret societies.

Gnosticism began with Eve's fall from active receptivity into the passivity of pantheism. Gnostics are children of Eve without Adam, but with the serpent instead. In the reign of Hadrian, c. 120 A.D., the Naassene Gnostics even worshipped the serpent as a symbol of wisdom that they thought the God of the Jews suppressed.

Alone, and without the theistic Adam, Eve is not able to recover the lost gift: the ontological, actively receptive, awareness of *being* as paradoxically both infinite and finite, yet one in Christ.

What is it that would explain such a wild, pessimistic phenomenon as Gnosticism throughout human history?

We humans seem to know something about ourselves that we try to connect with, do not know how, and really do not want to face. *God does not tell us directly, but only indirectly, what it is.* We alone can recognize, acknowledge, and admit it, if only we could discover it ontologically. Actually, the truth in the depths of us is in our face every breath we take. It haunts our common sense. Adam and Eve within us know what it is. And we, too, can know. (See Chapter 20.)

Because of the depth of our passivity, we lamely assume that God would have to reveal to us our ontological condition. But God gave us an agent will, as well as an agent intellect. So we are fully capable of facing and admitting the truth about ourselves. We ourselves, because of the freedom of our agent will, must be ontologically responsible for our own fall from active receptivity into the passive condition of being within us. Adam and Eve, while ontologically responsible with the rest of us, were first to become *morally* responsible, before they became our first parents.

So, in searching for an answer to the question about *Genesis* starting with the second, not with the first, creation, we do have an access to an answer, but it is not to be found in the deviant fling of the Gnostics. There is an ontological way of finding the light and warmth of *being*, in our agent intellect and agent will, and from there, finding the truth we seek.

Above all, the mysteries of our faith are not excuses for mental passivity. They are special invitations to active mental receptivity. Pondering is one of our noblest human occupations.

First, the Angels

We see angels showing up here and there across the pages of the Bible. But they are noticeably absent in the creation story. God must have created the angels in an original beginning other than the beginning revealed in *Genesis*. These personal beings were, and are forever, simple spiritual likenesses of the three divine Persons.

At the dawn of creation, all persons, created and uncreated, were *beings* together. They were communal and intensely intimate, without the least interference of space between them or time for any process of development within that space.

Persons, because they are *persons*, do not need impersonal space and time in order to *be*. Extensional and temporal conditions are necessarily imperfect. Space is essentially passive. Time is the result of impersonal motion in space.

Why would God, who is infinitely perfect personhood, create anything impersonal and imperfect like space and time? Could God even do so at all, unless space and time are involved in a creaturely movement of imperfection toward perfection?

Something must have happened in the original world of persons to bring about space and time. These imperfect conditions must have been caused *by*, *within*, and *from* finite persons moving from imperfection toward perfection.

But the angels, by being simply spiritual persons, are unable to cause a complex condition such as space and time. Only a more complex kind of person could have been involved.

Is it possible, then, that persons who were "a little less than the angels" (*Psalm* 8:6), or who were both spiritual and spiritually material by nature, actually caused the spatial-temporal conditions in the world of being?[36] If so, the original creation would have been a community of three major *kinds* of persons: infinite, finitely simple, and finitely complex.

Did We Pre-Exist this World?

According to the story told in *Genesis*, we did not pre-exist this world. The stars, sun, moon, earth, plants, and animals preceded us. This story, however, does not say *why* it omits the creation of angelic persons, and *why* it places other persons who are a little less than the angels at the end of a huge spatial-temporal process.

For an answer to these questions about *why*, *we* can look only to the transcendental structure of *being* itself. But how? By what light?

Aristotle in ancient times, Thomas Aquinas in medieval times, and Jacques Maritain in modern times (all metaphysicians) realized that the agent intellect causes our human knowledge. They called it a *light*. But none of them realized what this light actually is: an act of knowing the *is* of all that is by a pure act of *finite* knowing that was once perfect, and is now unconscious and preconscious. Ordinarily,

A Little Less than the Angels

we do not know *that* we are knowing in this way because we are alienated from ourselves.

The above-mentioned metaphysicians acknowledged our intuition of being and the transcendentals of being, but turned away from them and became concerned about objects: this and that. They failed to recognize the agent intellect as knowing the *is* of whatever the person is knowing. Consequently, they identified the transcendentals of being, but were unable to think consistently in a transcendental way. On their own terms, they were not person-based ontologists.

An ontologist knows *being*, and knows that knowing it is the *light* in which to think transcendentally about reality. Faced with the question about our pre-existing this world, an ontologist sees it quite differently from a metaphysician, or from a theologian who thinks about revealed truths with the help of a metaphysical philosophy.

An ontologist looks to *being* and to its transcendental structure for the light in which to see whether or not we pre-existed this world. On one side is Biblical revelation that shines its *transcendent* light on the transcendental light of *being*. On the other side is the best in metaphysics.

The transcendent side is supernatural; the metaphysical side is natural. Both, like two wings, help us to elucidate what we see in the transcendental light of *being*. Both the supernatural and the natural lights are included within the transcendental light, just as a bird's two wings are included within the bird itself. These other lights shining on the light of *being* help us to see the structure of *being*. But neither of them is, or has, the power of the transcendental light of *is*. The light of *being* is not just a power of our nature, but is a power of our being. This light is neither natural like metaphysics, nor supernatural like divine revelation; it is radically ontological and transcendental.

The first thing we notice about the structure of *being* is that we know the *is* of things whether or not we know that we are knowing in this way. So there is a noticeable gap between our conscious mind and our preconscious mind. We rarely, if ever, do our thinking from the transcendental viewpoint of *is*. Why this weakness? Why this fall from the clear light of *is* into the darkness of not knowing that we know it?

Looking to Biblical revelation, we find a clue. We discover in *Genesis* that we were "cast out," "expelled," from clarity into darkness. We were conscious, then we became largely unconscious. That is why our conscious mind is alienated from the agent light, and is thrown outward toward the objects of space and time.

According to the structure involved, we are beings *before* the existence of the unknowing world of space and time with its unknowing stars, sun, moon, earth, and all the rest. We are not beings that follow them in *being*. They "follow" us. We follow them in spatial-temporal *existence*, but not in *being*.

Being and Existence

Existence (*existere*) means "to stand out of." The Latin *sistere* means "to stand." Standing is a way of saying *being*. The Latin prefix "ex" means "out of." Existence, therefore, means a *being* standing in itself while being cast out of itself.

Thinking ontologically about *Genesis*, then, we can see that God created persons to *be*, not primarily to ex-ist. Our being did not necessarily have to ex-ist at all. Ex-istence in this space-time world is, therefore, a condition of being cast out. In the world of beings as being, we were fully conscious of *being* before we ex-isted and before we became unaware of what we now preconsciously know.

Fallen angels (not good angels) ex-ist because, within their being they spiritually imploded and "threw" themselves into their own being where they are hopelessly fixated forever. But their simple self-thrownness is a strictly spiritual result that could not cause spatial and temporal conditions by which material things ex-ist.

Only a complex self-thrownness could cause the outwardness of space and time. Persons who, in the beginning, were a little less than the angels could implode, but also could throw themselves outward, thus causing space and time. Their fallen ex-istence would become inevitably spatial and temporal. They could pre-exist space and time only as beings self-cast-out of themselves into an ontological coma. In that state of ex-istence, they were not consciously functioning persons.

Why Are We Here?

Because of our being-based (not moral) disorder, multitudes of persons (we humans) began to ex-ist in space and time. We are being outside of ourselves, that is, are self-expelled (*Genesis* 3:23) from our original selves. Our spatial and temporal existence is powered by God for aiding us to recover the perfection we lost.

With our usual way of seeing and thinking, we cannot understand how this can be so. But from a transcendental point of view, we can see that our ex-istence began in the world of being as a fall from *being*, and that it continues in this space-time world as the same ex-istence, but as one that is trying to return to full *being*.

We are accustomed to thinking from the viewpoint of space and time, not from the vantage point of the original creation. We settle ourselves in the perspective of this space-time world where we see everything from the outside inward.

If, however, we begin to see and think about things from the starting point of the original creation, we will have to go through a turnaround similar to the Copernican revolution. Then we will be able to see our beginning in this world from a person-based point of view, not merely from space and time. The cosmos, the redemptive universe, will be lit up by the light of the new perspective.

In that beingful light, we will be able to see what really happens at conception. That is when the ex-istence of our being begins to function redemptively.

According to our usual way of thinking, two cells (a sperm and an ovum) meet, unite, and God instantly creates our soul and infuses it into our one-celled body. God is "Johnny on the spot" whenever a man and woman conceive a new life. And we "observers" have confused this coming into functional existence with our very coming to *be*.

Why do we accept such a low level, stimulus-response manner of interpreting God's creation of human persons? Many times, the stimulus is a sinful act between a man and woman. God seems to be, in this centuries-old view of our existence, a *"deus ex machina,"* a kind of press-button mechanism. In the wake of this dualistic view of our origin, someone like Descartes understandably would come up with a mechanistic philosophy of the human person.

Our intelligence naturally looks for something more consistent with the infinite power of God. Seeing all of reality as person-based opens the way for a new, more mature, and more ontologically grounded, way of thinking.

To Receive or Not to Receive the Gift of Being

Active receptivity is the key to understanding something about the being of *all* persons, finite and infinite. Without infinitely active (pure act) receptivity, both within and between the divine Persons, their infinitely giving-receiving, interpersonal relating would be impossible. Giving without receiving is dysfunctionally relational, and is far from genuinely interrelational, especially for God.

Finite persons (pure finite acts) are also totally mutual in their powers of giving and receiving. But, according to the unconsciously univocal, spatialized way of thinking in much of our metaphysics and theology, receptivity is passive, not active. So, we need an insight into active receptivity to understand personhood in each of the three major kinds of persons.

Finite persons who are simply spiritual by nature (the angels) have one kind of active receptivity; they can receive the gift of being. Complex persons, however, who are both spiritual and spiritually material (humans) have two kinds of active receptivity; they can receive both the gift of being and the gift of their "little less than the angels" *kind* of being. Active receptivity for their human kind of being is their spiritual materiality that is not originally physical.[37]

In the very beginning of our being *out of nothing*, we failed to receive our being fully. So, our spiritual matter tended to become physical. Failing meant going into ontological shock and passing out as it were. As a result, our spiritual matter became passive (passed out) and feebly tended toward recovery.

The active receptivity of all persons is both intellective and volitional. All say within themselves, either infinitely or finitely, "I am." Immediately, the angels knew that they were finite and that God is infinite. Volitionally, these simply spiritual persons were free to receive or not to receive fully the *gift* of their finite being. Those

A Little Less than the Angels

who were happy to be finite said, spontaneously and fully, *yes* to the Giver, and they fully received the gift. Immediately, they entered everlasting union with God.

Other angelic persons, immediately and falsely willing (choosing) to be infinite together with God, said *no* to being finite. At once, their condition became hellish forever.

The less simple, or spiritually material persons (we), could also say, by virtue of our perfectly gifted agent will, either *yes* or *no*. Additionally, however, we could say, instead, *maybe*. We could *hesitate* about being finite. Our hesitation, by its very nature, caused spacing and timing. *Maybe* (partly *yes* and partly *no*) started an impersonal kind of situation not originally intended by God. But, by virtue of the *yes* in our maybe, God responded for the sake of redeeming us.

The partial *no* in our *maybe* caused a collapse of active receptivity into passivity in our spiritually material personhood. The partial *yes* in our *maybe*, however, was responsible for a vehement reaction against our passivity. The result became a passive-reactive state of being that caused (passive) space and (reactive) time.

Falling somewhere between saying, together with the angels, either *yes* or *no*, some (or perhaps most) of the spiritually material persons became hesitators. We said (immediately and freely) within ourselves, "let me think about this: *maybe* I will, *maybe* I won't agree to be fully finite." At once, we lost our pristine gift of active receptivity. We collapsed into an evolutionary process for resolving our *maybe* into either a *yes* or a *no*. Individually and together, we dropped ourselves into a state of reactive passivity that generated the energy (not the same as power) that can be associated with what physicists have called the "big bang." This ontological explosion was a *spreading-out* (in space) of a chaotic kind of energy that *tended to return* (in time) from ex-istence to be-ing: from being outside-self-and-others to being *within* self and *with* others.

By itself, however, this impersonal, evolutionary energy could not return to the personal state of being toward which it tended. It needed power. God's redemptive love became the creative *power* that transformed this wild energy into a creative process such as that described in *Genesis*: the spatial-temporal development of the imperfect, but good, redemptive universe.

"All Spaced Out and Doing Time"

God, in creating the world, responded to the *yes* in our *maybe* with power and love. We were given the space-time opportunity to say, finally, either *yes* or *no*. This "second chance" is the space-time world in which we now live.

Our original *maybe* spaced us out for doing time. Our hesitation to receive the gift of finite personhood reduced the power of our active receptivity into an extremely reactive passivity that generated the energy we needed for returning to our active receptivity. Within us, however, this energy cannot do so without power. Our intellective and volitional powers, together with divine grace, can transform our individual energy into a living *yes* to the gift of our being and to the Giver.

According to *Genesis*, the redemptive creation proceeded in time until human persons appeared on the scene. According to the subsequent revelation by God, the redemption was completed in the Incarnate Savior's death and resurrection. With the founding of his sacramental church, the *explicit activity* of salvation for *maybe*-sayers began. Those who would finally emerge (at death) from the redemptive creation with an emphatic *yes* in their personhood, but with a residue of *maybe*, would enter the process of expiatory purgation before reaching the glory they freely failed to receive in the original beginning.

From Spiritual to Physical Materiality

Our body began to ex-ist at conception. At that time-in-space, our passivized spiritual matter began to express itself in a physical way for our redemption. Our newly conceived body did not receive our soul; our soul received our body.

Our soul is not the same as our spirit. Our spirit remains actively receptive, though unconsciously and preconsciously so. Our soul is our spiritual substantial-form as fallen. Our body is our spiritual matter as fallen. Fallen spiritual matter is physicalized at conception for the sake of the redemptive process.

At death, then, our soul does not leave our body. Instead, our physical body leaves our soul as our personhood retains our body spiritually, not physically. This spiritual immortality of the human body makes re-incarnation into multiple bodies impossible, but resurrection of the *same* body possible.

The world of material elements, plants, and animals emerged in an evolutionary process that originated in the passive-reactive energy of our *maybe*. Together with God's redemptive power, this energy co-generated physical, organic, and sensient existents that are more like us than we are like them. All of them are person-based in the sense that *maybe*-saying persons caused their energy, while three divine Persons empowered this energy toward orderly and inter-relational formations.

When this physical-organic-sensient universe had evolved to an appropriate state of existence, our fallen beings began to express themselves in a physical-organic-sensient manner. This happened in a spatial-temporal sequence. All of us did not come at once into this redemptive universe. When our time arrived, the spiritual matter of our fallen being, by the activity of our parent's gametes, expressed itself in our redemptive matter so that we could say, eventually and finally, either *yes* or *no* to God.

Noticeably, everything in this redemptive universe has a *may-be* (maybe) kind of structure. Maybe I will take the next breath; maybe not. Maybe we will have good weather for the harvest this year; maybe not. Maybe the sun will shine tomorrow; maybe not. And on and on.

From Revelation to Explication

Revelation is not explanation. *Genesis* reveals, but it does not explain what it tells us to believe. It says that Adam and Eve were our first parents, and that they were created in a paradisal world, and that they were unsatisfied with their being as given to them. They wanted to be more like God than they were created to be.

This Revelation is a simple story that can be told to children. But it is loaded with ontological implications. The main implication is that there are two creations: one absolutely *out of nothing*, and the other *out of something* fallen from *being* into ex-istence, specifically out of the energy that exploded from the fall. These two creations interpermeate each other so densely that they seem impossible to distinguish from each other. An ontological act of intellection is required, therefore, to discern their difference within their unity.

Previous attempts to do so have resulted in various forms of Gnosticism or indulgence in stories, symbols, and images warped by a space-time point of view. Transcendental thinking that begins with a powerfully conscious awareness of *being* is required. From that point of view we can begin to see what the simple story of creation, and of Adam and Eve, implies. The result will not be some kind of Gnostic, Origenistic, occult, or new-age spin. It will be a clear-eyed ontological theology that can be developed through being-based pondering.

So, why are we all spaced out and doing time? We are here and now called to repent and to become more and more, a little less than the angels.

Sources: Robert E. Joyce, *Affirming Our Freedom in God: The Untold Story of Creation; Facing the Dark Side of Genesis: A New Understanding of Ourselves; A Perfect Creation: The Light Behind the Dark Side of Genesis; The Origin of Pain and Evil. LifeCom*, Box 1832, St. Cloud, MN 56302.

The main source is the forthcoming book by Robert E. Joyce, *When God Said Be, We Said Maybe: An Inside Story of the Creation, the Crash, and the Recovery.* (St. Cloud, MN, LifeCom, 2010).

Developmental Reflection D

"I know that my Redeemer lives." *Job* 19:25

"You shall see the Son of man ascend up where he was before." *John* 6:63

The Background Storyline

Why would the serpent want Eve to abandon her likeness to God? What was the fallen Lucifer's motivation? *Genesis* does not say, but clearly leaves this kind of question to be asked.

Why, however, would anyone want to "psychoanalyze" Lucifer? The reason is to understand better his influence on us, instead of not bothering about it and even denying that such an influence exists.

The result of searching through and beyond the wall between the two creations (the one described in *Genesis*, and the creation of the angels omitted by *Genesis*), is a serious speculation within the perspective of ontological theology. It is not, nor can it ever be, an historical report. Its authenticity depends upon its internal fidelity to clues within the context of divine revelation.

One of the main interests of an ontological theologian is the meaning of personhood as presented in Scripture. The meaning is implicit. Not until theologians were faced with the mystery of three Persons in one God did they begin to realize what a person is, as a person. The missing creation in *Genesis*, and the missing person in theology and philosophy, are co-results of the missing ontology.[38]

According to Biblical sources, everything in the created universe was good. But nothing was perfect. In fact, there was a tree of the knowledge of good and evil in the near vicinity of Adam and Eve. They were obviously on trial. But why? And an evil serpent was crawling around in the shadows. Who was he? Why was he there? That malign presence is the first scriptural hint that another world of creatures exists.

The First Creation

In the first beginning, all were finite; all were perfect. God could not have created immediately out of nothing anything that was less than perfect, since God was the only agent of this very first act of causality.

There were multitudes of angels. One was the highest and the closest to God. His name was Lucifer, the Light-Bearer. He was powerful and brilliant with the light of insight. But something he saw—or the way he saw it—presented a mighty challenge to him. What was it? Can we even know?

Revelations do not explain; they announce and proclaim. They are loaded with implications for our explication. We are called to raise questions and search for answers, especially from the viewpoint of *being* itself.

Something about the structure of *being* must have been a severe problem for Lucifer. Something agitated him ontologically. An explanation of what it was, though not explicit in divine revelation, would have to be implied ontologically, and also Scripturally.

Genesis does not say explicitly what Lucifer's challenge was. Its story, however, shows us that something about Eve, especially, "got on his nerves." He conquered her. But another woman, Mary, would conquer him (3:15). Something about Mary's involvement in the structure of *being* is implied.

Based on the previous reflection, "A Little Less Than the Angels," we can see that the two in Eden represented multitudes of persons who were beings like them. These (human) persons were with them in the original creation. All were lower and more complex in being than the angels. One of them could have been closest to the angels. Following the evidence of Scriptural revelation, we might assume that this person would have been Mary. None of *this*, however, would have been a problem for Lucifer.

The galling truth was something else involving these "little less than the angels" persons. One amongst *them* was much greater than Lucifer. His being reached from end to end, from God to the nature of the lowest created persons. He was *Being Triumphant*, Emmanuel (God *with* us), the consummation of the ontological, person-based

The Background Storyline

relationship between the finite and the infinite. He was the Wisdom-Word of God actively receiving within the divine nature the nature of the lowest kind of person, becoming one with *them*. He was, therefore, the King of the whole finite world including Lucifer himself.

When he, the highest, saw that he would be ruled by the greatest within the lowest, he said, "I will not serve anyone lower than I am no matter how great he is." The decision threw this highest of the angels into an obsessing turmoil forever.

Before the existence of space and time, at the very moment that God said "be," some of the angels said "no" to the gift of their finite being; others said "yes." The simplicity of their essence allowed only two choices. Those who said "yes" were confirmed in their perfection forever. Those who said "no" were confirmed in torment forever. Lucifer, now Satan, became the "king of the no-sayers," and "the father of lies."

Those who were a little less than the angels, and who were more complex in their being, could say, like them, either "yes" or "no." But they could also say, instead, "maybe." Mary, possibly the highest of the lowest, said "yes." Her "yes" would give notice to Lucifer-Satan that he could have made a supremely better choice than he did. The highest of the angels would not serve the King, but she among the lowest—Mary—would serve in his place.

Adam and Eve, along with many others of their kind, including ourselves, said "maybe." A few, or perhaps many said, like the good angels, fully "yes," and were confirmed in their perfection forever.

Those who said "maybe" about being finite fell into a reactive kind of passivity that reduced them into an ontological coma. But God responded redemptively to the partial "yes" in their "maybe," and to the explosion of passive-reactive energy that resulted as they fell from being into their ex-istence. In some kind of evolutionary manner, God used this energy to create the visible redemptive universe.

Only persons were created out of nothing. Passive matter, from which everything subpersonal originated, is the result of a person-based catastrophe in the structure of being itself, together with

God's redemptive response. None of these resultant creatures are evil. All are good, but none are perfect. Only persons, both infinite and finite, can be perfect.

Adam, Eve, and the Serpent

In due time, Adam and Eve entered the redemptive universe on earth. They, especially the woman, became a matter of concern for the serpent. After all, a woman, Mary, was in his face telling him that he could have made a perfectly good choice.

The serpent, because he hated the King who included in himself the lowly nature of Adam and Eve, wanted to make sure that these two in Eden would not regain what they lost by changing their "maybe" to "yes." He wanted an ultimate "no" from them so they could enter *his* "kingdom" and be *ruled* by him. So he lied to Eve about her likeness to God.

Eve had already said less than fully "yes" to her being, along with Adam and the rest of us. So she quickly fell for the serpent's deception, and easily convinced Adam to think and act likewise. Then she, together with Adam, became aware of their "nakedness," their self-projected objectness. They became conscious of their condition as being *"cast out"* of themselves and out of the paradise of the Kingdom of God (*Genesis* 3:23).

Adam and Eve became the parents of many others of their kind—those who needed to enter the redemptive universe. Lucifer-Satan kept his eye on all of them, hoping that all would join him in his kingdom of hatred. He wanted them all to change their "maybe" to "no" forever.

"Who Is He?"

Finally, according to God's redemptive plan, Mary came into this cast-out world. She escaped the watchful eye of Satan. She was so lowly he did not even notice her.

One day, an angel asked Mary to become the mother of the great King who would come into this world. She actively received him into her womb by the Holy Spirit. According to Simeon's words to her in the temple, her child, the promised King, was the suffering

The Background Storyline

servant described by the prophets. He had come into this world to be its redeemer.

But Lucifer-Satan took note of Jesus, and wondered who he was. "If he is the one I hate, what is he doing on the earth? If he is the King descended from the realm above, this is my chance to rule over him; and not only that, to destroy him if I can. If he is the King I hate, I want him to settle for a kingdom on earth where I will be in control of him." So he watched for an opportunity to manipulate Jesus as he had done so successfully before with Eve and Adam.

When Jesus was in the desert fasting for forty days before his public mission began, Satan approached him and tried to convince him to become an earthly ruler. The tempter was consummately clever with the fine art of deception. But Jesus saw through it all, and said to Satan, "Be gone."

Judas, one of the Lord's closest disciples, had a special interest, also, in the Messiah as an earthly king. Satan wanted to destroy this king, but Judas wanted to exalt him. Different in their motivations, the two had the same goal: a kingdom on earth. Without knowing it consciously, Judas became a worker of Satan's revenge.

This straying disciple had noticed the miraculous power of Jesus. He wished this power could be used to overcome the Romans who were making life really miserable for the Jews. He wanted Jesus to become, in a socially controlling manner, the promised Messiah. Jesus, however, showed no sign of fulfilling that dream.

So, Judas decided that he himself was chosen by God to force the matter. That is when the disciple, without knowing what he was *really* doing, walked straightway into the ancient "fired up" hatred of Satan for the King.

Judas knew the priests at the Temple were agitated by Jesus, especially by his threat to monotheism when he said, "Before Abraham came to be, I am." His miracles, too, especially raising Lazurus from the dead, were causing the people to follow him. So Judas went to these enemies of Jesus and offered to help them capture his Master. Jesus, he thought, would finally use his power to take over and become king.

But Jesus said to Pontius Pilate, "My kingdom is not of this world." Did Judas hear that?

Instead of becoming, on earth, the King he already was in another world, Jesus submitted to a terrible scourging, to death on a cross, and to burial in another man's tomb. Satan thought that he, himself, was finally victorious. Probably more than anything that happened to Jesus, Satan reveled in that hideous crown of thorns.

But he, like Judas, had a big shock coming. Judas was so stunned with dismay and despair at what he had done that he threw away his acquired coins and left town to hang himself.

Later, when Jesus rose from the dead, stayed awhile with his disciples to secure the foundation of his Church (his kingdom here), and ascended to his original world, Satan became more vengeful than ever. He decided that he would do all he could to prevent the redeemed "maybe-sayers" from receiving salvation by finally saying fully "yes." He would get them to say absolutely "no."

"Thy Kingdom Come"

Satan's eye on this world continued throughout the history of the redeemed. His subterranean social movements in his followers, like the serpent himself, crawled beneath the surface and headed for a climax. His goal has been, and remains, the formation of an earthly kingdom (*his*), with a global government in his control. A new world order would be the fulfillment of his obsession, his dream.

One of his final moves toward his goal has been his strike at the spousal-parental family by inserting his pill, or his plug, or his knife, and rending asunder what God has united. Like a slow-motion nuclear explosion, the consequences of attacking the cause of human life expanded against the effect of this cause: human life itself. And the explosion spreads widely into the culture, into its institutions, and throughout the Lord's Church.

But Mary, the finest daughter of Eve, continues to keep her beautiful, watchful eyes on the serpent. She has been doing everything she can to guide and protect the children of the Church. She, through the power of her Son, will crush the serpent's head (his plot) in the end. Then the Kingdom of God finally will extend into, and include, the earth. The wall between them will disappear.

For those who listen deeply, this coming of the Kingdom is what the prophets foretold. For those who, with transcendental insight and the grace of Wisdom, turn up the actively receptive light of their minds, this coming of the Kingdom is what the structure of *being* reveals.

Words and Meanings
as used in this book

Adam: The first (historical) man on earth; father of all human persons; also, the principle of the emphatic masculine (expressive) qualities in men and of the subdominant masculine qualities in women; the archetypal man.

Affection: The emotion that combines liking someone with the loving feelings of fondness and tenderness. Affection is a quality of the five kinds of love, especially: affirmation, friendship (*philia*), and family bonding (*storge*).

Affective: The emphatically feeling side of human nature, especially psychological and spiritual. *Affective* emotions such as love, joy, and sorrow relate to *being* as different from *doing*. The correlative *effective* emotions supply energy for actions.

Affirmation: A spontaneous response of the heart and will to the goodness of being. Gives another person to him/her self by an attitude of receiving the goodness of the other. Af-*firm*-ation includes firmness, the basis for the four strengths of character: good judgment, justice, temperance or moderation, and courage in the person's relationship with the natural and divine laws of love. Affirmation also includes affection and affinity.

Agape **(A-ga'-pay):** Greek name for the giving kind of love: caring and charity.

Agent (active) intellect: The power of the human person for a finite pure-act of receptively knowing the *being* of whatever is known. This ontological knowing includes an intuition that a being *has* an essence or nature; but it is not an immediate knowing of *what* that nature is. *Human* intellection is more complex than the way angels know beings. Angels know the essences immediately. We need to abstract and reflect. We are intuitive-rational persons; angels are purely intuitive persons.

Agent Will: The power of the human person for a finite pure-act of responsively affirming the *being* of whatever is known by the agent intellect. This power is the source of our ontological freedom for affirming or negating whatever we know. (The agent will is virtually unrecognized as such by classical and contemporary thinkers.)

Archetypes: Idealized images or models of intuitive insights formed by the relationship between the agent intellect and the imagination. Sources of power for wisdom in the mental-emotional life of the human person. The ontological principles of intuitive imagination. Powerful sources of transcendental inspiration.

Body: The physical expression of the soul, within the substantially receptive-expressive powers of the soul. The body is the organismic expression of the spiritual matter of the original human person. The human person is, in this sense, ontologically concentric: the body within the soul, and soul within the spirit. See also **metaphysical body.**

Buddhism: One of the oriental mentalities of the wandering Eve based upon various ways of escaping from desire, suffering, and mortality. These ways include a special kind of meditation that leads to enlightenment (*nirvana*) which is a state of personless peace and passivity. Nirvana is a return to the passive anonymity into which Eve was expelled when she willfully abandoned her gift of *active receptivity*.

Compulsive: Ignoring feelings and behaving in a driven way. An extreme that results when a person's sense of responsibility pulls away from that person's natural spontaneity, and takes over. An actively receptive kind of awareness helps to heal this unhealthy condition.

Conception (human): The single-celled beginning of expressive human existence in passive matter. The point at which a sperm and an ovum interact to cause the physical expression of the soul *within* the soul. Conception is not an imposition of a soul upon passive matter. Such is an overly masculine or a builder's way of thinking.

Culture: The values, attitudes, habits, and ways of doing things that predominate in any given group of people for the sake of consistent and harmonious living. The "personality" of a society.

Effective: The competent side of human nature. The opposite of affective emotions. Effective emotions such as fear, hope, anger and courage motivate the person to act in accordance with the various situations of life.

Emotions: Psychological feelings; those that are different from physical feelings such as hunger and thirst.

Eros: Greek name for one of the five kinds of love: desire caused by needs, wants, and wishes.

Eve: The first woman on earth: historical mother of all human persons. Also, the principle of emphatically feminine (receptive) qualities in women and subdominant feminine qualities in men; the archetypal woman.

Evolution: The development of potencies into actualities that have advanced powers for further development. The cosmological theory of evolution is matter-based. The ontological view of evolution, including the development of the earth and its organisms, is person-based.

Family: A social unit of father, mother, and children. A powerful, irrepressible archetype of human life and well-being.

Feminine: A receptive, inward, sensitive quality that is more connected with feelings and persons than with objects and projects. Feminine active-receptivity is a physical, psychological, intellectual, volitional, spiritual, and transcendentally ontological correlative of other-directed expressivity. Essentially integrative. An emphasis on receiving in a giving way. Integrates with masculine giving in a receiving way. The heart of integrative thinking and living.

Freedom: The power of a person's being to determine intentions and actions.

Friendship: One of the five kinds of love. The mutual sharing of feelings, thoughts, values, and interests. The four main qualities of friendship are equality, esteem, affection, and value-sharing.

252 Words and Meanings

Grace: Friendship with God. Union of our life with the Life of God. Inspires power for wisdom about love in everyday life.

Hinduism: One of the original mentalities of the wandering Eve in India, having sacred texts, such as the Vedas, the Upanishads, and the Bhagavad-Gita. Hindus adhere to a diverse mix of beliefs and practices characterized by belief in a supreme Self, reincarnation, a caste system, and liberation from matter (*maya*) by purification rituals.

Immanence: One reality remaining or operating within another. Withinness. The opposite of transcendence.

Impulsive: Disposition to act without reflective awareness and inner restraint. A response to impulses that neither affirms feelings nor guides behavior.

Individualism: An overly masculine ideology of self-affirmation by means of accomplishments and success. Prone to aloneness and loneliness.

Integrative: Able to unite opposites in a balanced completeness for acting together harmoniously. Active receptivity is the ontological principle of integration.

Logic: The science and art of thinking correctly from a starting judgment to its consistent implications. A logical conclusion is no better than its starting point. The logic of the objective *either-or* way of thinking is different from the paradoxical *both-and* way of thinking. The first is clarifying; the latter is integrative. The logic of wisdom uses clarification within the context of integration.

Love: A spontaneous and responsible response of the heart and will to goodness. There are five kinds of love: affirmation, friendship, caring, desire, and familial affection. Additionally, various kinds of feelings enhance love. But love means willing the truest and best for self and all others despite the cost, and so it exists beyond feelings.

Man: A male human person having a nature that is designed to emphasize *giving in a receiving way*, along with masculine other-directed qualities such as productivity, performance, management, exploration, invention, leadership, and at the same time including a masculine version of feminine qualities in an integrated manner.

Words and Meanings 253

Marriage: A lifelong commitment of a man and a woman to each other as the center of their otherness in space and time. The two are united as an image and likeness of God.

Masculine: An expressive, other-directed, assertive quality that is more connected with objects and projects than with feelings and persons. Masculine expressivity involves a physical, psychological, intellectual, volitional, spiritual, and transcendentally ontological correlative of inner-directed receptivity. An emphasis on giving in a receiving way that integrates with feminine receiving in a giving way. Differentiative more than integrative.

Metaphysical Body: The human soul's receptive potential for matter. This potential is actualized (immortally) by the physical expression of the soul. The physical body is within the metaphysical body. Therefore, rather than the soul being within the body, the physical body (within the metaphysical body) is within the soul. Death is the physical body leaving the immortal metaphysical body. The separation of body and soul is, therefore, *not metaphysically substantial*, but is physically real and natural. Here dies the "rational animal."

Metaphysics: Other than, and beyond, physics. Metaphysics is the objective science of being as being that was discovered and developed by Aristotle. It attempts to study the ultimate principles of reality that are common to both natural *caused causes* and the transcendent *uncaused cause*.

Ontology: Has an original meaning in this book, and is the context for all of its other meanings. In contrast to metaphysics, ontology is based on the intersubjective (being-with-being) union between the knower and the *being* of whatever is known. This union is an intellectual intuition that is not possible unless the agent intellect *knows being* immediately before, through, and beyond the senses. Such is not the case for the usual metaphysics that depends on sensory knowledge from which to abstract its concepts. According to metaphysics, abstraction is caused by an agent intellect that does not know being.

Pantheism: The way of thinking that sees everything as being God in different forms. All reality, or at least all created persons, are seen as being parts or functions of God.

Paradox: An interpermeating integration of opposites. Within each other opposites are enriched in meaning, each by the other.

Perfectionist: One who manipulates feelings and does not receive them as they spontaneously are. "Feel this way; don't feel that way," or else ignore feelings. Prone to repression and driven behavior.

Person: An inner-and-other-directed being who, by knowing *is*, is aware that "I am, you are, we are." Persons exist for the sake of loving communion with all that is. Loving communion is a mutuality of giving and receiving. *No person, as a person, is a rational animal.*

***Philia*:** Greek word for friendship. One of the five kinds of love: mutual sharing.

Playboy: An impulsive, self-centered individualist, who reacts against restraint of desires, especially against the Puritan version, and especially in relation to sexual privacy, but shares with the Puritan the masculine emphasis on performance and goal-striving.

Psychological: Relating to emotional and mental conditions and functions.

Puritan: Believes in being predestined as one of the elect in spite of being depraved by nature. He or she reacts by being overly self-proving as an individualist: devotedly productive, self-controlled, inventive, and performing.

Receptive: An inward response of mind, will, and emotions. Can be either active or passive. Active receptivity is a transcendental quality of all persons as persons, including the divine Persons. Passive receptivity is not possible for God because it involves imperfection of being. Passive receptivity is a principle of mathematics, matter, space, time, and logic. Because an insight into the power of active receptivity has been missing in both the Eastern and Western mentalities, ontological philosophy, such as that developed in this book about the future of Adam and Eve, is newly presented. Ontology of this kind requires a logic that is attuned to paradoxical thinking which is actively receptive, not based on the passive *tabula rasa* required by Aristotle's rational animal.

Repression: Refusing to let yourself *consciously* know or feel something you know or feel. Blocking intuitions and feelings from awareness; burying them alive.

Responsible: A caring response to thoughts, impulses, and feelings that affirms them with *firmness*, and that guides behavior with good judgment according to true standards of integrity.

Selfist: A subjectivist dedicated to the preferences and opinions of one's own self.

Sexuality: Maleness and femaleness of the whole self: physical, emotional, mental, moral, intellectual, social, and spiritual. Thus much more expansive than genitality, though inclusive of it. The giving-receiving capacity for sharing.

Sexual freedom: The ability to affirm sexual feelings as good, including genital feelings, and to suppress (not repress) these feelings until the person is ready to affirm them with firmness, and to let them be as they spontaneously are without physically or emotionally arousing them. This freedom makes possible the first kind of sexual life: receiving feelings and emotions as energy for developing manhood and womanhood without sex activity. Such freedom also makes possible the development of sexual integrity as the ability to say and live a healthy "no" to sex before marriage and a healthy (not driven) "yes" to sex only within marriage.

Sexually active: Not just genitally active. There are three ways of being sexually active in three kinds of sexual life. 1. Responsibly affirming sexual feelings, and receiving them as energy for developing manhood and womanhood. 2. Sexual friendship in emotional and mental sharing without genital activity. 3. Sexual (genital) life in marriage, sex, and parenthood.

Soul: The life principle of a living being. Animals have mortal souls; the spiritual souls of human persons are immortal.

Spontaneous: A natural emergence of feelings and thoughts before evaluating and expressing them. After the latter process, expression can become spontaneous in a developed way.

Storge **(stor'gae):** Greek word for familial bonding and affection; one of the five kinds of love.

Subsumation: an activity of soul that includes the lower *within* the higher by means of receptive integration.

Suppression: Regulating the expression of feelings by consciously and purposely stopping their arousal. Suppression is conscious and can be healthy or unhealthy. Repression is always unconscious and unhealthy.

Taoism: An ancient Chinese view that nature is the ultimate reality. An impersonal, universal Way that all things follow for the sake of harmony and peace.

Transcendent: The otherness of God that is compatible with the withinness (not insideness) of God. Transcendent otherness is not spatial beyondness or outsideness.

Transcendental: Attributes of being that are common to all beings, or to all persons, including the divine Persons. Rising above each while including all. Goodness, truth, and beauty are the classical transcendentals of being.

Trinity: The three Persons in one God. Ontologically, there is a spousal-parental, background-foreground way of interpreting the revelation of three divine Persons. Traditionally, theologians refer to what they call the "immanent" and "economic" Trinity, that is, God within God and God in relation to creation, respectively.

Voluntarism: An over-emphasis on the will and its part in decisions and choices that fail to follow the intellect in an interactive way.

Wisdom: The most important of the three intellectual virtues: knowledge, understanding, and wisdom. Sees the parts of a being within its wholeness. Intuitive insight that includes the mind of the heart and the heart of the mind. Essential to friendship and the other ways of loving. Wisdom orders all things mightily and gently (*Wisdom* 8:1).

Woman: A female human person having a nature that is designed to emphasize *receiving in a giving way* (active receptivity) along with inner-directed qualities of intuition, sensitivity to inner feelings and to those of other persons, while including a feminine version of masculine qualities in an integrated manner.

References

Ahlstrom, Sydney E. *A Religious History of the American People.*
New Haven: Yale University Press, 2004.

Aquinas, Thomas. *Summa Theologica.*

Baars, Conrad W., M.D. *Born Only Once: The Miracle of Affirmation.* Cincinnati: St. Anthony Messenger Press, 2009.
_____. *Feeling and Healing Your Emotions.*
Gainsville, Florida: Bridge-Logos, 2003.

Baars, Conrad W. & Anna A. Terruwe. *Healing the Unaffirmed: Recognizing Emotional Deprivation Disorder.* Rev. ed. Suzanne M. Baars and Bonnie N. Shayne (eds.).
Staten Island, N.Y.: St. Pauls/Alba House, 2002.

Bell, Daniel. *The Cultural Contradictions of Capitalism.*
N.Y.: Basic Books, 1976.

Bible. Douay-Rheims.

Bremer, Francis J. *The Puritan Experiment: New England Society from Bradford to Edwards.*
N.H.: University Press of New England, 1995.

Cole, Franklin, editor. *They Preached Liberty.*
Indianapolis: Liberty Press, 1979.

Collins, James. *A History of Modern European Philosophy.*
Milwaukee: Bruce, 1954.

Durden-Smith, Jo and Diane DeSimone. *Sex and the Brain.*
N.Y.: Arbor House, 1983.

References

Ely, John Hart. "The Wages of Crying Wolf: A Comment on *Roe v. Wade*," In *Yale Law Journal* 82, 1973, pp. 920–949.

Ferm, Vergilius, editor. *Puritan Sage: Collected Writings of Jonathan Edwards.* N.Y.: Library Publisher, 1953.

Frankl, Viktor. *Man's Search for Meaning.* Boston: Beacon Press, 2000.

Friedan, Betty. *The Feminine Mystique.* N.Y.: Dell, 1964.

Griffith, Bede. *The Marriage of East and West.* Springfield, Illinois: Templegate Publishers, 1982.

Haffert, John M. *Meet the Witnesses of the Miracle of the Sun.* Spring Grove, Penn.: The American Society for the Defense of Tradition, Family, and Property, 1961.

Hahn, Scott. *First Comes Love.* N.Y.: Doubleday, 2002.

Hilgers, Thomas, M.D. *The Medical and Surgical Practice of NaPro Technology.* Omaha, Nebraska: Pope Paul VI Institute Press, 2004.

Joyce, Mary Rosera. *Friends for Teens.* St. Cloud, MN: LifeCom, 1991.
_____. *How Can a Man and Woman Be Friends.* Collegeville, MN: Liturgical Press,1976. St. Cloud, MN: LifeCom, 1991.
_____. *Women and Choice.* St. Cloud, MN: LifeCom, 1986.

Joyce, Robert E. *Affirming Our Freedom in God: The Untold Story of Creation.* St. Cloud, MN: LifeCom, 2001.
_____. *A Perfect Creation: The Light behind the Dark Side of Genesis.* St. Cloud, MN: LifeCom, 2008.
_____. *Facing the Dark Side of Genesis: A New Understanding of Ourselves.* St. Cloud, MN: LifeCom, 2008.
_____. *Human Sexual Ecology: A Philosophy and Ethics of Man and Woman.* Washington, D.C.: University Press of America, 1981.

References

Jones, Ernest. *The Life and Work of Sigmund Freud.*
N.Y.: Basic Books, 1953.

Kilpatrick, William. *Identity and Intimacy.* N.Y.: Dell, 1975.

LaCugna, Catherine M. *God for Us: The Trinity and Christian Life.*
N.Y.: HarperCollins, 1992

Leaf, Caroline. *Who Switched Off My Brain? Controlling Toxic Thoughts and Emotions.* Rivonia, South Africa: Switch on Your Brain Organization, 2007.

Levinson, Daniel. *The Seasons of a Man's Life.*
N.Y.: Alfred A. Knopf, 1978.

Lewis, C.S. *The Four Loves.*
Boston: Houghton Mifflin Harcourt, 1971.

Lindbergh, Ann Morrow. *Gift from the Sea*
N.Y.: Random House, 1955.

Maritain, Jacques. *Creative Intuition in Art and Poetry.*
N.Y.: Pantheon Books, 1953.

Moir, Anne and David Jessel. *Brain Sex: The Real Difference Between Men and Women.* N.Y.: Carol Publishing Group, 1991.

Reisman, David, with Nathan Glazer and Reuel Denney. *The Lonely Crowd.* New Haven: Yale, 1964.

Terruwe, Anna A., M.D. and Conrad W. Baars, M.D. *Psychic Wholeness and Healing: Using All the Powers of the Human Psyche.* N.Y.: Alba House, 2003.

Tournier, Paul. *The Gift of Feeling.* Atlanta: John Knox Press, 1981.

Turkington, C. *The Brain Encyclopedia.*
N.Y.: Checkmark Books, 1996.

Vitz, Paul. *Psychology as Religion: The Cult of Self-Worship.*
Grand Rapids, MI: William B. Eerdmans, 1995.

West, Christopher. *The Love That Satisfies.*
West Chester, PA: Ascension Press, 2007.

Available from *LifeCom*

Books by Mary Rosera Joyce are found on the website, Lifemeaning.com.

How Can a Man and Woman Be Friends?

Friendship is based on qualities that present an unique challenge to persons who are sexually different and prone, by nature, toward *eros*, another kind of love.

Equality, esteem, affection, and value-sharing are essential qualities of friendship. Each of these attributes needs to be clearly understood before true man-woman friendship can become constant in our personal life.

In question-and-answer format, this 65-page book is easily readable.

Women and Choice: A New Beginning

Are women controlling their own minds? Not as long as they are influenced by the Puritan-playboy culture. This culture's original idea of the "comfortable concentration camp" and reactive notion of women's liberation from "the camp" has been structurally incapable of liberating women to be who they really are. Men, too, are suffering. Children are emotionally and spiritually abandoned.

Besides exposing the problem, the author shows why the true women's movement is yet to begin, what it involves, and how to live it. Women readers have said, "This book changed my life." One young man said, "I'll never be a playboy again."

Copied version of this book is available.

LifeCom
Box 1832, St. Cloud, MN 56302
www.Lifemeaning.com

Available from *LifeCom* in the **Two Creations Series**

The following and others by Robert E. Joyce, PhD

Facing the Dark Side of Genesis:
A New Understanding of Ourselves

This book claims that religious thinkers have overlooked a crucial aspect of the truth: God's creating act is necessarily interpersonal and immediately causes perfect creatures only. These persons, both angelic and human, necessarily respond instantly with full freedom. The new interpretation for understanding better who we are—and who we are not—integrates and deepens traditional belief in God.

Attention is given to the profoundly unconscious dimensions of the mind and heart, largely neglected, that emerge from the spiritual structure of being. This new theistic worldview suggests an expanded ground for understanding the conflict between creationists and evolutionists. The author discloses a general failure of theology to see the difference between creation absolutely "out of nothing" and the redemptive creation "out of something" fallen, as depicted in *Genesis*.

(LifeCom, 2008) 93 pages. For the general interest reader.

Chapters on The *Genesis* Gap; Originative Sin; A Theology of the Person's Being; Two Creations: Originative and Redemptive; Consequences for a Life of Faith, *et al*.

A Perfect Creation:
The Light behind the Dark Side of Genesis

This book challenges both creationists and theistic evolutionists to look deeper into the infinite intimacy of God in gifting us to *be*. We are called to acknowledge our hidden failure to be grateful for our own be-ing. We are seen to be not the only cause of darkness, pain, and evil in our lives, but the ultimate cause. We have spiritually repressed our absolute origin in God and have confused our coming to be in cosmic creation with our originative creation out of nothing.

The Book of Genesis and the rest of the Bible deal largely with the creation of rescue—done by God out of the void, darkness, dust, *et al.* caused by our pristine personal failure to say fully *yes* to the gift of being. The original history-making sin of Adam and Eve in Eden is seen as a major symptom of the originative sin of each one of us *with* Adam and Eve, *ex nihilo*. We are now awakening to the prospects and hope of living forever in repentant glory.

(LifeCom, 2008) 170 pages. Mainly for philosophers and theologians.

Chapters on *Cosmess* to Cosmos; The Missing Infinity of God; God's Intimate Act of Creation; The Meaning of Evil and Its Cause; Receptivity and the Will of God, *et al*.

LifeCom
Box 1832, St. Cloud, MN 56302
www.Lifemeaning.com

Endnotes

[1] Hyperactivity is reaction against passivity. It results from a lack of active receptivity.

[2] In his book *The Love That Satisfies*, 2007, p. 44-5, Christopher West quotes Hugh Hefner, saying that he started *Playboy* magazine as a "personal response to the hurt and hypocrisy of our Puritan heritage…it comes from the fact that I didn't get hugged a lot as a kid…." From Cathleen Falsani, "Hugh Hefner: Man of God?" *Soma: A Review of Religion and Culture*, May 16, 2006.

[3] For a description of selfism, see Paul Vitz, *Psychology as Religion: The Cult of Self-Worship*, William B. Eerdmans, Grand Rapids, Michigan, 1995.

[4] In this personhood vacuum, the *Dred Scott* and *Roe v. Wade* decisions by the U.S. Supreme Court denied personhood to black people and preborn children, followed by cultural "earthquakes" at profound national depths.

[5] *Summa Theologica*, 1-11, q.4, a.5, ad 5; 1a, Q 75-89.

[6] St. Thomas lived to be only 49 years old. Had this massively productive theologian lived much longer, we can only imagine what further insights he might have offered.

[7] In the case of twinning (identical twins), the newly conceived person either dies that two others might live, or the original one reproduces by a process somewhat similar to parthenogenesis (natural cloning) in which the original individual survives while begetting (in an asexual way) another or others. There is no reason for using the fact of twinning to deny that conception is the beginning of *at least one* individual person.

[8] 1) God is the primary agent cause. 2) and 3) Heterosexual parents, by previously acting together, are, at the moment of conception, the secondary agent causes. 4) and 5) The respective generative cells (ovum and sperm) are the instrumental agent causes. 6) The soul is the primary formal cause within the substance of the newly physicalized person. 7) The potency by virtue of the generative cells is the primary material cause: prime matter. 8) The physical matter of the generative cells is the secondary material cause of the bodily expression of the soul. 9) The new genetic information, instrumentally caused by the genetic information in the generative cells, is the secondary formal cause that is received by and *qualifies* the primary formal cause: the soul.

The soul receives into *its potency* for physical matter, the potency (prime matter) of the gametes, and, in so doing, physicalizes itself.

⁹ Cf. Henri Bergson, *Creative Evolution,* translated by Arthur Mitchell, Henry (N.Y.: Holt and Co., 1911). And also, Jacques Maritan, *Creative Intuition in Art and Poetry* (N.Y.: Meridian Books, 1955), p. 71.

¹⁰ There would seem to be three kinds of Thomism: Aristotelian, Existential (Maritain and Gilson), and Transcendental (Rahner, Lonergan, and others). Aristotelian Thomists are satisfied with the agent intellect as a cause of conceptual knowledge without, itself, knowing anything. Existential Thomists are more concerned about how the mind actually knows *is,* and they place this knowledge in a post-conceptual existential judgment. Transcendental Thomists realize that *being* is known in a pre-conceptual way, but they cannot resist a kind of deification of this primal human *noesis.* Their idea about human pre-conceptual knowing as "a dynamism to the infinite" misses the crucial point that it is also, and equally, a dynamism to the *is* of finite beings. Their simplistic "dynamism," therefore, makes them vulnerable to pantheism, which would be a philosophical disaster.

¹¹ Caroline Leaf, *Who Switched Off My Brain?* (Rivonia, South Africa: Switch On Your Brain, 2007), p. 17.

¹² For further development of this theme, cf. "The Paradoxical Logic of Wisdom," Developmental Reflection B, p. 223.

¹³ Recognition of the agent will is as new to philosophical reflection as is recognition of the agent intellect as our power for knowing the *is* of beings. Ontological insight into *being as being* implies ontological freedom to affirm or deny *being.* See the References for a list of books on this subject by Robert Joyce.

¹⁴ Conrad W. Baars, M.D. and Anna A. Terruwe, M.D., *Healing the Unaffirmed,* St. Paul's Publishing Co. Olathe, Kansas, 2002; and Baars, *Born Only Once; The Miracle of Affirmation,* St. Anthony Messenger Press, Cincinnati, Ohio, 2009; and *Feeling and Healing Your Emotions,* Bridge-Logos, Alachua, Florida, 2003.

¹⁵ St. John of the Cross.

¹⁶ Jo-Durden Smith and Diane de Simone, *Sex and the Brain,* (N.Y.: Arbor House, 1983); and Louann Brizendine, *The Female Brain,* (N.Y.: Doubleday, 2006); and Anne Moir and David Jessel, *Brain Sex: The Real Difference Between Men and Women* (N.Y.: Carol Publishing Group, 1991).

¹⁷ In their book, *Brain Sex; The Real Difference Between Men and Women, op. cit.,* Anne Moir & David Jessel see homosexuality as organically based. They are influenced by the East German scientist, Dr. Gunter Dorner, who "devoted his life's work to the theory that exposure to certain hormones before birth determines sexual inclination." p. 114-125. The authors also quote Sigmund Freud who had a

biology-based view of human sexual energy. A person-based view of human sexuality sees in the person a natural as well as a transcendent power-source that is not reducible to energy or to biology. This sexual power of personhood, together with divine grace, is a resource for the integrity of chastity and also for healing.

[18] Sources: Richard Fitzgibbons, M.D., principal contributor to *Homosexuality and Hope* (Wynnewood, PA: Catholic Medical Association, 1999) and a contributor to the book by John Harvey, *The Truth about Homosexuality* (San Francisco: Ignatius Press, 1996).

[19] In public demonstrations held in New York, Boston, and Minnesota in the fall of 1982, Dutch therapist, Franz Veldman, taught this technique to pregnant women. His *Life Welcomed and Affirmed* (Nymegen: Academie voor Haptonomie en Kinesionomie, 1976) describes his approach to affirming touch.

[20] According to Father Anthony Mellace, Sao Paulo, Brazil, a counselor of sexually disoriented persons, two men or two women in homoerotic relationships tend to be one submissive and the other dominant. If the submissive person becomes uneasy with the situation and seeks help by complaining about the dominant partner, some counselors attempt to help this person to become more comfortable in the relationship. Others might encourage this person to become more assertive and thus more other-directed toward healing. The dominant one would be likely, then, to feel challenged and uneasy, and might end the relationship only to wander away to "someone else like me" who is different and complementary by being submissive.

[21] Counseling sources: Focus on the Family, Colorado Springs, CO. Exitus (exitus.com). Courage (www.couragerc.net).

[22] Adam's theologians use a similar distinction between what they call the *immanent* Trinity (the three divine Persons and the relationships between them) and the *economic* Trinity (the relationships between divine and human persons.)

[23] Theologians say, however, that there is no sexuality in God. Thus, they imply that the sexual reality of man and woman is not *directly* like God, but only indirectly, that is, through their supposedly *neuter* spirituality. But this neutereity is an ontological problem of the highest order. It implies that there is no essential difference between the way in which a man and a man, and a man and a woman, were created in the divine likeness.

The implicit idea of neutereity in our likeness to God is neither Scriptural nor ontological. It is due instead to an intellectually fixated biological (genital) limitation on the meaning of sexuality.

Biological sexuality could not even exist unless it had an ontological source in the immanence and transcendence (withinness and otherness) of being as *being*. Thus every individual being, no matter what it is, expresses withinness and otherness, including each one of the divine Persons. Withinness and otherness, though not sexual, are the ontological source of sexuality. Human sexuality is the *personal* power to *share* withinness and otherness: biologically, psychologically, intellectually, spiritually, and primarily ontologically. This sharing power is an image and likeness of the divine Persons, who differently emphasize withinness and otherness.

The ontological meaning of human sexuality does not originate in biology, but in the structure of *being itself*. Masculinity and femininity are transcendental, not in biology, psychology, and metaphysics, but only in an ontology of human sexuality. Similarly, in the traditional theology of the Trinity, the word *generation* is used transcendentally in naming the first of the two divine Processions.

[24] Cf. Developmental Reflection A, p. 205: "The History of Personhood in Trinitarian Theology." This reflection shows the historical and ontological reasons why a spousal-parental interpretation of the "immanent" Trinity has not surfaced before.

[25] Sources: Dr. Thomas Hilgers, Pope Paul VI Institute, 6901 Mercy Rd., Omaha, Nebraska 68106. (popepaulvi.com) Billings Ovulation Method Association, Box 2135, St. Cloud, MN, 56302 (boma-usa.org). The Couple to Couple League International, Inc. Box 111184, Cincinnati, OH 45211.

[26] Jeff VonLehmen, a Catholic priest who works with Project Rachael, has said that women seeking abortions are influenced by various factors such as addictions, being abused as a child, poverty, selfishness, self-image, and more. These personal causes are different from a cultural cause for abortion such as the contraceptive *mentality*. This counselor's opinion is that the deepest source of the whole syndrome is alienation from God and the first commandment, and is not due only to the seven capital sins and those against the sixth commandment. He quotes Pope Benedict as saying: "A faulty concept of God leads to faulty moral behavior...." and "To sum up everything, then we can say the ultimate root of hatred of human life, of attacks on human life, is the loss of God. When God disappears, the absolute dignity of human life disappears as well." *The Essential Pope Benedict XVI: His Central Writings and Speeches* by John Thornton and Susan Varenne (N.Y.: Harper, 2008) p. 362 and 390.

[27] David Reisman, *The Lonely Crowd* (New Haven: Yale University Press, 1950).

[28] A source for filling in this ancient story is Charles C. Mann, *1491: New Revelations of the Americas before Columbus* (N.Y.: Alfred A. Knopf, 2005).

[29] Deepak Chopra, *How To Know God: The Soul's Journey into the Mystery of Mysteries* (N.Y.: Harmony Books, 2000), p 14.

Endnotes

[30] When we are sleeping, our natural *ability* to know and love does not sleep. At the moment of conception, we had the natural, not yet functional, ability to know and love. With time, nutrition, and love, this natural power gradually became more and more able to function.

Developmental Reflection A

[31] According to St. John Damascene, the last of the Greek Fathers of the Church, in his work, *The Fount of Knowledge* (Part 2), Mohammed seems to have conversed with an Arian monk, apparently influencing Mohammed to think that God is not a Trinity of Persons.

[32] Scott Hahn and others see the man-woman likeness to God in the psychological model of the Trinity: knowing (from Father to Son) as masculine, and loving (between Father and Son) as feminine. But how can love between masculine persons be a feminine person? It is true, however, that love is equally feminine and masculine (receiving and giving) in the Holy Spirit, a Person who *receives* personhood from two others, and is, in that latter sense, emphatically receptive.

[33] The image of the people of God as the bride of Yahweh is one of the most commonly used themes in the prophetic writings, such as *Is.* 54:1-8, 55:4, 62:4; *Jer.* 2:2, 3:6-25; *Hos.* 2:1-3:5; 5:3-7.

[34] *Eph.* 5: 25-33; 2 *Cor.* 11:2.

[35] Sources for the history of Trinitarian theologians and their theology: Catherine M. La Cugna: *God for Us: The Trinity and Christian Life* (N.Y.: Harper Collins, 1992). La Cugna opposes the paradigm of the economic and immanent Trinity, and emphasizes their inseparability. Also, Kallistos Ware: "The Human Person as an Icon of the Trinity," *Sobornost* 8 (1986), 6-23. Ware emphasizes God as a love-communion of Persons.

Developmental Reflection C

[36] According to 1 *Cor.* 15:44, St. Paul says, "If there is a physical body, there is also a spiritual body." That the spiritual (or metaphysical) body is not physical is explained above in Chapter 6.

[37] Cf. endnote 35.

Developmental Reflection D

[38] Ontology, in this sense, is not possible unless the agent intellect *knows* the *is* of whatever the human mind knows. Since no one of the preceding philosophers interpreted the agent intellect in this way, they were unable to develop, explicitly, this kind of ontology.